COLONIALISM DEVOURS ITSELF

GÉRARD PRUNIER

Colonialism Devours Itself

The Waning of Françafrique

HURST & COMPANY, LONDON

First published in the United Kingdom in 2025 by
C. Hurst & Co. (Publishers) Ltd.,
New Wing, Somerset House, Strand,
London, WC2R 1LA
© Gérard Prunier, 2025

All rights reserved.
Printed in Scotland by Bell & Bain Ltd, Glasgow.

The right of Gérard Prunier to be identified as the author of this publication is asserted by him in accordance with the Copyright, Designs and Patents Act, 1988.

A Cataloguing-in-Publication data record for this book is available from the British Library.

ISBN: 9781911723653

www.hurstpublishers.com

CONTENTS

Foreword ix

1. Genealogy: From Colonization to
   Decolonization: The Ambiguity of a Word 1
   The Chaotic Evolution of France Towards
   Decolonization 5
   Kamerun, Cameroons or Cameroun?
   Françafrique's *Ur-modell* is born in hybrid
   ideological confusion 16
   An "African" coup intrudes on a deeply
   disturbed colonial Metropole 30

2. Rough and ready: The *Françafrique*
   heydays (1960–81) 39
   Colonialism and the French political tradition 39
   Independences, counterinsurgency,
   assassinations and supporting friendly regimes Le 42
   Grand Charles as a political stylist 46
   So why *Françafrique*? 47
   Smooth sailing over rough waters 51
   In the wake of post-Gaullism, the beginnings of
   economic changes and structural
   transformations 64

CONTENTS

3. Mitterrand's non-reforms — 69
   Françafrique integrates the state: The Rwandese catastrophe and the oil scandal (1981–99) — 69
   Thomas Sankara's unusual political trajectory — 70
   Sankara's assassination — 74
   Virtue by prescription: The La Baule speech—and its unforeseen consequences — 76
   Rwanda: Tiptoeing to a catastrophe — 80
   Out of the door and back through the window: The French leave Rwanda and return through the Congo — 92
   France's African dilemma: Sharing energies between money and "grandeur": French oil from Elf to Total — 100

4. The Big Sleep (1995–2012) — 107
   Compounding disaster with failure— Trying to wrap up the Rwanda disaster via the Congo — 107
   Back to business as usual — 112
   Identity politics lead to a sporadic civil war in Ivory Coast — 123
   Trying to ride a wounded animal: *Françafrique*'s attempted romance with Paul Kagame — 130
   Libya: One intervention too many — 142

5. *Françafrique* is not dead, it is merely fading away (2012–21) — 153
   Ghaddafi dies, his Tuareg Praetorian Guard drifts southwards and boosts the Sahelian unrest — 154

CONTENTS

The Jihadi oil slick starts spreading out of Mali	161
Burkina Faso starts a coup cascade	167
Niger, *Françafrique*'s diplomatic Waterloo, collapses without a military defeat	173
Odd man out: The Coup in Gabon	181
The Chadian last redoubt	190
Oozing towards the coast: Will there be a last stand?	194
6. What is left after dismantling, spreading oneself thin, picking up the pieces and hoping to plug the gaps? (2021–24)	199
Francophone Guinea: The muted last hurrah of *Françafrique*	200
Gabon: The discreet low-key putsch settles in	203
The Alliance des Etats du Sahel (AES): An attempt to streamline the confusion	209
The pieces left behind	216
Full circle: In which France has to face decolonizing itself	223
Conclusion	239
Notes	247
Select Bibliography	273
Index	279

FOREWORD

Do not waste your time looking look up "*Françafrique*" in any dictionary (even a French one), because you won't find it. *Françafrique* is that barbaric lexical entity called a "neologism". But if you read any book or article about Francophone Africa published during the last half century, it occurs frequently in the text, which is unusual for a neologism. What is it, then?

Françafrique is a geopolitical construct which first made its timid appearance in the 1950s, at the time colonialism, then still in existence, had become a problem.

Between November 1884 and February 1885 the fourteen most powerful global political entities met in Berlin to decide what to do with Africa. Contrary to a frequently held view, they did not divide the continent among themselves; rather they established the ground rules by which the carve up could be carried out by the participants. While the latter was rather messy, contrary to the hopes of the Marxists of the time it did not trigger the massive face-to-face national confrontation

FOREWORD

revolutionary socialists were hoping for. When World War One broke out it had nothing to do with colonies, where very little fighting took place. Nevertheless, in June 1919 the Treaty of Versailles confiscated all of Germany's colonies and subcontracted them to the victorious Powers through a system of Mandates given to the League of Nations, the first attempt at managing international relations

Decolonization was a by-product of World War Two which had bequeathed the developed world a new architecture of international relations whose constituent states found themselves in various situations:

1. Victorious
2. Neutral
3. Vanquished
4. Controlled by the Soviet Union.

A number of "free" countries remained but they avoided slipping into number four only through United States protection.

France was in none of the above situations. Officially it was "victorious", in theory a number one, but practically it was really in position three, thanks to a "victory" acquired under Anglo-American auspices. In Reims on 7 May 1945, when the German representatives signed the capitulation of the Third Reich's forces, General François Sevez, the only French official present, was listed as an "observer", not as a participant. When he walked into the room where the German surrender was taking place Field Marshal Wilhelm Keitel, head of the German delegation, saw him and sighed : "*My God! even them!*" Roosevelt had prepared a structure for administering France as an "enemy-occupied territory", had had money printed for use in France and had planned to rule the country through the authority of (Vichy-nominated) *Préfets*. De Gaulle was dead-set against this "colonization" of France and managed a last moment flip-flopping (with the help of Winston Churchill who knew that the US idea was heavy with dangerous consequences) to prevent the Americans from going through with their plan. It was only in the last week before the Normandy landings that De Gaulle managed to countermand the instructions to Allied forces concerning the administration of liberated France, which, if applied would have brought France to the level of Italy. This had been a very close call and the danger of France being treated not as a victorious country but as an "enemy-occupied territory" remained a strong memory, especially since France was the only one of the of the five members of the UN security Council which felt in a somewhat wobbly position. The day the UN was founded (October 25th 1945) the French representation was only listed as "the Provisional Government of the French Republic".

Meanwhile France confronted a serious colonial problem which indirectly had a continuous and serious

FOREWORD

impact on its government's legitimacy. For France the Cold War was hot. Indochina had been freed from Axis domination with the Japanese capitulation of 15 August 1945, but De Gaulle was still weighed down by having replaced a pro-Axis government while seeking to re-establish French control over all its pre-war Empire. The first postwar French government was a tripartite coalition in which the Moscow-aligned Communist Party participated while the French Army was fighting Communists in Indochina. The Free French authorities had had to reset their control over a colony whose administration the Japanese had dismantled after their takeover of 9 March 1945 and the Free French almost came to blows among themselves over the question of negotiating with the Vietnamese Communists. Admiral Thierry d'Argenlieu took it upon himself to go for the jugular and on 23 November 1946 ordered the French Navy to bombard Haïphong, killing 6,000 civilians. The war was on and it lasted till the Dien Bien Phu disaster of May 1954, killing half a million people in the process and further undermining the legitimacy of the French government. When the Algerian conflict erupted in November 1954 the rapid intertwining of one colonial war into another compounded the anguish of the original "colonial" conflict and turned it into a national crisis. The problematic legitimacy of the French Republic had fluctuated all the way from the June 1940 collapse to the military putsch of May 1958. Indeed few people today would answer "France" if asked which contemporary European power came to fruition as the result of an army coup.

For De Gaulle's heroic bluff to win a seat at the victors' table to succeed, he had to throw in the added weight of the Empire. But France had just lost Indochina and was on its way to losing Algeria. The Algerian war raised the spectre of a civil war because *Algeria was France* (including in its population) and, in the wake of Dien Bien Phu, part of the Army was not going to let De Gaulle forget it just after putting him back in power to keep Algeria French. He needed an immediate buffer for the short term and it had to be put together quickly.

This is how *Françafrique* was born, a postcolonial extension of the lame duck state of French politics since 1940, a vital adjunct that could not be rationalized into an official system even if it was a vital necessity.

Françafrique was not an entity motivated by a neocolonial system of exploitation even if it was its most often mentioned *raison d'être*. Nor was it an imperial system even though it relied heavily on the French Armed Forces as its official arm. It never had a legal existence. The best way to describe it is as "an organic network". The men who took part in it—soldiers, legal experts, businessmen, journalists, civil servants and secret service agents—were all deeply convinced of serving the interests of "France" in the broadest sense of the word. Even though it resorted, unofficially, to the notion of "national interest" it also had enemies who saw it as an entrenched system of vested interests (which it also was). In terms of operational capacity, it was the real link between Paris and Francophone Africa for three quarters of a century. For better or worse *Françafrique* ran the Africa department of the French Ministry of Foreign Affairs and not the other way around. The Rwanda catastrophe was the first crack in the machinery and hastened its decline. All Africa specialists were aware of *Françafrique* but it never became an accepted intellectual category even if knowing about it and following its activities was both a sort of parlor game and an endless source of anecdotes ranging from the bawdy to the criminal.

The growing disarray of the dying empire is more apparent today as its bones and sinews are exposed to the elements. The received wisdom today is that "evil Muscovites" and "subversive Muslims" must bear the responsibility for this rapidly impending sunset. This is simply geopolitical myopia. The extraordinary situation which gave birth to *Françafrique* is not that of today. The Sahel insurgency belongs to another world that *Françafrique* was not designed to tackle. France is still trying to solve today's African problems with yesterday's tools, and it is less and less able to do so.

Most of "the West", as seen from a NATO perspective, was complicit with the unorthodox way France was dealing with the continent and the demise of

FOREWORD

Françafrique is a serious problem, particularly for Washington. The Americans looked away from Africa for many reasons and were glad that the French always seemed ready to get stuck in, even if it was at times embarrassing. Being the world's largest global power has its limits and leaving Africa to the Russians is not a viable alternative. The fact that Africa can operate independently of the Great Powers is for the time being a pious piece of political correctness—even if the idea of Kenyan troops battling Haïtian gangs is new and the symbol of a different way of looking at the continent. *Françafrique* is now on the junk heap of history but in spite of its questionable record, this remains a mixed blessing.

1

GENEALOGY

From Colonization to Decolonization: The Ambiguity of a Word

The relationship of Europe and the rest of the world has passed through two distinct periods of conquest preceding today's complex "globalization". Both periods are considered to be "colonization" although the first one should be seen more as "empire-making" hence the ambiguity of the word. In the sixteenth century this first wave of European conquest of the planet, mostly by Spain, Portugal and Britain, ended between 1776 (US Independence) and 1825 (the independence of Bolivia). This was entirely linked to European politics where the first mature European nation-states had projected their territorial ambitions beyond their hard-fought borders. The colonies of this first wave of European imperialism were disputed according to victories and losses in European conflicts, without any participation by the colonized. The main losers were the French whose first colonial Empire—some parts of India, Quebec, Louisiana and its outliers towards the Great Lakes—disappeared, to the benefit of Great Britain. Here we will not consider this archaeology of imperial colonization because its features—especially demographic—were radically different from those of "modern" colonization, whose Weberian "ideal type" was essentially visible in Africa.[1] This was followed by a period of transformation before the word "colonization" began to be used.

The British Empire as a symbol of world dominion opened in triumph in 1815 while the French lost the real first world war, namely that launched by Napoleon Bonaparte. Its later "Empire" (the colonial one) was a consolation prize for France after losing both the first Empire (Napoleon's) and, to cap it all, the national defeat to Prussia in 1871.

Both were part of that crisis of cultural megalomania which the West had embarked upon in the sixteenth century, after the discovery of America. The Treaty of Tordesillas (7 June 1494) was an act of diplomatic hysteria which divided the entire world between Spain and Portugal. Can we imagine today a treaty that shared the planet between the United States and the People's Republic of China? Someone imagining such an outcome today would run the risk of being bundled off to a psychiatric clinic. But in that case it was sanctified by Pope Alexander VI speaking in the name of God. The Pope was Spanish and the world addressed by this distinguished member of the Borgia family was considered juridically to be *res nullius,* a land belonging to nobody, a status which would lead to both the genocide of the Native Americans and the onset of the Slave Trade. The British and the French soon contained such Iberian delusions to South America and got down to the serious business of contesting who would be the true master of the world. After several unexpected reversals, the fall of Napoleon in 1815 decided that no, it would not be the French. But then, in a situation somewhat reminiscent of the pre-Tordesillas dilemma, there was the problem of Africa. Contrary to America, Africa had always been there. Its northern Mediterranean fringe belonged successively to the Greeks, the Carthaginians, the Romans, Byzantium and finally to the Ottomans. But it was only the peel of the fruit because south of the Sahara lay, in the new European view, another huge area defined as *res nullius*: Africa, the "real Africa", which till the nineteenth century had been considered only as a source of gold or slaves bound to work on America's plantations.

Sea battles between the Europeans and the Turks had resulted in a draw because the Europeans were too busy fighting each other to embark on a new round of Crusades. The key to world domination was located more on the Danube and later in Flanders than in

Algeria. But European world expansion was boosted by a massive demographic boom and, increasingly, by the new phenomenon of the Industrial Revolution. European industry produced both quinine and excellent weapons. Africa was now within reach. The new African game was launched by yesterday's losers, the French, when they landed in Algiers in 1830 and compensated for their attenuated geopolitical ego by massacring thousands of Arabs and the assimilated population. For a while this did not lead to much till the rising star of European imperialism—Germany—began to worry about this new dimension of the great imperial game. Strange explorers with strange origins began turning up in droves in the most unexpected places[2] and Chancellor Bismarck who had been satisfied with saying: "Let the French rooster scratch the sands of the Sahara" began to worry about his European plans being undermined by the rival growth of European expansion in Africa. To stem that threat he convened a conference in Berlin aimed at bringing order to European imperialism in Africa (November 1884–February 1885) so that Germany would stay, if not on top of the game, at least on the pitch. Another chunk of *res nullius* would get new owners. It lasted about a hundred years, with Namibia in March 1990 being the last black African territory to declare its independence, in this case from South Africa. The consequences are still with us and the French, who had been the first on the continent, are now taking their leave, stumbling backwards.

The Chaotic Evolution of France Towards Decolonization

The Second World War was the turning point for decolonization and for France the outcome was far from crystal-clear. The French had always been the European odd man out in terms of imperialism. 1815 had closed a chapter in imperial rivalry, with France having lost everything after having conquered everything. But there was one thing which had survived, a kind of prestige, a special aura, which led to what David Todd called "Velvet Imperialism".[3] French women were the most beautiful in the world and their perfumes the sexiest. Buy these perfumes and imitate their couture. When the French Army landed in Algiers in 1830, French merchants already had control of the harems. Paris bypassed defeat on the battlefield by exerting influence through other means, even though the military dimension would be added later.

The crushing of the French Army by the Wehrmacht in 1940 opened a period of comparable ambiguity. Part of turning that post-defeat lack of means into something operationally useful came from Africa, from France's "African Empire". The starting point was unpropitious because the entire colonial structure had opted to throw its weight behind what seemed at the time to be the legitimate government of France, the one led by Marshal Philippe Petain's Vichy-based regime. The first modest turning point began in July 1940 when the Governor of Chad, Félix Eboué, sent his second in command to Nigeria to get in touch with the British. With British support, at the Brazzaville Conference, held in early February 1944, De Gaulle created the so-called "Bloc Français de l'Empire" whose novel feature was a promise of autonomy for the post-war dispensation. It was not any kind of "self-government" as some historians have hastily written. Eboué himself was the embodiment of the "autonomy" being proffered. A Black person from Guyana, he had risen through the ranks—a hard-to-achieve success for a "native"[4]—and become a colonial administrator, first in Guadeloupe (West Indies) and later in Africa. He was absolutely loyal to the idea of the Republic and considered Pétain to be a usurper, which was morally courageous and politically daring for a Black man. But he could not conceive of any self-government when his own status made him a black-skinned Frenchman with no geographical base. The Bloc Français de l'Empire grouped together Cameroon (Cameroun), Moyen ("Middle") Congo[5] and Oubangui Chari (the future Central African Republic). Pétain sentenced Eboué to death and De Gaulle made him Governor of Equatorial Africa. This split considerably influenced the later administration of the French African colonies. De Gaulle tried to take AOF (Afrique

Occidentale Française)[6] by storm but his attempted military landing in Dakar was opposed by Vichy's Governor Pierre Boisson and his small fleet sailed back under fire to Great Britain. The "secession" of AEF (French Equatorial Africa) and the mini-civil war in AOF had a major impact on the French Colonial Civil Service because these events indisputably affected their planning for the post-war era. Everybody knew that the eventual shape of French Africa would depend on the victors' dispensation and if the Axis powers won it would obviously be quite a grim outcome. But things were more hopeful—and also much less clear—in the case of an Allied victory. A simple return to the pre-war situation remained a possibility but there was a general feeling that it was unlikely. In June 1943, after the Allied occupation of North Africa, a stark choice became apparent because the future of the European colonies was a source of discord between the Americans and the British. Roosevelt wanted to sweep away the colonial empires while Winston Churchill favored their preservation. De Gaulle's position was an ambiguous one since his own relationship with the French Empire was in itself problematic; he depended on the French Empire—the majority of his troops were colonial—but he had no autonomous financial or military means that would have made him free of the Allies whose support was discreetly conditional. Choices had to be made and to make his quandary worse, the very tools he was forced to use were not coherent. The progressive slide of French Africa from Vichy to London was accompanied by an internal transformation. A "new colonial elite" rose as the old colonial administrators were pushed aside by the Gaullists and demands for "a new empire" after victory were raised because it seemed that traditional colonialism had few chances of a smooth survival and would have to confront native unrest. In military terms, whatever little equipment the Free French had till late 1943 was of British origin and the British were themselves short of armaments. De Gaulle himself had to make a decision, which prompted him to organize the Brazzaville Conference (January 30 to February 8 1944). Brazzaville had been picked by De Gaulle to be the capital of Free France and the conference had been organized by the Comité Français de Libération Nationale (CFLN), which was the outline of a temporary French national government. But although the CFLN pretended to prepare what a "New Empire" would be it began by creating a "Council for the Defence of the Empire", the key element of which would be "Defence". The only civilian measure it took was the abolition of the Native Code.[7] The real issues at stake with continued colonization were discussed but the liberals and the conservatives were evenly balanced. A few months later the Brazzaville discussants were in Paris dealing with the realities and had to embark on some kind of legislation supposed to define the status of the

Empire. The gap between theory and practice was brought to a bloody head at the time of the Thiaroye massacre, in which up to 300 Tirailleurs Sénégalais were killed.[8] A key moment in the move towards decolonization (which had not even been vaguely hinted at during the Brazzaville Conference) was the change in the *apparentement* of the *Rassemblement Démocratique Africain* (RDA).[9] *Apparentement* in the French Fourth Republic was a system by which MPs who were members of small political parties had to be apparentés (linked to, or word for word, "made members of the same family") to a larger political group sharing similar political tendencies. The small RDA was *apparenté* to the Communist group, the Communists being the only political party which had a clear-cut anticolonial position in its program. The RDA leader, Félix Houphouët-Boigny, was a very sedate middle-class person from the Ivory Coast. He was a cocoa planter and a member of the mostly white planters' association but as the only Black member of the French Constitutional Assembly in 1945 he had felt that the RDA *apparentement* to the Communists was the only option for a colonized African. De Gaulle, who was a conservative but a pragmatic one, understood the difficulty Houphouët-Boigny had to deal with and approached the RDA leader through moderate sympathizers who thought colonialism was outdated but felt that France had to keep ultimate control of the

"Empire". But by then, what had "the French Empire" turned into? It is hard to say because the nature of that huge and empty word was changing not even month by month but week by week. To begin gauging the transformation bear in mind that the period when the new constitution of what was going to be called the *Union Française*, which was supposed to replace *l'Empire Français*, roughly coincided with the opening shots of the Vietnam War. At one end the RDA (Senegalese) MP Lamine Guèye was shaping a new law supposed to extend French citizenship to all colonized people (April 1946) while at the other end Vietnam had risen against its French masters (March 1946) and heavy artillery was used to bring the "natives" into line. We cite the Vietnam example because that conflict would grow to huge proportions and become a key element of the Cold War, given the Soviet involvement. But who was paying attention to the Madagascar uprising of 1947 or the growth of violence in Cameroun? Almost nobody. The problem was that France had been humiliated (and ruined) by Germany and was trying to compensate that loss through the exploitation of its Empire which it had promoted to a symbolic "Union" status. From the beginning France had been in an ambiguous situation concerning "its overseas". The parallel with the British Commonwealth, at times cited by political scientists, is inapplicable. The 1949 birth of the Commonwealth was seen, in typical British fashion, as a kind of gentlemen's club. Global complete control of the empire was not really envisioned. The only parallel with the radical French situation applied to the loss of India. India, the oldest British colony with Ireland, had been a metabolic constituent of the British (English) world view and its loss had been a painful blow to the British image, both towards the world and—perhaps worse—towards itself. The word "Raj", i.e. an administrative interiorization of a Hindi/Sanskrit word into the core of the British structure of government in India, would have been unthinkable for the French. For France *L'Empire* was an outward extension of something fundamentally, essentially French. It had to be defined by decrees emanating from Paris and to obey norms issued from the heart of the Gallic worldview. Colonial views in France could never be the native policies practised by the British, Somali in Somaliland, Hausa in Nigeria and Baganda in Uganda. The joke about the school programs which were defined by Paris alone and where Bamileke, Dioula or Malinke children had to learn about "*our ancestors the Gauls*" was that it was not (only) a joke, it was also a tragic reality. The dispute at the beginning of the *Union Française* between the "centralists" and the "federalists" was already decided, some kind of "federalism" could be deployed but it could only be a way of humoring the natives, not of heading towards some kind of actually applied self-government. The fact that today Paul Kagame can be the Chair-in-Office of the Commonwealth seems to the French like a bizarre perversion of the structure the Rwandese President is supposed to serve. The intertwining of interests, fears, self-glorification and money-making in the creation of the *Union Française* was a strange blend of *à propos* arrangements but it was in any case Franco-French.

If we want to understand how *Françafrique* is now dying, we have to go back to its beginning and appreciate how congenitally essential it was to the essence of France. This remark opens my rejoinder to the accusation of essentialism. This accusation—today an almost obscene word—is the product of historical ignorance. Essentialism applies in some cases even if its relevance is historically limited. But within these limits, it does not mean it does not exist. Let me explain. In Spain *la generacion del noventa y ocho* (the generation of 1898) was represented by the best intellectuals of the turn of the century (Miguel de Unamuno, Pio Baroja, Angel Ganivet, Ramon del Valle-Inclan). It was the last post of a slowly dying international world culture which had ended in agony when Simon Bolivar liberated Caracas in 1813. The loss of the colonies, confirmed through the US victory in the Spanish–American War of 1898, was the end of Spain as a world power. It took Spain almost a century to readapt to its new situation as a mid-size world power and Madrid finally only accepted its "essence" with the death of Franco in November 1975, the final hiccupping of dying imperial Spain being the failed *coup d'etat* of Colonel Antonio Tejero on February 23 1981. This example provides a warped parallel with the French situation.

The confusion within which the French Fourth Republic was born, soon to be shorn of its Provisional President when General De Gaulle resigned on January 20 1946,[10] prompted reflection about what the Empire/Union Française/colonies were and should become. "The colonies" were never a peripheral "addendum" but remained, for a wounded country, a central element where the very soul of the nation was at stake. The course of the nineteenth century had been for France a period of growing involvement in international affairs where its 1815 defeat was slowly resorbed. An interesting moment when the past almost came hurtling back to life was the tension almost leading to a major war at the time of the Fashoda Incident.[11] In Great Britain the two central (foreign) questions of the post-war years were how to tame the rebellion of the First Colony, Ireland, and how to deal with the annoying agitation of the Franco-German continentals who insisted on resuscitating a democratic version of the 1806 Continental Blockade to annoy Her Majesty's Government. They called it the *Communauté Européenne Charbon-Acier* (CECA) and when that did not seem irritating enough for HM's Government the rebellious continentals pushed through via the agency of the Belgian Paul-Henri Spaak[12] the creation of the Rome Treaty signed in 1957 which created the European Common Market! This (with the Cold War as a dignified icy underpinning) was the world vision of British public opinion. India had been lost in 1947 and the Franco-British occupation of the Suez Canal in November 1956 was a reminder that, no matter how crazy the French could be, walking in step with them could only cause the staunchly dignified United Kingdom to stumble into Gallic confusion and end up with the Soviets uttering nuclear threats. To sum up, when the French vacillated between Gaullist haughtiness, military restlessness and bloodshed and when French MPs tried desperately to cobble "something" together (what was it?) called *Union Française*, this was a desperate game by ungentlemanly persons with whom it would be better not to share anything of any substance. Meanwhile the French were still frantically jumping up and down in a tropical swamp called Indochina where the Americans, the Korean War notwithstanding, refused to put boots on the ground. They delivered ammunition, some GM trucks, a few C-47 "Dakota" transport planes and World War Two surplus Navy fighter planes, the "F6F Bearcats"; but no jets and definitely no nuclear weapons. Children should not be allowed to play with dangerous toys, Cold War or no Cold War. Meanwhile, back in Paris the hapless French MPs were desperately playing with the legal framework of what they feared was slowly turning into a catastrophe. The RDA, in the process of separating from the Communists by re-setting their *apparentement,* put the left wing of their party on fire. Houphouët-Boigny was a Black bourgeois but his main rival in the RDA was Gabriel d'Arbousier, the son of a West Indian White aristocrat whose family had possessed plantation slaves in La Martinique. Strangely enough the father of this rich *Beke* (Creole) had travelled to Senegal and married a Mossi princess who was a descendant of the Senegalese Sheikh El Haj Omar.[13] The son had become an ardent Marxist and led the left wing of the RDA. He fought tooth and nail against the split between RDA and *Parti Communiste Français* (PCF). Even more so when he realised what was going to be the alternative. Houphouët's choice for a new *apparentement* was the *Union Démocratique et Sociale Républicaine* (UDSR), an opportunist gaggle of politicians which was playing the field so as to occupy the right wing of left-wing cabinets and the left-wing of right-wing ones. The UDSR was a political chameleon with a right-wing leader (René Pléven) and a left-wing leader (François Mitterrand).[14] The result was the RDA's switch into a pro-establishment party which French political circles could begin shaping to occupy "post-independence" positions. The bowels of *Françafrique* could then begin to digest the African independence movements, albeit with one exception: Cameroun, which was the one African problem De Gaulle later admitted to be more difficult to handle than Algeria.

But he had a marginal advantage in the Camerounian crisis: this was a pure colony with no White Francophone population. A few well-aimed bullets and political murders could do the job. But why was Cameroun so much more difficult to handle than other territories of Black Africa? Because it was not a "genuine" French colony.

Kamerun, Cameroons or Cameroun?
Françafrique's Ur-modell *is born in hybrid ideological confusion*

Kamerun was a German colony of about 750,000 sq km. Postwar (1918) it had shrunk to 432,000 sq km, after being split into two colonial zones (a big French one and a small British one) "devoluted" (a nicely uncertain word) to the Mandate and Territories Commission of the League of Nations in Geneva. The French had a "Mandate" over Cameroun and so did the British who had half-forgotten their Cameroon one because they had a real job in neighboring Nigeria. Surprisingly, the best document to understand the strange quality of political life in the Mandate territories of this ancestor of the UN is not a report but a novel, the marvelous book by Albert Cohen[15] who used to be a League of Nations employee and experienced life in the front seats of absurdity. He wrote about it thirty years later when that particular absurdity had been succeeded in 1944 by another war and then another—but spiritually and financially more generous—absurdity called the United Nations Organisation. The book was considered—due to its avowed topic and to the excellence of its writing—to be a romantic novel, whereas it was also an undercover political pamphlet. The problem for the local African populations was that they were living *under that cover* and had no possibility of switching publishers. At a time when the gaggle of Fulbe Muslims, Kirdi Animists and Bassa Catholics called "*le Cameroun*" was trying to decide what it was, General De Gaulle had more pressing problems and, to limit to what Paris called "*the overseas*", it was the situation in Indochina which gave the leader of the Free French sleepless nights. There in March 1945 the Japanese decided that they could ensure the survival of their own imperialism by empowering the Vietnamese Communists and bequeathing to the French an almost unmanageable part of the *Union Française* puzzle called "Indochina". As a time-bomb (and a fuzzy ethnic concept) this worked perfectly and poisoned first South East Asia and then the rest of the world for the next quarter of a century.[16] Compared to this poison *Kamerun/Cameroons/Cameroun* was a minor irritant, except of course to its inhabitants and to their French masters. Especially as there was a channel of communication between Indochina and Africa and that was the French Army itself. A component of the slowly growing deep origins (hence my choice of the very pregnant and ambiguous term, the German *Ur-Modell*) of *Françafrique* was the nationalist revolutionary soldier.[17] These men would be the ones who, after another bloody defeat in Dien-Bien-Phu in 1954, would four years later bring De Gaulle back to power. For them, just as for their Nationalist German forebears (many of whom they had fought against during the Second World War) the key slogan was "never again". But for them it referred to the Dien-Bien-Phu defeat. After the fall of Indochina many of the officers were brought to the next colonial catastrophe in the making, Algeria, and also to the largely neglected external theater of operations, Kamerun. After De Gaulle's fallout with his former backers who tried to assassinate him, the French war concept walked away (officially) from colonialism.[18] The French soldiers, including the African ones, were not interested in nuclear dissuasion. It bore no relationship to their lived experience. Nor did they follow their white brethren into the bitter dissension (sometimes violent) that shook France between 1958 and 1963. But they stuck to the colonial mentality, some of them going all the way to the top positions of the slowly germinating *Françafrique*.[19] Cameroun was the laboratory where formal independence systems were set up and progressively tested so that an informal neo-imperialist one could be set up. The reason was basically that the League of Nations (and later UN) mandate system coupled with loose colonial connections allowed for a wider margin for the operation of an Army that its recent "revolutionary war" experiences had shaped into a politico-military organism of an entirely new nature. Cameroun was the locus where the new *Françafrique* creature began to spread its rhizomes, zigzagging between the last days of World War Two, the first days of the Indochina war, a temporarily disconnected Gaullism and—at the time—some fairly solid economic interests.[20]

Part of the oddity of the French presence in Cameroun was the aggressive militancy of a large segment of the colonists. Strangely enough, ordinary white-on-black racism melted into Germanophobia given the fact that *Kamerun* was a former German colony and that early proto-nationalist movements were immediately suspected of being manipulated by the Germans. In 1940–41 this was an easy way of justifying racism, even at the official level, such as when the Douala Prosecutor Luciardi declared publicly "as long as I will occupy this position, I will not allow a black man to be declared right and a white man wrong".[21] The local colonists created a militia called "*les colons combattants*" (the fighting colonists). Of course, the word "fighting" was there to characterize a group of Frenchmen standing up against Vichy. By 1945 they had ideologically recycled the very words that Vichy regime had used but justified doing so by claiming to be anti-German. The problem was that when genuine Gaullists arrived in Cameroun at the war's end, they had to deal with the *colons combattants* who attacked an African demonstration supporting De Gaulle, shouting slogans against Nazism, racism and colonialism. That last word was clearly one word too much! The *colons*, counter slogan was quite radical: "Let's kill the blacks to restore order".[22] The police and Army brought them under control before they could go too far. In practical terms the Cameroun anti-Nazis focused on huge scale tropical plantation agriculture, growing palm oil and cocoa, which were resources for France. To facilitate their export, the Gaullists put the natives back to work on the Douala–Yaounde railway, the construction of which had been started between 1904 and 1927 but later abandoned. In the early days the human toll among the laborers was massive: 61% of them died, a rate which reminds us[23] of the industrial scale massacre of Africans who built the Congo–Océan railway. Things were less bad post-1947, but strangely enough there seem to be no statistics on fatalities for the more recent period.

1947 saw the creation of the UPC (Union des Populations du Cameroun) which was at first simply a branch of the bigger Rassemblement Démocratique Africain (see above). The entire Western attitude towards its colonies was ambiguous: of course there were nice "nativist" organizations which worked in collaboration with the colonial authorities. But there was also the war in Indochina which was openly a Communist operation, militarily supported by the

Soviets. In 1950 another war exploded, the Korean one, now a joint endeavor between Moscow and Beijing, since the Chinese Communist guerillas had become the new government in power in China (1949). There was a choice between colonialism and communist-sponsored decolonization. NATO (and even the now-forgotten SEATO) had just been born. Containment—and now with Truman, roll back—was on the books. *Françafrique* was not yet born but all its components were in the toolbox, readily available. As the Algerian war broke out in 1954, in the wake of the Dien-Bien-Phu defeat, President Truman was consumed with resisting pressure from General MacArthur to use nuclear weapons in Korea. The Cold War had started in Berlin in 1948; it slowed down after a year but its resulting shadow now extended over the whole planet. In Cameroun the UPC led by Ruben Um Nyobe[24] had been created in 1947 and if we look at the *colons combattants* literature, his nickname was "The African Ho Chi Minh". In 1950 a weak post-war Europe had created the CECA and brought forth the political concept of Europe, a political non-starter hiding under an economic tarpaulin. But France had an ace up its sleeve: Eurafrique. The word had been created in the 1930s as the kind of fabrication France confusedly brandished to try scaring Hitler away.[25] After the birth of CECA, "Eurafrique" was recycled to try to push France ahead of its competitors in the group of post Second World War survivors,

Eurafrique being a trump card for the anti-communist side. Here is a good summary of the situation at that time:

> Eurafrique was a modish concept during France's 4th Republic, a forerunner of what was later called "Françafrique" during the 5th Republic. The only reality in Eurafrique was simply the unanimous will of French political leaders of all sides to keep, in somewhat "adapted" form, the ties between Africa and the now integrating "Europe" in order to keep away the wave of decolonisation that was shaking Asia. Behind this Eurafrique concept there was the hope of mobilising Africa in the strategic battles of the time, of reaffirming the ontological superiority of European civilisation and, first of all, to maintain the political and economic superiority of France over the African continent.[26]

"Kamerun" was the tiny pebble in the French colonial shoe. In those post-war years there were many more such pebbles at the UN level, and several were more preoccupying than the former German colony. But in New York, Africa, so long taken for granted and protected by the colonial carapace, still remained something of a question mark. And everybody knew the world was changing, but in directions that were difficult to gauge. In early 1955 Ruben Um Nyobe had been invited to New York as a tentative possible representative of Kamerun/Cameroons/Cameroun. The French were displeased but the UN delegation had been briefed by the "liberal" Cameroun Governor Robert Delavignette and Paris was perhaps discreetly interested in getting a picture of the Mandate Colony from an international viewpoint. The UN was somewhat lost but so was Paris and Ruben Um Nyobe was obviously intelligent and straightforward. The result was grim if potentially manageable. On the hard side, the Catholic Church had excommunicated the UPC members for being "communists". There was not a shred of evidence to back up this accusation but being anti-colonial was enough to be characterized as being an atheist (wasn't the White Man a God, or at least his local representative on planet earth?). Given both the dominance of the Catholic Church ("French") and the importance of Protestant denominations ("German"), the political struggle extended to religion. Excommunication was not a one-way street given the fact that the mandate economy was structurally divided between the co-mandated. Colonial propaganda was not even logical but it was exacerbating an already complicated situation where for the French— Germany having been eliminated by its 1945 defeat— the enemy had become the British, harking back to a kind of simplified Fashoda + Mers-el-Kebir syndrome.[27] Far from simplifying the situation, the 1956 Suez Crisis had harmed the relationship further and the anticolonial war went on at the religious level. Um Nyobe was a

Protestant, and the head of the Presbyterian Church in Douala forbade him from receiving the holy sacraments because "being faithful to Communism is incompatible with being faithful to Jesus Christ".[28] Similarly the one thing the French administrator of Bassa, a devout Catholic, declared fifty years after the fact, was that "as far as Um Nyobe was concerned the only thing I knew about him was that he had gone to university in the Soviet Union".[29] This could have been relevant had it been true, but it was completely wrong. These shifting political/social/religious rifts were abundant in Cameroun because its ambiguous legal status opened the door to positions that probably also existed elsewhere but could not be given free rein given the tight control of the Ministry of Colonies. What was to later become *Françafrique* was beginning to take shape in the interstices of a hurried and confused half-baked ideology. But even though economic interests were present, they were not the driving force. It is interesting to note that in the intellectual atmosphere of the time (and in the agitated political climate of France's post-war years) even the conservative right was unwillingly influenced by a communist-tinged form of reasoning. So many views—both supportive or critical—were shaped by the global "soft Marxist" reasoning that economic factors were essential. With the communist-led war in Indochina as a background this could be understood. But the problem was that this "Red obsession" was involuntary. Regarding Ruben Um Nyobe as a "Cameroonian Ho Chi Minh" was unhelpful because it hid the man's reality which was perhaps primarily Protestant and bureaucratic, i.e. sensitive to a kind of balanced inflexibility which belonged more to the world of Max Weber than to a Leninist position. The Bassa dimension was also forgotten and it is an interesting trait of this "*France-à-Fric*" (cash-pumping France) then in the making that it denied its roots in economic imperialism and latched on to a global theatre of "culture" where the only culture that mattered was French.

The only French Africanist obsessed by African tribes is Bernard Lugan, and he is considered by most of his French colleagues as an oddball. There are few good French Africanists who include "tribalism" (a dirty word nowadays) into a realistic political perspective.[30] This was to be later the (dangerous) trump card of the actors of *Françafrique* whose best high wire artist was Robert Bourgi. My late friend the novelist Denis Tillinac was a more modest and more frankly Gaullist practitioner of the same fine art of influence. Robert Bourgi was decorated with the *Légion d'Honneur* by President Sarkozy in 2007 but President Macron "deprived him of the right to bear the Légion d'Honneur insignias" on 18 March 2019 "for a duration of five years". Such convoluted twist-and-turns of statist dignity are typical both of French culture, and even more, of their application to such a complex and shadowy domain as *Françafrique* where ambiguity is trying to cheat *sous-entendre*. Why were men like Robert Bourgi or Denis Tillinac useful to the concept of *Françafrique?* Because—for better or for worse, depending on the nature of their friendships—they knew that African societies were tribal. We won't go here into tribalism and its varieties of regional declensions.[31] But a ministerial office is not very good at dealing with tribes, which would later, when it was it was fully deployed, make of *Françafrique* a "special interests" hive of tribalized Frenchmen.

But if we return to the word/concept of archeology, the key moment was the time when François Mitterrand had recuperated Félix Houphouët-Boigny and his RDA in the dark undergrowth of *4ème Republique* politics. Cameroun, ever the political laboratory of trying to get the natives to support their "half-colonial" French government, gave birth to a new political acrobat,[32] Alex Manga Bell, to whom Paris gave the job of getting the UPC—still the Camerounian branch of the RDA—to cross over and support the RDA conversion from Communist *apparenté* to UDSR fellow-traveler. Manga Bell was a Douala from a prominent family and his father had been hanged by the Germans in 1914 for having resisted their land-grabbing. The French Socialists (SFIO) got him elected and brought him to Paris.[33] Bad luck. The man—intelligent as he was—was also a political dilettante and instead of reinforcing RDA/

UDSR he chose to throw in his lot with the Christian Democratic MRP. The submarine had surfaced in the wrong place and the struggle to bring UPC under control still had a long way to go. The French Governor Roland Pré had to admit: "The means we use at present to fight the UPC are incapable of succeeding". Just as in Algeria at the same moment, the era of the nationalist military of the Colonel Lacheroy model was coming. In 1955 the UPC was outlawed. The shock wave in Cameroun was huge and in May there were massive UPC-led demonstrations. The Nationalist section of the French Army, with its bleeding back to Indochina and its bleeding front in the Algerian Djebels, reacted according to how it perceived the situation: 79 civilians were killed "officially", with twice the number having died in the bush where they had fled. Outlawing UPC boomeranged among the intellectuals and it took control of the Camerounian student community in France.

The British situation in evolution in the Gold Coast since 1951 and later the electoral victory of the *Comité de l'Unité Togolaise* (CUT) in February 1958—Togo was also a former German colony under SDN and later UN Mandate—kept the Camerounian population focused on the UPC whose program, contrary to French colonial propaganda, was in fact open to collaboration with the Mandate powers.

In December 1956, a number of UPC dissidents, fed up with French manipulation, held a conference in the

Camerounian British mandate part of the territory. Their meeting prompted them to launch an armed insurrection under the leadership of the so-called *Comité National d'Organisation* (CNO) against the French presence. Rather hurriedly they decided to start fighting on December 18. After a few days of delay the insurrection began. The military means were pathetically insufficient: some stolen German Second World War sub-machine guns, some hunting rifles and some machetes. The starting point was the town of Ekite in Sanaga Maritime district, in Bassa country, not far from Ruben Um Nyobe's birthplace.[34] The Army counterattacked and let itself loose. The administration admitted to "tens of victims" but the most prudent researchers reached a very different conclusion.[35] The post December repression was massive, carried out by elements of the French military who had served in Algeria (and in some cases Vietnam). The *ratissage* (raking) of Sanaga Maritime by the French troops was a bloody affair. But what made it worse is that the colonial authorities panicked given the fact that the CNO had been created in the British zone and that it had a non-negligible English-speaking component, some of it from Nigeria. So the French embarked on widespread arrests of Bamileke chiefs in the English Zone in spite of the fact that there was no serious UPC presence there. These arrests galvanized the spread of UPC elements in the West and led to the creation in October 1957 of the

Sinistre de la Défense Nationale du Kamerun (SDNK).[36] SDNK started a not negligible guerilla war in the Bamileke region, creating a second front away from Sanaga Maritime. The SDNK fighters managed to buy guns from Nigeria and as a result killed enough French Army soldiers to start taking weapons from enemy corpses. The West was ablaze, especially after French commandos attacked the UPC headquarters (3–4 April 1957) in Bamenda, in the British zone, and burnt it down before the British Army could intervene. By mid-1957 the Cameroun uprising had developed into the only organized guerilla war ever to take place in Francophone Africa and the practise of torture, already a notorious phenomenon in Algeria where it had led to a national scandal in Metropolitan France, was deployed. The "revolutionary war" theories of Colonel Lacheroy began to spread under the aegis of Nationalist officers who felt they were involved in a new theater of operations in a world-wide conflict against Communism. There was extreme tension in Algeria where the French population had created self-defense commandos and where part of the regular army was plotting an anti-government putsch. In December 1957 the Mandate Authorities created a special *Zone de Pacification* (ZOPAC) where the army had a free fire zone. The Africans suffered massive casualties, the details of which are still held in restricted French Army files. The manhunt for Ruben Um Nyobe was on and he was shot dead by an Army commando on September 16 1958. But in the meantime, the long expected Army putsch had taken place in Algiers on May 13, overthrowing the government and bringing General De Gaulle from internal exile. For the General the boiling pot on the fire that demanded his immediate attention was Algeria which had brought France to the edge of civil war. What happened in Cameroun, important as it may have seemed to the local authorities, was far behind in the list of priorities. The star reporter Max-Olivier Lacamp, from *Le Figaro*, reproached the Colonial Judiciary for ... being too lenient! De Gaulle was in Paris, hovering on a slice of power which had been cut on the raw in contradictory circumstances,[37] and he had other matters to focus on that were merely a sideshow to the main event, namely the coup d'état that was tossing the Republican regime born at the end of the Second World War Two into the wastepaper basket of history.

An "African" coup intrudes on a deeply disturbed colonial Metropole

We were in Europe, caught on the hook of a colonial conundrum which had ramifications reaching out to various parts of the empire, one of which was Cameroun. But these convulsions of the French political soul harked back to the interwar years, when the system that later tried to piggyback on the Wehrmacht had established itself in order to benefit from a possible defeat. The defeat had come, De Gaulle had risen as a response to its impact and in May 1958 France suddenly found itself trying to understand whether this moment was a remake of 1940 or something new. In 1940 the right wing French political leader Charles Maurras had hailed the unexpected rise of Marshal Pétain to the head of the French government as "a divine surprise". In 1958 the equally unexpected rise of General De Gaulle to a similar position was both a soft replay of 1940 and a radically different type of political surprise. There were two points in common: both were unconstitutional and both of these unconstitutional changes were desperate efforts to staunch a bleeding wound in French society at large. But what gave it a different significance for French society the second time around was the link between the problem and the metropolitan center: in 1940 the French state had been vanquished in battle by a victorious enemy which was seriously considering abolishing France as a country or—more probably—reducing it to a kind of colonial status on the model of what it had just done in Poland. De Gaulle's refusal to accept the French military defeat was a social and cultural response which at the time had no national military basis to underpin it. It was an existential defiance of military reason, an act of faith. The situation in 1958 was quite different. De Gaulle had an Army, albeit a divided one. The difficulty for the French "strongman" was that he was, contrary to June 18 1940, not facing a national catastrophe but trying to repair an illegitimate political entity. The only element in common was that "the overseas" was again at the heart of the problem. Contrary to June 1940 he had no legal competitor; it was the nature of what could be called "legitimate" that was now in question.

There was a considerable degree of agitation between Paris and Algiers during the late part of May 1958, trying to plug the legitimacy gap. In June 1940 De Gaulle had had to challenge the legitimate seat already taken by Pétain. But in May 1958 while he enjoyed the type of legitimacy Pétain had in 1940—military, heroic, historical—he lacked any formal shaping of his situation. It was the onset of a process of trying to extend his historical legitimacy such that it bolstered his constitutional legitimacy. De Gaulle was not a putschist himself but he was the beneficiary of a putsch engineered by other military men.

The President of the Fourth Republic was now being asked by Gaullist militants and, behind them by the Army in Algiers, to take the reins of power in what would be an unconstitutional process—De Gaulle had not won an election—and become the Prime Minister of that very same 4th Republic he had walked away from in 1946.[38]

Given the profusion of plots, subplots and counterplots that surrounded him in that month of May 1958[39] he needed a hidden dagger, not to swing things in military or political terms, but in deep practical ways. He had one, a near complete unknown at the time: Jacques Foccart. Foccart was depicted as a loyal Gaullist. This was true but one could say that this was an acquired taste. He was an "overseas" Frenchman even though he had been born in metropolitan France. His father had been an important banana planter in Guadeloupe, in the French West Indies and his mother was a Beke (Creole) from a very rich planter's family. During the war he had worked with the Germans not for ideological reasons but to make money. He sold them charcoal to be used for the gazogène system,[40] used for civilian vehicles. Gazogène distribution was the job of the Todt Organization, a German government body in charge of logistics for the Wehrmacht which was then building the Atlantic Wall. Foccart was arrested by the Germans on suspicion of cheating them and had been freed on bail. One witness to Foccart's charcoal business had later been murdered in suspicious circumstances but the police closed the file for lack of evidence. In 1942, probably feeling the wind of defeat for the Germans after Stalingrad, Foccart joined the Resistance.[41] In 1944 he "saved" two USAF crew members who had parachuted to safety when their plane had been shot down and used them as a go-between to approach the advancing US forces. As soon as Paris had been liberated he joined the temporary government's secret service and forged links with historical Gaullists. He soon developed a specialty of overseas operations in the West Indies through old family links and used these to arrange for the reimbursement of the bail paid to the Germans in 1942. The bail legal process had been handled by the Vichy administration and Foccart got the provisional Gaullist authorities to reimburse the money in December 1945.[42] This freed him legally to create a company which specialized in imports of tropical agricultural products from the French West Indies. After the war he became a member of UDSR, Mitterrand's hinge political party, a post he combined with being co-opted as a member of the Gaullist group of the Union Française Assembly. In 1953 he had accompanied De Gaulle on a tour of French West Africa where he met Félix Houphouët-Boigny, later to become the key leader of the RDA. After this trip, Foccart developed his new field of endeavor and became a fixer and propagandist for the Gaullist movement in French Africa. In May 1958 he acted as a key linchpin of the so-called *Opération Résurrection* where politics were blended with business to support De Gaulle's legal return to power.

The legality gap was plugged when *Président de la République* René Coty addressed the country on May 29 1958 to declare that he had asked "the most famous of all Frenchmen, General Charles De Gaulle", to form a new government within the framework of the existing constitution. As soon as De Gaulle was back in transitional power, he appointed Foccart as his technical advisor for African Affairs. On June 1 De Gaulle presented his cabinet to the Parliament where it was immediately endorsed, with the unspoken backing of the putschist Army in Algiers. In the event of a military clash De Gaulle had the support of an Army which was ambiguously behind him, above the heads of the civilian population. What the Army wanted was to win the war; what the civilian population wanted was to end the war. The two objectives would not obviously synchronize. On September 28 1958, as part of the complete legalization of the Army putsch, Prime Minister De Gaulle put the draft of a new constitution to a referendum. The results were symptomatic of the situation: in Metropolitan France about seventeen million voted yes and about 4 million voted no. In the overseas territories about fourteen million voted yes and 2.5 million voted no.[43] The referendum was a large victory for De Gaulle who was soon elected to the Presidency on October 28 1958 with 78.5% of the vote, in polls held in Metropolitan France—which at the time included Algeria.

But by then it was obvious that "the overseas" mattered enormously, and represented almost 50% of his victorious vote. By January 1959 De Gaulle was the President of France and he made Foccart Presidential Secretary for African Affairs. In fact Foccart was a kind of Secret Service second head (with the unofficial but real advantage of being in a permanent position). He talked with the President once a week, whatever happened (or did not happen) in the purview of his work. Another advantage was that the Secretariat for African Affairs was an independent unit, depending directly upon the Presidency of the Republic rather than being part of any ministry. It was unique in being devoted purely to Africa (and Madagascar which was considered as "African", creating a cultural and political special case which practically escaped the authority of the Ministry of Foreign Affairs). In fact it could have been "the Secretariat of Francophone Africa", a point to which we will return in Chapter 3 when we assess the Rwandese crisis. Since the presidency of Giscard d'Estaing Rwanda had been included as a part of the French zone of interest/influence even though it had been a German colony, later a SDN and UN mandated territory and never a French colony.

But while these portentous events happened in the French Metropole, the Cameroun war went on unaffected.[44] After Ruben Um Nyobe had been shot in combat his corpse had been put in a cement slab which had been buried at an unmarked spot in the bush. The RDA section in Cameroun (which had survived in spite of UPC) had declared that "independence means happiness" and Governor Jean Ramadier had concluded that "we need to make an independence which is not really one". After the French had granted the territory a form of internal autonomy to please the UN, Governor

Ramadier had manipulated things so that Ahmadou Ahidjo, a former clerk, had become a key figure in the autonomous cabinet.[45] But this concerned only the area where the French Army exerted control in the territory. On July 10 1959 five SDNK members had been shot in public in Bafoussam in the British Mandate Zone. The French government had started to create militias on the model of the *Harka* it had organized in Algeria and in Paris Foccart had started a bitter struggle against Constantin Melnik[46] with whom he fought to be the "man in charge" of unofficial matters. Melnik was a member of Prime Minister Michel Debré's Prime Ministerial cabinet where he coordinated his activities with two rival secret services, the DST and the SDECE. As De Gaulle increasingly became a target for the radical Nationalist officers, Melnik's "gloves off" struggle to negotiate with the radical officers put him in direct competition with Foccart. In Cameroun independence was planned for January 1 1960. On December 30 1959 SDNK rebels occupied Yaounde airport which the French Army had to bring back under its control through a serious armed clash, leading to a death toll of around forty people. In February 1960 the constitutional referendum was largely approved but with a split mandate. In the Muslim North the French Army was more entrenched and managed to impose a "yes" vote through rigging while in the South, where the clandestine UPC had more influence, the "no" vote prevailed.[47] Constantin Melnik had one up on this one but he was linked to Debré. With the end of the Algerian War in March 1962, De Gaulle, who did not consider gratitude to be a political virtue, asked Debré to resign (April 1962). Melnik had to leave with him but Foccart stayed on. The bloodstained businessman had replaced the ideologue. *Françafrique* was born.

2

ROUGH AND READY

THE *FRANÇAFRIQUE* HEYDAYS (1960–81)

Colonialism and the French political tradition

Algeria, the main problem from the French point of view, emptied itself of about one million non-Arab people[1]—the so-called *pieds noirs* or "Blackfeet"—between 1962 and 1965. But for *l'Afrique Noire* the situation was much more complex, in spite of the fact that, apart from Cameroun, there was no more fighting anywhere. Cameroun, a UN Mandate and not a French colony, was a special case. But the "real" French colonies of *l'Afrique Noire* were quite another case. The September 28 1958 referendum had set up the principle of self-determination for these territories but what that term actually meant had no reality for the French. Familiar with brutally losing territory either colonial (Canada and India taken by Great Britain at the end of the Seven Years War) or national (Alsace and Lorraine annexed by the German Second

Reich in 1871), France had never known the slow and legally complex processes that had led Canada and Australia to become Dominions, or the neat sword cut that overnight had turned the British Raj into two distinct completely independent countries, India and Pakistan,[2] which could then remain members of the Commonwealth. From the McKenzie-Papineau rebellion of 1837 to the accession of Canada to Dominion status took a mere thirty years. The case of Australia was even slower: between its establishment in 1788 to its accession to Dominion status took 112 years. But the 1958 upheaval during the French Republic which, the Second World War notwithstanding, had tried to restore its prewar political culture, had proved a failure. And given the organic relationship France had developed with its colonies, that failure extended to the colonies. The general situation was also a product of French culture which seems to have a taste for periodical face offs between revolutionary rupture and bare-fanged conservatism. The British slow-motion sliding from conserving the outward tropes of the past, such as the monarchy, to small increments allowing for change, does not seem a natural part of French culture. *Vide* the fact that in the 1930s the strength of the Trade Union Congress never led to a strong Communist movement in the UK while the British appetite for Oswald Mosley's fascist political philosophy seemed to have remained quite limited. Such prudent attitudes seem foreign to French culture.

The Nazi occupation caused strong political local reactions all over Europe but perhaps nowhere so strongly as in France. In spite of the frantically brandished concept of *Libération*, 1945 was not a turning point leading away from the pre-war Third Republic but rather a continuation of that regime which had violently oscillated from the Social-Communist 1936 Popular Front to the Nazi-compatible "*Etat Français*" four years later. It was this frightening continuity which had driven De Gaulle to his irritated 1946 resignation. What followed seemed to justify his *mouvement d'humeur* [3] and his return had the looks of a desperate dash to save the country from the threat of civil war. De Gaulle, the very symbol of anti-Nazism, was brought out of storage, paraded on the political stage and asked to fix things up. But by then in 1958 De Gaulle himself complained about "the rush towards independence". It was of course a product of *Zeitgeist*, the 1945 "spirit of the times" and it made the process of a slow-motion British-type move from Empire to Commonwealth hard to conceive. In 1837 in Canada, it had been a post on a distant horizon. In 1919 in Amritsar it had become a pressing difficulty. And by 1947 it had become a complete impossibility to avoid, even for Great Britain. But for France, a country where such a process had never been known, the very concept was an oddity. The French had two main relations to political reality: conservatism or revolution. De Gaulle's return was a desperate grab for a lifejacket but, contrary to what had briefly surfaced in 1945, there was no revolution in sight in 1958 (and in the French Empire, where, apart from Cameroun, there was no such prospect anywhere). It meant that the only alternative would be legislation from the center and a revamped conservatism, which is exactly what De Gaulle had had in mind as an alternative since 1945. French centralism dates back to King Philippe Auguste (in the twelfth century), the very period when the British nobility had imposed the *Magna Carta* on their own king and created a Parliament. In France, White French decentralists ended up on the *guillotine* in 1792 and there seemed no reason to appease their political family in order to offer the same type of freedom on a silver platter to Black colonized subjects. This led to a situation where Houphouët-Boigny, a British type progressive conservative, complained: "I was left waiting at the door with my bouquet of wilted flowers". He had invented the slogan of *Françafrique* as a motto for a slow transition from colonialism to interdependence but the name turned under his eyes from a friendly bouquet of flowers into the hissing head of a Gorgon.

Independences, counterinsurgency, assassinations and supporting friendly regimes

In January 1959, the Mali Federation was given autonomy[4] and in January 1960 Cameroun was given a

UN-satisfying independence while behind it another Mandated former German colony, Togo, managed to slip by in April. 1960 was the year of independence: Mali Federation and Madagascar (June), Niger, Upper Volta (later Benin), the Ivory Coast, Chad, Central African Republic (former Ubangui-Chari), the Congo Republic (Brazzaville) and Gabon (all in August), Sudan (September) and Mauritania (November). Two small territories would wait another fifteen years: the Comoros in July 1975 (minus Mayotte, kept as a "French" piece for reasons of metropolitan politics) and Djibouti (June 1977) which De Gaulle, conscious of its considerable strategic importance, had never wanted to abandon.

As for the other islands, The Antilles (West Indies) Polynesia, French Guiana and last but not least New Caledonia, the other confetti of the Empire which had missed the 1960 Decolonization Express entered a complex twilight.

But the Cameroun war took a long time dying down. No official statistics exist for the deaths in Bamileke country till late 1961 when the violence began to subside. The estimate of the Ahidjo regime, hurriedly put in power by the French shortly after independence, vary between 12,000 and 120,000 fatalities, mixing ANLK, the surviving military arm of UPC, and the civilian population.[5] In the traumatized French colonial consciousness, UPC and its "Marxist revolutionary" image remained the main enemy. Since the death of Ruben Um Nyobe, the main leader of UPC had been Félix Moumié. In 1960, having taken refuge in Conakry Guinea, he contacted Chinese agents and arranged for arms purchases to strengthen the guerrilla fighters. This is when the French Prime Minister Michel Debré, a fanatic anti-UPC activist, decided to eliminate him. As he wrote in his memoirs:[6] "Ahidjo asked me to keep the French administrators in place after independence. I agreed. But this first decision was insufficient. I decided to undertake a real and complete reconquest." He threw himself into the task and, as a part of this grand operation, he ordered Jacques Foccart to eliminate Félix Moumié. The intended killer was a Dutch national who worked as a part-time agent for the French Secret Service, the SDECE. Moumié was careless with his security and became friendly with the future hit man with whom he had lunch in Geneva where he was supposed to meet his Chinese contacts. The hired killer poisoned him during lunch and Moumié succumbed to an agonizing death on November 3 1960 in a Geneva hospital. The autopsy revealed that he had absorbed a high dose of Thallium.[7]

This assassination was supposed to protect friendly regimes. But if friendly regimes did not exist they could be created. In Togo President Sylvanus Olympio, a nationalist hostile to the French, was attacked in his palace by an armed commando unit led by former

French Army Sargeant Gnassingbe Eyadema during the nights of January 12 and 13 1963. The President took refuge next door in the American Embassy and the commandoes returned the next morning and finished him off, without any interference from the US Marines. This was a coup organized by pro-French Nicolas Grunitzky who had run against Olympio for the presidency and who took power as soon as Olympio was dead. But four years later Eyadema overthrew "his President" and set up an even more aggressively pro-French dictatorship which lasted thirty-seven years, marred by constant human rights violations. Rigged elections were held five times during these thirty-seven years and opponents were routinely massacred and their bodies thrown in the Atlantic Ocean by the hundreds. Other human rights violations were a matter of routine. Eyadema died in 2005 of natural causes[8] and his son Faure Gnassingbe immediately took over from his dead father in a constitutional vacuum. At the time of writing he is still "President" of Togo and has just introduced (April 2024) a constitution abolishing presidential elections. From now on the president will be chosen by the Parliament which, given its complete subordination to Faure Gnassingbe, is unlikely to choose anybody else. While cracks can be observed elsewhere Togo remains safe within the system. This has been the political pattern set up by this diffuse network of former soldiers, businessmen, secret agents, diplomats, French civil servants, journalists and even scholars (a few) who made up *Françafrique*. Eyadema, a thug, was a limit case.[9] But the Bongo dynasty in Gabon—fifty-six years in power in total—Paul Biya in Cameroun (forty-one years in the presidency) or Ismail Omar Guelleh in tiny Jibuti (twenty-four years in the presidency), had similar reigns. There were no rules—only habits—and unspoken manners. The vote-rigging was bilateral, with French citizens overseas filling voting proxies that could be used in any constituency where the Gaullist party felt it needed a bit of extra support.

What did that all mean?

Le Grand Charles[10] *as a political stylist*

Charles De Gaulle (1890–1970) rigged the *Françafrique* machinery as an instrument of power and in agreement with what he felt to be the spirit of the times. He had been born in 1890, had fought in the First World War and later in Poland with the anti-Bolshevik French expeditionary force. The social philosopher of his time was Herbert Spencer (1820–1903) whose summary Social Darwinism was perceived as the *nec plus ultra* of contemporary thought. As was often the case for De Gaulle, as for many others before and since, he thought along the parameters of what was at his time broadly popular even if it had meanwhile become already obsolete. Notwithstanding his monarchist sympathies,[11] his realism prevented him from being a monarchist. His class origins precluded his being a socialist. But he knew enough to perceive his world as being in transition from a creaking post-socially hierarchical system to an unknown future that was still definitely national but where private capitalism had to be kept under national control. Politically he was ideologically non-ideological and personally an egoless egotist. He was mystically married to France the way the Holy Virgin was married to the Holy Spirit. He had great personal courage but very little private respect for human beings who did not belong to a certain intellectual class, such as one of his rare personal friends, the writer André Malraux. In 1968, when the police wanted to arrest Jean-Paul Sartre (whom he rightly considered to be a political enemy) he had refused and said: "It would be silly to arrest Voltaire".

So why Françafrique?

First of all let us eliminate racism as a political motive. De Gaulle was far too clever to consider biological factors as being the main cause of a person's intelligence, what was discussed in the preceding chapter considering Félix Eboué being proof enough. He had no scruples about promoting a talented Black person over a less capable White one. And here let us deal once and for all with a propaganda canard: Eboué was never "bought" and De Gaulle was not interested in buying anybody (except of course if there were precise political reasons to do so, which was not the case with Eboué). There were other people at hand for this kind of practical maintenance—hence the use of Jacques Foccart—and De Gaulle was typically uninterested in these tasks himself. He was not immoral; he was amoral and considered politics as a job neither for idealists nor for criminals, although he was ready to use both types if there was a good (i.e. an efficient) reason to do so. This did not mean of course that he had to become friends with such housecleaners. The General's pragmatism was total and the ethnic group that collectively paid the highest price for this were the *Pieds Noirs,* the White Settlers of Algeria who had believed in May 1958 that the coup they had sponsored and supported had brought them a durable North African abode. Four years later they had to pack and flee to France which many of them hardly knew. De Gaulle had cold-bloodedly betrayed them in the interest of his eternal mistress, France.

So was there an overriding reason to favor the creation of a kind of African wolfpack to serve the interests of France? First of all it had to be a wolfpack and not an identifiable specific element of the state apparatus. This allowed for deniability and employing the services of beyond-the-pale characters such as "Bob" Denard.[12] Second, it enabled the financing of irregular forces through budgetary lines that were linked to the Secret Services and hence fell outside the official budget, subject to Parliamentary scrutiny. Third, the objective of the entire venture was distilled in the words of Minister of Foreign Affairs Louis de Guiringaud: "Africa is still within our reach: it is the only place in the world where, with perhaps five hundred men, France could change the course of global history".

De Guiringaud was a realist and so was the General-President. De Guiringaud belonged to an old noble family that had served the French political state in various capacities for the last two hundred years. He knew where France was at and what it could and could not do. And he knew what he, as a French Minister of Foreign Affairs, could possibly achieve or not achieve. He shot himself in cold blood on April 15 1982, abandoning *Françafrique* to its fate somewhat too early.

De Gaulle was immune to such depression but he could see things with realism. Yes, Africa was probably the only place where France could remain in a game-changing position with limited means. And the General believed (and said) that there had been "a timeless pact between our country and the progress of humanity". He meant to put his game-changing capacity where it could make a bigger impact as a symbol of France's influence, showing it was still an earth-shaking power capable of moving things in the right direction.[13] The General's official display of pragmatism harked back to the Brazzaville Conference in 1944 where he used the Africans by never promising them what they thought he was there to give them: independence. This was precisely the opposite of what later took place in Algiers in 1958 where the opposite (protection) was supposed to be on offer and was also betrayed. The times had changed but *la Patrie* ("the homeland", with its feminine life-giving connotation in the French language) and its interests remained the rallying cry. In 1944 the preservation of the Empire had been a key element in the resuscitation of France whose Empire had been a compensation after the disaster of the 1815 Congress of Vienna. But in 1962 becoming a Great Power meant having to shed a collection of out-of-fashion political clothing but—and this was an important but— having created a wardrobe full of dead imperial rags and stitched them into an eleven-piece quilt—eleven being the number of post-colonial Francophone states—that impressed the UN General Assembly. But for the system to work, it would be necessary that the same ground could become an executioner's field in case of need. Of course dead bodies should not be too numerous after "independence" had been achieved. There was a certain standing to keep in the main reception and dining room (New York), never mind what happened in the kitchen. Now the *common ground* was a way-of-life that went from three hundred types of cheese to the same variety of wines, and from beautiful women to lovely landscapes. De Gaulle was ready to share all of this with an African hand-picked elite.

Amusingly enough, De Gaulle ("from the Gaul") whose very name seemed like an embodiment of the oldest incarnation of what France had been, was probably a non-French name of Flemish origin, Van der Waal, meaning "of the ramparts". France definitely used him in that particular capacity but he had enough *panache* to walk away from power when his role as a rampart was no longer helping take France to where he wanted it to go.

Smooth sailing over rough waters

Gabon: the jewel atop the crown

The *Françafrique* ship was built between 1958 and 1960. But it was only after Algerian independence in July 1962 that it set off on its Paris-chartered course. Its launching fanfare took place on February 17 1964 when a *coup d'état* in Gabon organized by the popular political leader Jean-Hilaire Aubame, who accused President Léon M'Ba of vote rigging, was put down by the French army to reset M'Ba back in power.[14] There was no pretense of "reestablishing democracy", just a declaration about "keeping order". This created a delicate situation because Léon M'Ba had terminal cancer and the problem was how to keep Gabon—a gem of "Franco-African cooperation" with a minuscule population and huge natural resources—on the "right side of the Force". The obstacle was circumvented by the creation of a Vice-Presidency, with a Vice-President who would automatically assume the presidency in case of the death or resignation of the President. A nice post office clerk who had been noticed by the French ambassador to be "a good boy", Albert-Bernard Bongo, was promoted to this new Vice-Presidency. President M'Ba was reelected in March 1967 and died obligingly of cancer the following November. Albert-Bernard Bongo immediately became president without a hitch. And from then on, he remained the president of this model of a neo-colony with almost no people, no communists and huge natural resources (timber, gas, uranium, petrol) without any visible difficulty. Of course as in the best of families there can always be problems, but the French were always there to fix them.[15] In 1968 Albert-Bernard wanted an audience with the Pope, for political reasons, in order to cement the Catholics behind him. He could not find his certificate of baptism so he had himself re-baptized in a splendid public ceremony and Paris arranged for him a private audience with the Pope. Fine. But the Pope had no oil and in 1973 came the oil crisis. So Albert-Bernard converted to Islam forthwith and became "Omar Bongo". This allowed him to be well received at OPEC and hence to negotiate with the mostly Muslim OPEC countries on even terms. Outside of its oil dimension, he never bothered too much with his new religious status even if he preferred to drink water at state dinners. But politics predominated. In 1970 two French mercenaries had killed his opponent Germain M'Ba, a member of the late president's family. There was a superficial inquiry, the killers were jailed for a while and later disappeared. In 1977 another opponent, Ndouna Dependaud was shot too. The following inquiry proved beyond any reasonable doubt that the killers had had nothing to do with the president.

In this pearl of the single party system, Bongo had Soviet-style election victories, with over 99% at each poll, in 1973, in 1979 and in 1986. But paradise can go too far and after another opponent was "mysteriously" killed in 1993, this resulted in a student revolt and an end of the single party system. Multi-party elections were held, with French support. It was a hard slog at first—even if Bongo stood as a single candidate he won with only 51% of the vote in 1993. Abstentions and spoiled votes occurred on a massive scale. Later he slowly climbed back through better and better rigged polls and his "victories" regularly improved: 66% in 1998 and 79% in 2005. Not being immortal he had to die, which he did in 2009 in Barcelona.[16] A host of French dignitaries attended his burial and the game among the journalists who had come to Gabon was to put a price tag on the head of every powerful Frenchman present. Bongo was rich, quite generous and *Françafrique* was a two-way street. Omar's oldest son Ali ascended to power immediately upon his father's death, in kingly fashion. Gabon had been treated as the private property of the Bongo family since 1967 and when Ali was recently overthrown by a putsch a quick assessment of the family fortune reached £12.8 million, including a luxury car collection (parked in France) and €800m of foreign real estate properties, mostly in Paris's smarter districts, along with with several villas on the Riviera. The per capita income of the country was $6,577 with a population of 2.3m people. This is a deceptive figure because of the usual negative plastic surgery of statistics in rich poor countries: statistics are an average because those few who earn several million dollars a year are "averaged" with those many who earn less than $4 a day. The Gabonese "earn" 8% of "their" oil, foreign oil companies "earn" 92% (but they have high production costs and many things to worry about). The Gabonese are poor Africans living in a small natural resources paradise and this made it the core of *Françafrique* and its (half empty) cashbox.[17] As a starting point for operating *Françafrique* Gabon had been a piece of cake with no Communists in the game[18] and France's neo-colony enjoyed a soft-landing.

Making war in various places:

Françafrique was, first and foremost, a combat unit. And combat was also an economic factor. *Françafrique* inherited a colonial mentality, but also realized that there were Africans who could be part of the show. It took its first steps during the Cameroun counter-insurgency, in a French quasi-colony then stirring when the Algerian war model (itself a phantasmatic sequel to the Indochina conflict) counted as "a classic". But this was not an autonomous development.

The first time *Françafrique* operated on its own was in Biafra. When Colonel Ojukwu had proclaimed the independence of the Republic of Biafra in May 1967, it was in the wake of a very complex situation that had been unfolding for over a year. The Igbo, who were at the core of the new secessionist state, had been buffeted between Fulani, Hausa and Tiv politicians and soldiers, carrying out coups and counter coups, till Ojukwu proclaimed a secession trying to get out and away from the unbearable situation that had developed in Nigeria at large. The main tribes making up the Army were northern Muslims. But in those "close to colonization" early days everybody was trying to do what *Françafrique* was trying to achieve but in a more traditional manner. Foreigners in Nigeria regarded Biafra with an international geopolitical outlook which sold the African side short.[19] This is how on the French pro-Biafran side mercenaries, humanitarians and the oil giant Elf Aquitaine ended up rubbing shoulders with Jacques Foccart delivering guns while Bernard Kouchner was getting the on the ground experience that would lead to the creation of MSF two years later. On the opposing side there were Russian Ilyushin Il-28 bombers flown by Egyptian pilots and British shells provided for the Federal Army's artillery, a bizarre genocidal cohabitation. The common points were simple: on the Federal side, for the British it was let's try to support this future giant of Africa and help maintain British postcolonial influence over it, while for the Soviets it was let's try to get these people to come over to some kind of Angolan pro-communist line. On the French side, it was let's fight communism in Africa and bugger the British who by a mixture of paradoxical geopolitics and chance happened to find themselves on the same side.[20]

On the *Françafrique* side the humanists eventually wound up realizing that they were involuntarily working for Elf Aquitaine, trying to slip under the barbed wire and help the oil giant drink a bit of British oil. *Françafrique* was not responsible for the war but it helped prolong it. Its interventions were always off the record, done through mercenaries and never involving any official military forces. It was also a rare case of French intervention in a former British colonial zone.

Biafra had been an exotic excursion outside the comfort zone of the usual "among us" *Françafrique* operations. Too big, too hard, fighting with gun smuggling and mercenary forces against a regular Army sponsored by two other Great Powers, the United Kingdom and the Soviet Union, this was too much. The game was too high-stakes for gifted amateurs only partly supported through remote control by an Army tired out by seventeen years of official colonial combat. France lost the Biafra oil to the "Anglo-Saxon mafia" and returned home licking its wounds. But nothing deeply "French" was lost in a struggle where Foreign Africans were battling other Foreign Africans; it was more like a geopolitical parlor game of *Risk* where defeat remained something that never deeply mattered, sounding just like another tome in the epic geopolitical production of Gerard de Villiers.[21] The human losses are still unknown today, with "back-of-the-envelope" statistics giving a bracket of between 500,000 and 3,000,000.[22]

The exact opposite of the Biafra conundrum was the Chadian case. After its August 1960 independence, Chad was the place where the greatest number of French military interventions in any former French colony took place, and therefore we can say that while Chad was not the target of frequent interventions, it was in a situation of permanent military operation[23] as far back as 1965. There *Françafrique* became a national chameleon fighting all by itself for its own little chunk of the Cold War against Soviet ally Muhammar Gaddafi, using all means available, everything from standard regular troops to mercenaries and from French Special Operation Commandoes to "native auxiliaries". Everything but the kitchen sink, definitely a French comfort zone where the boundaries were endlessly designed and redesigned in Paris, at times so fast that the local actors had difficulties in keeping up with the changes. To be honest the local actors were acting the same way: the Christian Southerners fighting against the Northern Muslims but everybody having a strong taste for betrayal, Christians allying themselves with Muslims to thwart the dark designs of fellow Christians, Muslim anti-Christian rebels fighting each other (the Hissen Habre versus Goukouny Weddey infernal couple, swapping regularly their positions as Prime Minister and rebel leader), the worst enemy of the French becoming the closest ally of the French before betraying them to the Americans who—because of Cold War Anti-Communist imperatives—had belatedly become involved.[24] Chad was a witches' cauldron, its situation prompting Marielle Delbos, a specialist on the country, to describe it as a "zone of permanent military operations" developing into a full-fledged "war as a living situation".[25] War had become the quotidian norm of an entire society, without any end in sight.

In 1990, as the Hissène Habré-Goukouny Weddeye couple was going through its usual political dance and the Libyan government had betrayed its third Peace Agreement, the French Secret Service (DGSE) found a new element to inject in the situation, a former French Army officer called Idris Deby Atno who had been an assassin on behalf of President Hissène Habré. He had decided to double cross his boss and had taken refuge in Sudan, then ruled by Islamist Mohamed Omar Beshir. He was a Zaghawa—an ethnic group representing 3% of the Chadian population, not another member of the northern Tubu trouble-makers—he had a flexible ideology (centered on himself)—and the support of the Islamist regime in Khartoum. He did not take seriously the Islamic paraphernalia of the Sudanese regime and he was right not to do so. But there were two things that made him go all the way: First, Islam was—through the Muslim Brotherhood's support—a good financial bet with money coming not only from Khartoum but also (with highly profitable intermediary steps) from Saudi Arabia. Second, the DGSE representative in Sudan, Paul Fontbonne, was a good *Françafrique* man, a member of the Service but painting himself (and actually being) on the loose and playing a kind of Lawrence of Arabia role, with the tag "I am officially an unofficial". Fontbonne pushed the right buttons in Paris and in Khartoum and then let Idris Deby loose on Chad. The blitzkrieg was highly mobile and fought entirely with Toyota 4x4 Land Cruiser battle wagons; it lasted about ten months. In December 1990 Hissène Habré fled to Senegal, Idris Deby occupied Ndjamena (with *Monsieur* Paul Fontbonne in tow[26]) and got to work setting up a cozy little dictatorship which lasted thirty-one years, with at first the support of Omar el-Beshir (who later switched to trying to kill him but did not succeed, something which tainted the Islamist option), then the exit of Gaddafi (he took the Soviet collapse badly and renounced his plan to acquire nuclear weapons or embark on continent-wide subversion) and throughout the entire period with solid and continuous French support. When Deby was finally killed supposedly fighting rebels,[27] President Macron rushed to his funeral and tenderly held his son's hand. He was the only head of state present and Mahamat Idris Deby Itno had ascended to his father's throne without any election or even the pretense of holding a meeting of a Council of Elders. We are looking ahead here somewhat but in the 2020s, as *Françafrique* started to fall apart, Chad was probably the only piece of the Empire which still felt solid.[28] It still is the case but the pot of iron is itself perched on top of a fragile earthenware cup; Chad is solid but not unbreakable. President Macron's patting Mahamat Deby's hand was a tender gesture, obviously supportive and welcoming; but it also looked like an expression of both anguish and a renewed commitment to the last leader standing of the French post-colonial Guard, as fires raged all around.

But we are anticipating here the half-glimpsed end of Empire without having finished dealing with its heyday.

War indeed but diplomacy too:

The inaugural "Franco-African Summit" was held on November 13 1973. Nobody knew what it was since President Pompidou had billed it as an "exceptional event". In fact it repeated itself twenty-seven more times and became the annual gathering of an official yet unofficial event. The most recent reunion took place in October 2021 and we'll see in Chapter 6 whether it was the last.

ROUGH AND READY

The senior figures present in November 1973 were representative of the paradoxes of Francophone Africa:

- Jean-Bedel Bokassa, a French Army veteran of the Indochina war now president of Oubangui-Chari recently renamed the Central African Republic. He had recently accessed power through a military coup in 1966 and in December 1977 he proclaimed himself Emperor before being deposed in 1979 by a French airborne invasion. To seek revenge he declared (and provided proof) that he had given President Giscard d'Estaing a bag of industrial diamonds (albeit not the really expensive type). He also admitted that his wife had become Giscard's lover. The French electorate being realistic, it was the diamonds that prompted Giscard's defeat at the polls notwithstanding his amorous success. The result was the presidency of the Socialist François Mitterrand and an unofficial promise of reform of *Françafrique*.[29]
- Félix Houphouët-Boigny had been five times a minister in various cabinets of the Fourth Republic prior to 1958. Now he was President of the Ivory Coast and seemed part of a timeless view of French politics.
- Albert-Bernard Bongo was still the (unelected) President of Gabon before trying to turn it into a hereditary Muslim Sultanate.

- Aboubakar Lamizana had been brought to power by a coup in 1966 and was going to be removed by another coup in August 1984, his country's name Upper Volta then being changed by the next President, Thomas Sankara, who called it Burkina Faso, "the country of honest men". It did not work out well because Sankara himself was murdered, together with twelve others on October 15 1987 by a group of putschists organized by his closest friend Blaise Compaoré, who then declared himself President.
- Hamani Diori, President of Niger since 1960, had to disobey *Françafrique* because being Djerma he had created in Niger a cabinet made up of Djerma, Fulbe and Hausa. The Hausa of Nigeria were at the core of the anti-Biafra Nigerian Army so Hamani Diori had had to reject Jacques Foccart's friendly remonstrances and refused to help the Biafran cause. He was later removed by a pro-French coup in 1974.
- Last but not least for Francophonie's morality, there was also Léopold Sedar Senghor, then president of Senegal, world intellectual and future member of the Académie Française. He ruled a country where there had never been a coup d'etat, where elections were clean and when he thought he had been in power long enough, he abdicated the Presidency and passed the reins of power to his Vice-President. But then he had never been considered a *Françafrique* man.

This was November 13 1973. The ritual was repeated annually, with a growing attempt at broadening and inclusiveness. Paris remained a key place for African politics but it remained *French*. In spite of its diplomacy *Françafrique* never extended its empire beyond Francophone limits. It was not for lack of trying, especially by seeking new openings in Belgian Africa.

France jumps on the former Belgian Congo:

That process was suddenly forced by an emergency situation on May 13 1978 when Congolese President Mobutu Ssese Seko sent a worried message to President Giscard d'Estaing asking him for his immediate military help after the FNLC had invaded Kolwezi by way of Zambia.[30] Mobutu added that he had sent the same message to Belgium, Morocco, China and the US. Six days later Paris had a whole para-commando regiment flown to Kinshasa and soon air dropped it on Kolwezi where FLNC had taken the whole foreign population (about 3,500 people) hostage. The emergency was brief and extremely brutal: 170 Europeans and 430 Black Congolese civilians were slaughtered by the invaders who lost 250 of their own. It was finally a clear-cut victory for the French troops and their Belgian allies,[31] even if its political consequences were peculiar because the next step was the deployment in June of an African force that was deployed to "protect Shaba".[32] It was made up of troops from Morocco, Gabon, the Ivory Coast,

Togo and Senegal, practically a *Françafrique* military parade. The message was clear both for the Russians (don't come) and for the Americans (we are already here[33]). The Fifth *Sommet France-Afrique* was held in Paris while the military operation was taking place and had Mobutu as a guest of honor. The next summit (1979) was organized in Kigali, Rwanda having joined the Franco-African family four years before. A continental triumph for French diplomacy even if nobody could have guessed at the time the future catastrophic consequences of that particular success.

In the wake of post-Gaullism, the beginnings of economic changes and structural transformations

Given the way the expression "*Françafrique*" crept into common parlance in the 1970s, it has been linked to large and illicit financial operations. This is a delicate point. Saying that this was not the heart of the matter immediately raises the suspicion of a "cover up". In fact, in its early years (1962–1974), i.e. the De Gaulle and Pompidou mandates, the shapeless entity later known as *Françafrique* was basically a continuation of the earlier French colonial economic relationship characterized by military security treaties, unequal economic exchanges, French state oversight, control of and favoritism for French enterprizes and a very large number of French *coopérants* (advisors) at many levels of education, health and technical research. This was known in Paris as "*notre pré carré*", "our own backyard". In other words, what international organisms called "development" and militant left-wing movements stigmatized as neo-colonialism was an acknowledged fact. This was an overall phenomenon, analysed, criticized or praised, largely as a function of the observers' positioning on the world chessboard of the Cold War. But if it had a "French touch", it was definitely not something out of the ordinary and/or a source of hyper profits for ravenous French economic interests. It counted in world geopolitics but hardly at all on global stock exchanges because this was first and foremost a French government matter, linked with state sovereignty, not (primarily) a source of financial reward. While French companies were helped and favored, they were not the engine of the machine, good or bad. What was special for the humiliated and suffering country was France's wounded national pride as it sought to re-establish its national glory. The fact that this cloud of self-regarding greatness was partially puffed by Africans blocked in a painful position of halfway independence was seen as secondary: had not the French brought civilization to Africa? Had not the support of the Empire been essential to the recreation of greatness while the Wehrmacht was parading on the Champs-Elysées? The Empire, renamed *Françafrique*, was a fundamental lynchpin of French identity, the matter was political, cultural and even psychological. But up to 1974 it had never been the engine powering the relationship of France to "its" Africa, "its brotherly backyard". This changed with the arrival of Giscard d'Estaing, a half-non-Gaullist[34] to the constitutional kingship of the French Republic.

Giscard was surfing on the liberal wave transforming global capitalism as the Cold War was beginning to turn a corner as that great world geopolitical farce was on the wane. It would take another twenty years before globalization would push Franco-African economics away from the state's embrace and onto the floors of the stock exchanges. But the process which, strangely enough, came to visible fruition during the "socialist" government of François Mitterrand, had started during the mandate of Giscard. We will see in Chapter 3 how the Mitterrand "Reform" concerning French policies in Africa was a hinge period which saw the epoch-defining publication of François-Xavier Verschave's *La Françafrique: le plus long scandale de la République*,[35] finally giving a name to what had been an unacknowledged reality for forty years. The problem, as often happens when a certain political truth becomes public, is that it has already transformed itself significantly between its birth and exposition. The animal had shed its skin during these forty years and the state had seen its place shrink in favor of transnational private finance. The continuity between the two periods had a name: Vincent Bolloré who, at the head of Africa Logistics had, between 1986 and 1991, become the largest transport and logistics contractor in the entire continent.[36] But what had happened meanwhile to the "scandal of the Republic"? It was de-financialising itself without losing its scandalous aura which was on the verge of becoming even more scandalous and less financial. Money and the French African world had merged before denationalising themselves as they headed towards the final exit (see the following chapter). The pattern evolved from French government control to French diplomatic (and even military) "protection", essentially in the mafia sense of the word.

French involvement in the Biafran war had largely occurred as part of an attempt to help Elf Aquitaine, the French oil giant, acquire a new and profitable source of crude oil. But it was not the sole reason, De Gaulle's strategic vision being broader than simply how to make money. Given the predation of external actors, Africa provided an opportunity for making large amounts of money and settling political feuds in secret and illegal ways, all this via an unofficial government organization which had the great advantage of not even existing. During the 1993–95 period during which Elf was privatized, some of my friends worked on that process.

When René Journiac[37] died, *Françafrique* was twenty years old and its founding father had been forcibly removed. The "Quasi-Gaullist" President Giscard d'Estaing was caught in a *Françafrique* scandal with the former CAR "Emperor" that he had himself deposed.

The fear—that proved prescient—was that the Socialist Mitterrand was going to be elected and would upset the apple-cart. Well, Mitterrand won the election but did not upset the apple-cart, as we will see in the next chapter. Africa-wise, the focus of Mitterrrand's campaign was targeting apartheid South Africa, a nicely consensual positioning at the time and years before the murder of Dulcie September in Paris[38] and the freeing of Nelson Mandela from Victor Verster prison. As far as France's role in Africa is concerned, Mitterrand had remained in his position of Minister of Overseas Territories during the Fourth Republic, when apartheid had remained a topic comfortably un-French. Now that topic had turned into something politically useful in a recently globalized world while it had remained mostly innocuous in France. As for *Françafrique,* it was not going to be targeted by Mitterrand; it was going to be tactically overhauled so that it functioned better. The result of that clever overhaul was going to be the killing of from eight hundred thousand to over two million people.[39] *Françafrique* did not cause this; it facilitated it without even realising what it was doing.

3

MITTERRAND'S NON-REFORMS

Françafrique *integrates the state: The Rwandese catastrophe and the oil scandal (1981–99)*

Françafrique had been one of the factors in Mitterrand's victory at the polls and in the French exasperation with a Gaullist regime which had lasted twenty-three years, *Françafrique* had played its part. In a move unusual in a Western liberal democracy, Gaullism had over the years colonized the French state and *Françafrique* was its African pseudopod. With the socialist victory it was more than two decades of politically programmed "good behavior" which—many French thought—had come to an end. They were wrong. The suit of armor of the French Fifth Republic was so well devised—and so useful and seductive for any system of power—that Mitterrand, far from reforming the state,[1] intervened increasingly and tied the leather straps shut so that the two finally became one. He claimed command but the state structure was stronger than its new incarnation. Mitterrand was largely run by what he claimed to be running. This development extended to *Françafrique* which far from being brought under control, influenced the state apparatus on African matters more than ever, till it eventually (and typically) overreached itself and plunged into a monstrous storm it had not seen coming and in which it nearly floundered.

Thomas Sankara's unusual political trajectory

Who was Thomas Sankara, the Upper Volta (today's Burkina Faso) President assassinated on October 15 1987? In the *Françafrique* context of the time, he was basically a glorious misfit. But how had the man who upon his death would be hailed as "The African Che Guevara" assumed power in the first place? In a muddy and confused manner that was typical of the Francophone "decolonization" period; that's how. In November 1980 a coup took place in Upper Volta with publicly-stated reformist ambitions but within months the new regime had turned into an authoritarian, typically putschist, military *junta*. Thomas Sankara, who had been taken on board this initially popular regime as "Secretary of State for Information"[2] and had resigned in April 1982 in protest at the banning of the workers' right to strike, was dismissed from the army. Six months later another coup took place and the coup-makers offered him the position of Prime Minister which he had refused initially. Briefly detained by his own politically mixed government for having invited Gaddafi to Ouagadougou on a state visit,[3] Sankara was freed through massive popular demonstrations, supported by Army units disobeying their own officers. Sankara's release from detention ushered in a period, in his own words, of "democratic revolution". He formed a cabinet with two extreme left-wing militant movements but never organized elections.

Sankara then abolished the administrative authority invested in traditional chiefs and kept by the French, replacing them by Revolutionary Defence Committees (CDRs). This initiated a drawn out process in which the CDRs enforced government decisions but also began to abuse their powers. The fluctuating relations between Sankara and the Committees he created would last to the end of his rule.

On May 28 an attempt at a conservative putsch was nipped in the bud and the attempted putschists sent to court where seven of the twelve were condemned to death and shot while the others received heavy prison sentences. There was no broader repression. Sankara's reign was thereafter defined by the following points:

- Regular state expenses were cut in order to shift spending towards productive investment. Symbolic measures were taken such as when all ministers,

Sankara included, had their luxury sedans decommissioned and replaced by ordinary little Renaults.

- Fruit and vegetable imports were prohibited and help given to increase their production in Upper Volta. The CDRs were mobilized to create new distribution circuits and facilitate women direct shopping and delivery from their stores. By 1986 the UN Special Delegate for access to food declared: "The Government of the (renamed) Burkina Faso[4] has eradicated hunger: in four years Burkina has become self-supporting in terms of food."[5]
- In April 1985, Sankara, the first African head of state to be sensitive to ecological issues, introduced a whole system of measures, including:
  - Banning loose and unregulated deforestation, together with help for those switching to using bottled gas rather than charcoal;
  - Prohibiting bush burning;
  - Ending uncontrolled cattle grazing;
  - Promoting water catchment schemes including direct help to peasants who wanted to build them themselves;
  - Halting large-scale infrastructure projects which he accused of offering more benefits to the French construction companies involved than to their supposed African recipients.

- Attention to the problem of women: the government created a "vital salary" where husbands were supposed to repay some of their income not to the state but to their wife or wives. He created new legislation to end forced marriages, outlawed dowry, which he considered to be "a *merchandization of women*", created a minimum age for marriage, introduced consent, prohibited excision and tried (unsuccessfully) to prohibit levirate and prostitution.
- He repudiated the IMF loan system and refused to accept any further financing from the Fund. In 1987 he sought from what was then still called the Organization for African Unity (OAU)[6] a global rejection of IMF loans which he denounced as "a cleverly organized system for growth and development being based on norms and values which are completely foreign to our needs".

Sankara defined his own politics as "basically anti-imperialist"[7] and directly critiqued France. He developed an "anti-imperialist" diplomatic network by increasing contacts with Cuba, Libya, the ANC,[8] the PLO, Rawlings' Ghana and Nicaragua's Sandinista Movement. Interestingly he never tried to develop relations with the Moscow-aligned Warsaw Pact regimes, seeking an exclusively "Third-World" diplomatic alignment distinct from a "Communist" one. French aid decreased by 80% between 1983 and 1986.

This did not stop President François Mitterrand from visiting Ouagadougou in November 1986. To the French President's considerable surprise, Sankara directly accused him of "imperialist designs", citing practical examples, resorting to undiplomatic language while also avoiding bombastic militant rhetoric. He also never alluded to the declining level of French aid and never complained about it nor asked for a penny more. This greatly impressed Mitterrand, who was used to *Françafrique* heads of state making routine trips to Paris with a standard stopover at the Ministry of Finance to negotiate further aid packages. He had received an extremely negative briefing about Sankara from his old friend Houphouët-Boigny but retained a kind of puzzled sympathy for the young African revolutionary firebrand.[9]

Sankara's assassination

On October 15 1987 as Sankara and several of his advisors left a meeting, a group of armed men waited outside and machine-gunned all twelve of them to death. A little bit of background would be in order here. *Françafrique* was not of one mind concerning Sankara. Since May 10 1981 France had been governed by a nominally socialist i.e. left-wing government and one of the (unofficial) theoretical objectives of this government was closer and more transparent relations with Africa. But nothing was official or enshrined in a clearly-stated policy.[10] Oddly, if we recapitulate Sankara's policies set out above they read almost like a wish list of Mitterrand's advisors on Africa. Or do they? Having been one of those advisors—even if in a low-ranking role—I would say "not really". And the next section on Rwanda will show in greater detail how divided, incoherent—and powerless— we were. This brains trust—particularly in the case of Africa where French influence was at the time real, not only symbolic—was deeply divided between the "realists" and the "idealists". This last subgroup was later to realise how deceived it had been by the *realpolitikers* who were definitely closer to the President's outlook on world affairs. But the Sankara situation was more ambiguous. As the possibility of an anti-Sankara coup was mounting Mitterrand sent Sankara a discreet warning of what was afoot.[11] But the Burkina President refused to act on that alert. Actually several of his closest advisors (some of whom were killed on October 15) wanted to arrest Blaise Compaoré before it was too late. But Compaoré was an old childhood friend of Thomas Sankara and they had ventured into politics together. They shared principles. The Burkinabe leader *refused to acknowledge* what was coming. Compaoré was married to Houphouët-Boigny's niece who was angry at being marginalized, especially as her uncle was the leader of the anti-Sankara lobby in the African wing of *Françafrique*. Compaoré was playing along with the "realists" in Paris pushing a line according to which Sankara hated the French and was chumming up to Gaddafi. This was for ordinary consumption. For the "secret" side, Guy Penne, head of the African cell at the Elysée, was the leader of the realists. I remember him telling me that Sankara was plotting to create a centralized Marxist-Leninist party which would take absolute control of Burkina Faso, arresting or killing the country's entire political elite. Did he make that up all by himself or did he listen to music composed by Houphouët-Boigny? But in any case, even though the French did not kill Sankara, knowing what they knew about Compaoré's plans, they allowed him to be murdered. A major bridge had been crossed. Violence had existed during the decolonization process, particularly in Cameroun. Half counterinsurgency—still partly legitimate—and half political assassination—the Moumié murder was an example. But being complicit in the killing of a full-fledged head of state with a seat at the UN, this was something which in a court of law would have had to be labelled as "state terrorism". This was the kind of event only a well-known dictatorship would not have shied away from. In a way this violent episode can be seen as the closing event of the *Françafrique* "classical" period. But much worse was about to come

Virtue by prescription: The La Baule speech—and its unforeseen consequences

This politically normative speech was delivered by President François Mitterrand at the 16th Franco-

African conference in La Baule on June 20 1990. It was a pean to democracy by the representative of a radically anti-democratic association in the African context, a *chef d'oeuvre* of virtue by an apparently repented sinner:

> France will link all its contributions to the efforts accomplished to go towards more freedom. There will be normal aid to African countries but it will be evident that this aid will only be lukewarm for those whose behavior will be authoritarian and more enthusiastic towards those that will step forward faster to reach democratization ...

Then the president moved on towards what was happening in Eastern Europe and added:

> this wind will obviously blow clear across the planet. ... France will not intervene in the internal affairs of our African friends since this subtle form of colonialism based on giving lessons to the states of Africa would be as perverse as the other forms of colonialism.

The origins of this speech went back to 1989, when Mitterrand realised that the Soviet system was on the cusp of radical change that would send vibrations throughout Western Europe and, indirectly, all the way to the *Françafrique* post-imperial sphere. He tried to adapt himself to the new situation but was constrained by his understanding of Communism, which was framed by his experiences from the 1930s to the 1960s. He wanted to recognize the August 1991 Moscow putsch before the coup had even succeeded because for him the USSR was a given, a reality he could see oscillating but not disappearing. As for the lesson he meant to give Africa in 1990, it was an appendage to an incomplete and misunderstood decolonization process. He renewed it through economic aid threats and promises to Africans during the Sommet de la Francophonie (November 21 1991):

> When you ask me how should every country determine its rhythm, do you expect me to dictate how each country should do it? This is not at all the role of France ... We should leave to all the people the way to determine their path and the manner in which each should do it.

At first Mitterrand talked about "official multipartism" and "free elections". Several heads of state (Paul Biya in Cameroun, Juvenal Habyarimana in Rwanda) disliked these "instructions" which France insisted upon but soon backed out from. All that remained were vague indications emanating from Paris about "a direction" and "a rhythm". In fact Mitterrand had no idea of the political developments in the different countries of the global *Françafrique* and nor did his son Jean-Christophe[12] possess the knowledge required to clarify the situation. For the past thirty years Paris had skippered an unofficial—but powerful—ship. Mitterrand abruptly decided on a new course without being aware of the waters in which he was sailing and of the fact that the ship was now rudderless.[13] The rocks on which it foundered were in the mountains of East Africa, near Lake Kivu in Rwanda. Rwanda was not an "official" member of *Françafrique* being a former German colony mandated to Belgium by the League of Nations in 1924. Decolonized in 1959 in chaotic circumstances[14] it had been softly annexed to *Françafrique*, during the presidential administration of Valéry Giscard d'Estaing in the 1970s. Ruled by a Hutu ethnic administration since then it endured a brittle normalcy under the pretense of *Rubanda Nyamwinshi* which was an ethnic expression of majority rule.[15] Beneath this superficially quiet reputation as a kind of African Switzerland the place was a potential time bomb. The Belgian (post-German) recolonization had exasperated the Hutu/Tutsi dichotomy. For the Belgians, exploiting Rwanda's ethnic bipolarity had been a comfortable shortcut in the colonial administration of what was for them a kind of back door logistical depot for the Belgian Congo. The French had only the vaguest notions of the country's real situation and the La Baule speech was given as it was about to explode. It did not itself trigger the explosion but it happened without the French having any serious notion about what was underway as they became enmeshed in a situation which was completely alien to their previous experiences in France's African colonies.

Rwanda: Tiptoeing to a catastrophe

In 1964, when the last vanquished Tutsi took refuge in Uganda, they were walking not into a real haven but a temporary refuge. As time went on their children, including the man who is today the president of Rwanda, Paul Kagame, grew up as Ugandans. They were embedded into the Ugandan reality of their time and place and "became Ugandans" as is normal for the children of any refugee population which remains for years in another country and is educated in that society. But they were bordering their country of origin and the man who became president of Uganda in 1986 was an "ethnic cousin".[16] This gave the militant refugees considerable clout in their adopted country of refuge. The Chief of Staff of the Ugandan Army, Fred Rwigyema, was the son of Rwandese refugee parents and he played a key politico-military role during the civil war and in the subsequent localized conflicts that plagued the early years of the Museveni regime. He considered himself a real "integrated" Ugandan. But these "Ugandanized" Rwandese had succeeded too well, to the point of antagonising the old Baganda pre-civil war political elite. In the years after the war, the antagonisms grew between the old elite and the new one, recruited largely among refugees, even though they had made

MITTERRAND'S NON-REFORMS

common cause during the war. The war being over, the competition grew for jobs and economic benefits between the old traditional elite and the new post-war one. Museveni is a native Ugandan and regardless of his links with the Rwandese—Fred Rwigyema and he were not only political allies but also close personal friends—he had to listen to the complaints of the old Ugandan native elite. The Rwandese were progressively pushed aside and started to listen to the siren voices of those emigres who had formed armed insurgent columns—using their strong links within the Ugandan military—and were now calling for a "return to our homeland." When Rwigyema was sidelined from his top role in the Ugandan army, he, the "integrated Ugandan", turned to the newest of these Rwandese political movements, the Rwandese Patriotic Front (RPF). At the time I was both a member of the International Secretariat of the French Socialist Party and living in Uganda. I could keep these two segments of my identity safely apart but it did not last. On October 1 1990, RPF forces conducted a major attack on Rwanda while I was on holiday in Paris. For the past year I had been getting to know several Tutsi exiles in Uganda and my nickname for them was "The White Russians". This came from the stories I had heard from my parents about Paris in the 1930s where White Russian refugees kept plotting confused conspiracies aiming at killing Stalin and overthrowing the Bolsheviks. My Rwandese exiled friends in Uganda discussed similarly bizarre methods for attacking the Rwandan government but in October 1990 I realised how wrong I was when these "White Russians" invaded their home country with deadly intent (using weapons "borrowed" from the Ugandan Army) and made a serious dent in the Forces Armées Rwandaises (FAR). On October 5 1990 I had an appointment to see Jean-Christophe Mitterrand in order to gauge French policy towards the Sudan where the civil war was on the uptick. Given the recent Rwandese attack, I chose to engage him instead on that more recent topic. I found a confused man who told me that the French ambassador in Kigali had written a short note on the question but that he had not had time to peruse it yet. "One of these border clashes I suppose." I tried to explain to him the "White Russian" syndrome all the way back to its origins and how unsafe was the ground beneath our feet. He seemed to have only some vague notion of the situation. And then in the middle of the conversation the phone rang: it was President Habyarimana calling from New York.[17] There was a short conversation in which Habyarimana seemed to try to find out what the French position was and how President Mitterrand would react. From what I understood as a listener Habyarimana was worried about the French reaction which he wanted to see turned in to a French expeditionary force, mobilized to support his government. As he seemed to describe an attack by the RPF on Kigali[18] itself Jean-Christophe Mitterrand's

MITTERRAND'S NON-REFORMS

answer was noncommital but when he showed me to the door he added: "Well, we'll send him a few boys, to old man Habyarimana. Within a month or two everybody will have forgotten about it".[19] Such was the prescient commentary that accompanied the French involvement in Rwanda.[20] In my later testimony to the official Commission of Inquiry I tried to reframe the intervention into its real landscape:

> The country into which Operation Noroit had been launched in 1990 had nothing to do with those France was familiar with [in Africa] such as friendly Senegal or our Ivory Coast partners and in reality France had no notion of where it was coming from, a glaring evidence for those who knew [the Great Lakes]. The actors of French policy, if they did not know the country, should at least have been conscious of their own ignorance and of the dangers of the terrain on which they were setting foot.[21]

The French operation in Rwanda merited the usual media coverage of African politics, a back page mention in the international press. This was to remain so during the next three years, when, prior to the genocide, the UN absent-mindedly voted Resolution 872 (October 5 1993) creating the United Nations Assistance Mission to Rwanda (UNAMIR). Three years after the war had begun the international community began marginally to take it into account. The French were on their way to evacuate their troops and it was out of the question that French soldiers could be incorporated within the global embrace of a UN operation given the fact that the RPF guerillas were set against it. Since the beginning of Noroit, the *Détachement de l'Aide Militaire et de l'Instruction* (DAMI), an *ad hoc* French military mission to Rwanda, had brought massive help to the *Forces Armées Rwandaises* (FAR) which had grown in three years from 5,200 men to over 50,000.[22] The recruitment was spottily carried out and many members of the extremist militias later globally called *Interahamwe* ("Those who work together") were recruited by FAR. It was these *Interahamwe,* some of whom were French-trained, who later carried out the genocide. The French involvement was unofficial and was immediately questioned by some of the very men who were in charge of Noroit and others propping up the regime in Kigali. As early as mid-October 1990 Ambassador Georges Martre wrote in a note to Paris that "the Rwandese population of Tutsi origin is hoping for a quick victory of the RPF which would allow them to escape a genocide."[23] This was not an inflated expression of the French Ambassador; it was a prescient evaluation of the on the ground reality. But at the same time it was an assessment that anybody familiar with Rwanda—its society, its history—could possibly have made. The problem was that Mitterrand did not have such people at hand to warn him of the excessive danger France was now at risk of because of its own ignorance.[24] This went back to the sacking of Jean-Pierre Cot. Cot had been appointed in the first socialist cabinet in 1981 as Secretary of State in Charge of Cooperation and Development. The whole mess of *Françafrique* landed on his desk and within months he realized he had been made Secretary of State in charge of a monster. He embarked upon an attempt to reform "the thing" that would have meant resetting one of those cornerstones that underpins a whole branch of a regime, one of these elements nobody ever speaks about because they are silently felt to be completely consubstantial to a country's politics. He tried gamely but was finally forced into resigning in December 1982, to the great relief of the military lobby which was going to play such a large role in the Rwanda catastrophe. There were periodic warning signs as the vehicle chugged its way towards the abyss. The first one was the massacre of the Bagogwe in early 1991. The Bagogwe are an untypical Tutsi clan which had shunned the modern world and still lived the way explorers and anthropologists describe the "Tutsi way of life", i.e. nomadic herders wandering through highland pastures with their long-horned cattle. In early 1991 the RPF briefly occupied the town of Ruhengeri, humiliating both the FAR and their French Army allies. The Bagogwe had nothing to do with it, most of their young men having even neglected to join the RPF. But they lived not far from

Ruhengeri and the regular FAR troops soon retook Ruhengeri. The local civilian authorities, using the *Interahamwe* militiamen, launched a massacre, randomly killing Bagogwe whose only fault was of being in the wrong place at the wrong time. In three weeks over 1,000 Bagogwe were slaughtered, the Rwandese government denying the killings, even pretending that the RPF had killed them, an evidently absurd proposition. The Belgian League for Human Rights carried out an inquiry and wrote a report. The French looked the other way.[25] Since the poor Bagogwe were marginals in their own society, their deaths remained a marginal phenomenon in Rwanda at large. But the DAMI (the French Army detachment advising the Rwandan military) kept recruiting personnel of questionable character and in Byumba a French soldier had the unpleasant experience of seeing some of these new recruits arrest local Tutsi—and even Hutu who were members of opposition political parties—and after a night when he could not sleep because of the screams coming from the barracks where the recruits were torturing their prisoners, he contacted officers of the French *Gendarmerie* deployed in Kigali and told them that in the morning he had seen trucks with dead bodies leaving their compound. One of the *Gendarmerie* officers took the soldier's account very seriously and during his next leave to France reported the story to his superiors and wrote a report. The outcome was that his deployment in Rwanda was terminated and he was recalled to France.[26]

Some of the civilian personnel working in the administrative offices evaluating the deployment in Rwanda such as Pierre Conessa of the *Délégation aux Affaires Stratégiques* began to worry. Gérard Fuchs, Secretary of the Socialist Party International Secretariat for International Relations,[27] and a few legislators familiar with African affairs tried to sound the alarm. The Army was not very cooperative. When I made a clandestine visit to the front in early 1992 I came under Rwandese artillery fire directed by French instructors (we listened to them on their radio frequency). Upon my return to Paris I went to the Ministry of Defense and joked about this with the office in charge of DAMI, saying "you guys nearly killed me". The answer was short and blunt: "Pity we missed you". That was not a joke. They meant it.

There was worse to come. The Minister for Cooperation, Marcel Debarge, went to Kigali where he gave an incredible speech (February 1993) in which he asked Hutu opponents of Habyarimana's MRND regime to "make common cause with the regime" against the RPF, that is to create an ethnic Hutu coalition against the Tutsi. At the time the democratic opposition to the government MRND was growing, including from Hutu majority parties. If we look at the La Baule speech delivered by Mitterrand, he had asked for a democratic reorganization of the African political landscape so that authoritarian former single party regimes would accept real elections and the democratization of their countries. Thus the message carried by Mitterrand's minister was the exact opposite of the President's official policy. Soon after I met with one of the leaders of the Parti Social Démocrate (PSD), then the second largest opposition party in Rwanda, who grim-facedly told me: "Did this man [Debarge] realize he is condemning us to death?" Was this an exaggeration? Not in the least. At the time there was a wave of killings of people involved in politics and this was because, trying to obey the La Baule line defined by Mitterrand, the autocratic Rwandese regime had been trying to open up. New parties had sprung up and the capacity to negotiate the Arusha Peace Agreement had been a byproduct of this new liberty. But this was not a direct jump from dictatorship to open-minded politics. In the historically polarized situation of Rwanda, deconstructing an oppressive killing machine could not be achieved by the miracle of a peace treaty when at the same time the representative of the peace guarantor was supporting a policy not of peace reinforcement but of militant aggressive alliance. The Hutu who wanted to keep opening up and who agreed with the provisions of the Arusha peace agreement were taking enormous risks. Indeed my interlocutor was killed just as the genocide began. He had opposed to the last "making common cause with the regime". His party survived him, to become a partner in the first coalition government after the genocide, later to be totally brought to heel by the victorious RPF.

But then why was Mitterrand so radically engaged in supporting a regime he did not know, about which members of his own party were not very enthusiastic and to which no big strategic, diplomatic or financial stake was attached? The answer is key to understanding one of the essential features of *Françafrique:* hostility towards the "Anglo-Saxons". Behind that bizarre expression lies one of the underpinnings of French geopolitical thinking: hostility towards this weird Anglophone "tribe" which used to be basically "English" but which had sprouted in the last hundred years into a multiplicity of subgroups, all suspected to be hostile to the "French way of life". In our globalized times, this cluster has become a world-wide phenomenon. Of course it started with the "near-English" such as Americans, Australians, English-speaking Canadians and so on. But with the "Anglo-Saxon" victory of 1945 and the vast and rapid expansion of "Globish", Global English, the world turned into a vast anti-French conspiracy. The October 1990 attack on Rwanda by an English-speaking guerilla group was felt by Paris to be another forward move of the "Anglo-Saxon" anti-French conspiracy. Never mind that these "English-speaking" intruders were hardly English-speaking (they operated in their mother tongue Kinyarwanda and occasionally used Swahili, Luganda, Runyankole and yes, even English) but they represented the opposite of what De Gaulle had wanted to use Africa for and to which Giscard d'Estaing had later latched on when *Françafrique* was extended to the former Belgian colonies. The enemy was at the gates and had to be stopped regardless of what the so-called "specialists" might think about it. Rumours of American help were inflated beyond belief, some pro-government analysts even going back to Museveni's years in the bush (1981–86) and inventing a US plot to put him in power "to extend 'Anglo-Saxon' imperialism to Eastern Africa". For people who remembered how hostile Washington was to Museveni when he achieved power[28]—the Americans considered him to be a dangerous leftist—in terms of creative political delirium it was not dissimilar to the type of intellectual construction Vladimir Putin later made us familiar with. But even if the RPF attack on Rwanda in October 1990 had nothing to do with the somewhat paranoid perception the French had of it, it was indeed an act of war emanating from an "Anglophone" country onto a "Francophone" one. If the nucleus of the RPF had been formed in the Congo or in Burundi, two other countries where many 1960s Tutsi refugees lived, the whole perspective would have been quite different and it would have been unlikely to have prompted the *Françafrique* behemoth to spring into action. The perception the French had of the RPF did not change once they finally evacuated Rwanda militarily, long before the genocide. The Arusha Peace Agreement (August 4 1993) was supposed to end the war and therefore made the French Noroit presence redundant. During this pre-genocide period (August 1993 to April 1994) which the Rwandese called *igihirahiro* (the time of uncertainty) there were no doubts on the French side. Retrospectively it was easy to "know" that something awful was in the offing. That the Arusha Peace Agreement was fragile, even perhaps unworkable, was more or less clear. But that its failure would end up in a genocide was stretching the limits of the French political imagination, including mine.[29] The French had—discreetly and illegally—left behind a small DAMI contingent to help the FAR in case of trouble. They went beyond the call of duty and kept working with the Rwandese Army even as it was distributing arms to civilians publicly in the streets. The bulk of French troops had finally departed in December 1993 but the French did not put any pressure on local political forces. The whole region was strongly concerned about the non-compliance of President Habyarimana with the terms of the Peace Agreement but Paris did not seem to share this concern and nor did it exert the influence it could have had on some of the region's governments (Kinshasa or Bujumbura, even Dar-es-Salaam where Julius Nyerere was probably the most concerned of the various heads of state) to try to force Habyarimana into complying with the treaty he had signed. I remember Nyerere telling me shortly before his death (1999): "what a lunacy for the Allies at Versailles to have given a Mandate to the British over Tanganyika and to the Belgians over Ruanda-Urundi. Another case of inter European diplomatic balance, a footnote to the Berlin Conference.[30] In one bigger ensemble these volatile kingdoms would have been melted down, like in Nigeria". Mitterrand, in his French-centered vision of Africa, tried his terrible best at keeping a country whose history he did not know in a situation he knew even less about. But *Françafrique* was behind and even ahead of him. The result scarred East Central Africa to this day, making it partly unmanageable, separating it into a neo-monarchist dictatorship in Rwanda and a suppurating zone of permanent tribal anarchy in the Eastern Congo.

Out of the door and back through the window: The French leave Rwanda and return through the Congo

In late 1993, the French had militarily evacuated Rwanda to comply with the provisions of the Arusha Agreement, leaving behind a very complex situation but one where France was not part of the problem, at least officially. On April 6 1994 Habyarimana's plane was shot down and the genocide, evidently prepared beforehand, immediately exploded. We were on for ninety days of hell and glad to be out of it.[31] Which is why I was unprepared when my phone rang on June 30 1994 with a call from my friend Jean-Christophe Rufin, who had recently been appointed by the Minister of Defence François Léotard as his special advisor. He asked me: "Can you come with me to Rwanda? We have to meet Paul Kagame. The French Army will soon return to Rwanda on a humanitarian mission." Humanitarian mission! I was flabbergasted. Now I was being asked to step in as an unofficial intermediary of the same French Ministry of Defence whose artillery shells I had been dodging to negotiate with the RPF, where I knew a lot of people but not their leader Paul Kagame. I said: "We have tried our best to get out. Why do we have to go back in when there are hundreds of thousands of corpses?" "To facilitate a humanitarian mission", Rufin answered. Given the fact we were in the midst of a genocide, this sounded like a useful endeavor. But at this point we have to assess whether there were deeper motives explaining why the French wanted to go back in. They are all the more intriguing given several journalists cooked up a complicated scenario trying to demonstrate that the French plan was to help the members of the former government to escape detention. But by whom? The UN had no mandate to do this. The RPF was not even trying. The French? One had to construe an aberrant scenario according to which 2,500 men complete with artillery, air cover and a huge logistical apparatus would be dispatched to Rwanda for the sinister purpose of helping a few war criminals to escape justice (even though they had already done this through their own means), concealing this "secret mission" under the official objective of creating a safe zone for potential Tutsi victims to find a refuge (an almost impossible job for which the French troops did not have the necessary transport or medical equipment). Basically the job of Operation Turquoise was, as one civilian Tutsi friend told me in Cyangugu on the Congo border, "to wash Mitterrand's bloody hands under a humanitarian tap". Rough but basically true. The problem was that some of the French military were waiting for what they saw as an opportunity to get even with the RPF. I accepted the job and we flew to Uganda. I had the feeling of being one of these "useful idiots" who prompted Lenin's mirth. I had ended up being a *Françafrique* instrument because I knew that both on the RPF and on the French side there were men who were spoiling for a fight. It was now a distinct possibility that Mitterrand's effort to look as if he were extricating himself (and *Françafrique* behind him) from the horror and the bloodshed would fail. Worse, it could play into the hands of those who were waiting in ambush to create another mess to compound the previous one. To add more victims to a genocide, again through do-gooding clumsiness, was the continuation of the job *Françafrique* had launched in Rwanda four years earlier in the name of democracy and progress.

MITTERRAND'S NON-REFORMS

We got to the hill overlooking Byumba and met Paul Kagame. The encounter was icy. His main worry was the scale and operational and logistical capacity of Turquoise. It looked more like an invasion force than a humanitarian one. I had asked General Mercier in Paris why he had put it together in this manner. His answer was simple:

> my instructions are clear: we are not going in to fight. But I just came back from Bosnia, living under the fire of Serbian artillery for weeks. I swore to myself: never again. And when I accepted the leadership of Turquoise I thought that if these RPF guys had a kind of Serbian view on what we were, I wanted to have the means of shoving it back into their throat instead of seeing them slaughter my men. If I don't use what I have, better. But I want to have it just in case.

We then engaged in a dialogue with Kagame, the man who was in a position to probably defeat those we had never claimed as allies, and that we could even less claim today as they were busy killing hundreds of thousands of men, women and children. We had to pre-negotiate an armistice with mass killers who, through their mobilization of popular opinion, were no longer even an army but more a shapeless horde. We had an overview and Kagame had even a better one, but the chain of command was far from clear. The French Army was coming with a "humanitarian" overcoat and also light and medium artillery and a dozen fighter-bombers. Plenty of teeth for a humanitarian mission even if the precautions taken by general Mercier made sense from the point of view of his Sarajevo experience. In the midst of our discussion a messenger brought a sheet of paper to Kagame. Colonel Tauzin who was in Gicongoro had issued a communique: he was digging trenches around the town's perimeter to prepare his defence against a possible attack by the RPF. "... *and if they attack 'je ne ferai pas de quartier'"*. Kagame, who was educated in Uganda, had only a spotty command of French and so turned to the officer who had brought the paper:

"What does it mean 'pas de quartier'?"

"Sir, it means he will kill all the wounded ."

Kagame turned his head to face us and said with a crooked grin:

"This does not sound like a very friendly remark for a humanitarian operation."

Rufin, me and a secret service officer who had come along with us looked at each other. Rufin, our "official leader", shot back a quick answer:

"Sir we are equipped for such an emergency. Can you please give us a couple of hours?"

We (or rather two sturdy French Marines) had carried with us what was then the technological top-of-the-line instrument of communication, a satellite telephone with a folding dish antenna and a thirty-kilogram battery. We deployed our prehistoric equipment and dialled Paris, soon getting to the heart of the matter: how to prevent a clash between the advancing RPF forces and the deploying French "humanitarian" expedition. We sketched out something, Colonel Tauzin[32] was recalled to Paris and Kagame took us to Kigali to enable us to assess the situation. Somehow it was worked out (many calls to Paris and probably other calls by Kagame to his commanders) and we later tip-toed back to Kampala amid advanced mayhem.

Later I went to Kivu and found French troops again, busy burying the tens of thousands of victims of a raging cholera epidemic. *Françafrique* had reached a limit its wise men had never imagined: dealing with the practical consequences of their own omniscience. Was Rwanda a typical *Françafrique* operation? Definitely not: it was worse. It was *Françafrique* having taken over the French state and imposing—particularly the military lobby—summary "solutions" to problems they had not the faintest idea about. Beyond its post-colonial perimeter (and I am being generous) *Françafrique* did not know Africa: it was Chester Himes' blind man with a gun and the result was appalling. It had been particularly clear when the French border police had arrested Kagame a couple of years earlier as he was transiting between two flights at Roissy airport. At the time Rwanda was barely present in the news and the DAMI operations in the country were very far from anybody's mind in Paris, except the DGSE's. But once Kagame was being held nobody knew what to do with him. I learnt later about his brief detention and expulsion which showed that the French government, far from planning any kind of genocide, treated its main enemy as a wrong piece in a puzzle nobody understood. Kagame was freed after a desultory interrogation. Thus in the summer of 1994 the French "humanitarian" comeback was just the latest episode of a case of mistaken identity. I remember attending a very large planning discussion to prepare the logistics of the operation in June. The main landing point for the troops was supposed to be Goma in Congo, practically on the border with Rwanda. I asked if I was right in understanding that the coming operation was set to create a safe area for fleeing Tutsis. When this plan was confirmed to me I said it was impossible because there were no more Tutsis to save in the northwest because they had all been killed in the first week of the genocide and if you entered via Goma you would have nobody to save and the RPF waiting in arms on the other side of the border, convinced you are about to attack and preparing to defend Rwandese territory. I told them you must land in Bukavu and come in from the southwest, not the northwest. This prompted a heated discussion among those present, the gist of it being that long range transport planes could land in Goma but not in Bukavu and that deciding on Bukavu as an entry point would oblige the expeditionary force to unload all its equipment in Goma and transfer it to smaller planes that could land in Bukavu. "Too expensive" was the military consensus. The Secretary General of the Ministry then slowly took the floor and said icily: "Shifting cargo is cheaper than a war". The military complied and I blessed in my heart the principle that subordinated the Army to civilian authority; this was a few days before our little trip to meet Paul Kagame.

Turquoise did not exfiltrate any war criminals[33] and saved a few Tutsi amid utter confusion. France had entered Rwanda in 1990 "to help out old man Habyarimana" as Jean-Christophe Mitterrand had said. Nearly a million people were dead, Habyarimana was dead too and the French Army was inefficiently picking up a few survivors. Of course this cannot be attributed to the French. They did not do it but they made it possible through a mixture of ignorance and arrogance that represented the nadir of geopolitical engagement. *Françafrique* had reached a certain limit from which its subsequent decline was unavoidable. But in the popular outlook, *Françafrique* was first and foremost a financial mafia, a judgement I consider an enormous oversimplification, even if not entirely wrong. So while the confusion reigned and the blood was flowing, what was happening to the financial dimension of *Françafrique*?

France's African dilemma: Sharing energies between money and "grandeur": French oil from Elf to Total

The basic problem facing critics of *Françafrique* is language and particularly the confusion French slang made between *Françafrique* and *France à Fric;* i.e. on the one hand the cultural, political, diplomatic and military quasi government concerning Africa in France (1) and on the other hand the coarse expression France-à-Fric meaning France-with-cash (2). The tendency, particularly among French government critics, was to smear option 1 with the muck and corruption option 2 presupposed. Not that option 1 was particularly glorious but it had a respectable background having been coined by Félix Houphouët-Boigny himself who meant by it a cooperative blending of France with "its Africa". As we have already seen, the marriage had been on the wrong footing since its early days.

Critics of *Françafrique* have had a tendency to equate 1 with 2 in ways that do not help us understand the problem. First of all, yes there was blood on *Françafrique*'s record but it was what we already looked at from before 1994, during the decolonization process. Let us dispel any ambiguities: the Rwandese genocide had nothing to do with making money—in fact it cost France money in the option 2 sense—but it had a lot to do with the option 1 meaning. François Mitterrand hastily sent an expeditionary force into Rwanda in 1994 for the option 1 type of reasons—protecting France's

African sphere against the "Anglo-Saxon" enemy, reasserting our authority *vis-à-vis* our little flock of continental allies, fencing off Uganda—but strictly not for financial reasons. There was not a penny to be made from this expedition, even before it went insanely wrong and led *Françafrique*—and beyond it even its state institutional base—into a bloody quagmire. But that did not mean that while this tragedy was unfolding there was not money to be made elsewhere in Africa, particularly in "our" oil lands in Gabon and the Brazzaville Congo, very far from the Rwandese slaughterhouse.

Oil has had a very peculiar history in France, starting in 1940 when the French government created an entity in charge of oil. After several transformations this entity gave birth in 1960 to a state company called *Union Générale des Pétroles* (UGP). As soon as it was born—the impetus came from General De Gaulle himself who was eager to place under French control the oil France had discovered in Algeria—there was a media campaign headed by US and British oil majors—those Anglo-Saxons at it again—trying to disparage the whole UGP project, in fact trying to get their hands on the Algerian oil. Algeria being part of metropolitan France at the time, French law applied and the continuation of its post-independence status was a sizable element of the negotiations at Evian, prior to Algerian independence in 1962. The problem was that for a whole bevy of reasons UGP was not a proper structure to centralize all the oil production controlled by France. As soon as Algeria became independent, work started in Paris on creating a mega oil company De Gaulle thought France needed for political and strategic reasons. More in France than in any other economically advanced country in the world, oil became from its very beginnings a political element, some said "a weapon". Elf, born in 1967, was the result of that deliberate government policy. "Naturally" oil discoveries in the decolonising French Empire immediately became "Elfland" and the oil basins were fenced off against mostly "Anglo-Saxon" predators.[34] Elf's first CEO was Pierre Guillaumat, a former Minister of Defense and Director of the French Secret Service (DGSS by their mid-sixties acronym) and he felt no moral qualms at marshalling Elf employees into becoming agents for the Secret Service. As former Elf Chief Executive Le Floch-Prigent has written[35]: "Nothing happens in oil-producing countries, especially in Africa, without Elf being involved". This was a bit exaggerated: Le Floch-Prigent meant of course mostly French Africa. And then in 2003, after years of inquiries by Judge Eva Joly, the whole French Oil Empire collapsed into what the *Guardian* called "the biggest political and financial scandal of any western democracy since the Second World War" (Ah! Those Anglo-Saxons!).

The basic accusations were that millions of Euros were overcharged to various entities so that Elf could divert illegal funds in order to give bribes to mostly

African—but not African only—beneficiaries. The roster of the accused was impressive: businessmen from various nationalities, top Elf management, Mitterrand's former Minister of Foreign Affairs Roland Dumas, his mistress Christine Devier-Joncours who unabashedly published her memoirs under the title: *The Republic's Whore,* Loïc Le Floch-Prigent (he got the state to finance the legal costs of his divorce), former CEO of Elf and his "African" team heads Alfred Sirven and Andre Tarallo who had the job of dispatching the corruption bonuses to various beneficiaries. Smelly remnants came out at the same time: fake jobs to distribute easy money to Elf "employees",[36] former Minister Roland Dumas who billed the government for his luxury shoes, bribes given to senior German politicians for buying a refinery in Leuna, the whole thing perhaps corresponding to the *Guardian's* scandal-mongering title.

Strangely enough the only beneficiaries who were never charged with anything were the African ones: they had accepted corrupt French money but this was not an offence under French law. As far as the law in their own countries was concerned, they could take care of it. Everybody in France knew who was heading the list: President Sassou Nguesso of Congo-Brazzaville and Omar Bongo of Gabon who died as the trial was coming to its end.

Both "grandeur" and the role of money between Africa and France were dented in 1994 but *Françafrique* was holed beneath the waterline, not sunk. Its framework—the word "décor" would be more appropriate—was dented. In a way the main beneficiary in France was the right-wing National Front whose electorate began to grow at exactly that time. Seen from France, anything "African" now looked bloody and corrupt. To cap it all, Elf took out an OPA to buy Total, a smaller French oil company. But given the judicial circus of the previous six years, discreet political interventions redirected the buying off and led to the exact opposite: with discreet public support Total bought out Elf (September 1999). Did it mean anything in terms of how Total operated in Africa? Not really. The two companies were "married" with the approbation of the French government. In direct French tradition, "grandeur" had reasserted itself over money. The new CEO Thierry Desmaret first smoothed out the domestic dimension of what soon became a fusion so that external activities would not be harmed by what had happened in the home base. For some time the name Elf had been a burden to carry and Total cleansed the Augean stables of the public image of French oil in Africa. For France the Rwandese genocide and the Elf scandal had comparable public impacts but not on the same segment of the public. Elf was a Franco-French scandal whose impact was played out on the domestic stage; the Rwandese genocide was a global scandal and France had to dodge accusations of responsibilities that were both true and not true: yes, France had painted itself into a corner in Rwanda because it had not known where the limits were. The reality of the Rwanda involvement that I have tried to paint in a scholarly way before[37] is sketched here in a more lively pictogram. But the French will never admit it, and never admit either to its deeper meaning: when I returned from my encounter with Paul Kagame in July 1994, I attended a hurried meeting in Paris for all those involved in the post-genocide situation. The exchange concerned the RPF:

> Now they have locked the Congo border. Next we'll find them in Kinshasa with American backing. This is intolerable. We have to check with Mobutu. We can't give the Congo to the Americans. We have to use the Rwanda crisis to put Mobutu back in the saddle.

The speaker was Bruno Delaye who had followed Jean-Christophe Mitterrand at the head of the Africa Unit after the President had fired his son. *Françafrique* had survived the Rwanda earthquake and was going through a post-traumatic stress hangover. It denied its responsibility and expected that things would remain "as usual", i.e. with a faithful Africa that it began to realise it did not really know. Jacques Chirac had been elected President in May 1995 and *Françafrique* was rallying around him. The first job was mopping up.

4

THE BIG SLEEP (1995–2012)

Compounding disaster with failure—
Trying to wrap up the Rwanda disaster via the Congo

I would like to salute here the presence of an old African, the representative of a long African tradition, who worked alongside general De Gaulle, then with President Pompidou, then with me; this is Jacques Foccart. I am very glad that he could make this trip with me, as he did earlier with the General and with Georges Pompidou.[1]

The recently elected President Jacques Chirac launched his relationship with Africa by recycling a man who was not "the representative of an old African tradition" but the ghost of a certain attitude towards Africa and who soon lived up to his awful reputation. Following Chirac's election, the (official) Africa Unit 2 Rue de l'Elysée had been assigned to Michel Dupuch who had spent fourteen years as Ambassador to the Ivory Coast as a faithful Foccart man while a second unit was set up at no 14 in the same street under Foccart's personal authority, with his office space installed next door to where the President's personal staff worked. The resuscitated ghost clearly had the upper hand on Africa. As for the Ministry of Cooperation it had been assigned to Jacques Godfrain, a faithful associate of Foccart and a close friend of Omar Bongo. The Africa-oriented power structure in Paris now looked like a cartoon of *Françafrique* and it had a few scores to settle. The first effort was to try to save Marshal Mobutu, the embattled Congolese President, from the consequences of the Rwanda horror. Mobutu had sent troops to help Habyarimana and when the regime collapsed after Habyarimana's death he gave political asylum not only to over one million Rwandese refugees but also to about 50,000 ex-FAR soldiers with their weapons. Foccart and his right-hand man Fernand Wibaux went to Kinshasa and discreetly coordinated with Mobutu the treatment of the "Rwanda-out-of-Rwanda" regime led by former Habyarimana officials under the symbolic aegis of Agathe Kanzinga, the former President's widow. They sent a delegation to China to purchase weapons, which incensed the new Rwandese authorities. In April 1996 Mobutu was received at the Elysée, without any official agenda and no final communiqué was issued. Kagame prepared for war. In October he launched the *Alliance Démocratique des Forces de Libération* (ADFL) under the nominal leadership of Laurent Désiré Kabila, an old opponent of Mobutu who had been in semi-retirement for the last six or seven years. ADFL was joined by a slap-dash "transnational force" cobbled together for the anti-Mobutu cavalry charge by Uganda—which brought a strong contingent[2]—and joined by armed detachments from the armies of Burundi, Tanzania, Zimbabwe, Angola and even from far away Eritrea and Ethiopia who all provided a smattering of at least symbolic forces. They also had the moral and diplomatic support of South Africa which had recently acquired a world-wide prestige rare for an African country with the dismantling of apartheid and ascent to power of Nelson Mandela.

This amounted to a pan-African crusade with Julius Nyerere as its visible head and Mobutu, the common enemy, as a symbol of all that was wrong in Africa. It was a bit naïve but for once at least free of sordid financial calculations.[3] On the French-supported side there were the rags of the Zairian Army[4] and the survivors of the Rwandese *génocidaires*. These were hardly seductive in terms of positive international relations—especially given the US position—and not very effective militarily. This made for a rather uneven balance and in November 1996, as the ADFL and the Rwandese Army progressed westwards, Paris asked the UN for a pro-Mobutu intervention to which the UN agreed. Francophone African countries all supported the intervention but the ADFL surrounded the refugee camps and herded about

370,000 refugees back into Rwanda. The Americans, who were pro-ADFL, seized the moment and the State Department declared: "The mass return of nearly half a million Rwandese Refugees from Zaïre obliges the US to review its plans in the African Great Lakes crisis". Support for the Multinational Intervention Force (MNF) in Zaïre began to fade and the US put all its weight into stopping its deployment. At the end of November the UN cancelled the MNF before even creating it and Paris remained isolated. Unwilling to deploy French troops to protect the *genocidaire* former FAR, it resorted to the bizarre stratagem of recruiting mercenaries who were hardly in a position to stop the momentum of eight African armies led by the RPF.[5] The mercenaries, a contingent of 280 mostly Serbs with a Belgian commander, were few and poorly armed. They landed in Kisangani at the end of 1996 but by March 1997 the ADFL had moved into position, putting Kisangani under siege. So Paris resorted to an even more desperate and militarily useless measure: it asked the UN and the European Union for a military intervention in order to occupy the Kisangani airport "*for humanitarian reasons*". This was presented by the French as mandatory in order to land humanitarian supplies destined for the whole region but the real reason was because the mercenary contingent had a small number of planes, hardly an air force, which could at least keep the ADFL at bay. The French wanted to keep the airport but their proposal was turned down and on March 15 the rebels took Kisangani. The last of the Serb mercenary contingent was evacuated towards Kinshasa in total confusion by French Air Force transport planes. Mobutu hung on for two more months and then fled to Morocco where he died in September 1997. Foccart had died in March and with the Congo collapse, more in ridicule than in tragedy, these events seemed to mark the end of an era. Jean-Christophe Rufin wrote in December 1996: "The events in Zaïre mark a serious failure of our African policies and will probably be seen by history as the beginning of its end". In fact, a quarter of a century later, as we now witness the death throes of *Françafrique,* we have to see that his diagnosis was both logical and premature. Why? Because when President Chirac put Foccart back on the stage he did not realise—and few observers did either—that *Françafrique* was an anachronism but one that through force of habit still had the means to perpetuate a wafer-thin structure and keep it running for some time. The relationship of *Françafrique* and its environment had changed massively and the "neo-feudalism" of France's new president towards Africa could not be obviated for long by recycling a mummy. What was perhaps more surprising was that the consequences were not manifested following Rufin's diagnosis. Quite the opposite: *Françafrique* went on working for the next twenty-five years in a state akin to sleepwalking. The agitation in the

République Centrafricaine, which occurred in parallel with to the Zaïre debacle was seen as the usual vicissitudes of a permanently troubled country and not as the forerunner of any kind of deeper transformation of Francophone Africa.[6] Meanwhile, the show went on with a few adaptations here and there, with the money being still the apparent focus. But one thing was missing: the "*grandeur*".

Back to business as usual

The nature of the French Fifth Republic is that of a Republican elective monarchy and the general outlook of the regime gives a special role to the personality of the President. Under that republican monarchy stands an enormous body of administrative offices ensuring the imprint of the state on the civilian population.[7] But *Françafrique* was on a different course. It was an improvization which was at the same time *practical,* a rude word in the French political vocabulary which loves lofty generalizations. The year 1994 with the twin catastrophes of the Elf public collapse—a national dimension—and the Rwandese genocide—an international horror—affected *Françafrique* differently. President Mitterrand was buffeted by both but in very different ways. The Elf scandal, large as it was, was part of a certain French type of politico-financial scandal. For readers with an interest in history, the first thing that springs to mind is the 1892 Panama Canal scandal where financial misdeeds were closely linked to the functioning of public affairs. The beneficiaries were domestic even if the setting was exotic and it was business as usual, except on a much larger scale than usual. The Rwandese horror belonged to another world, one where the most direct and personal political choices had no financial dimension but carried a large civilizational and historical one. It was a mysterious culture where the French, as usual secure in their "knowledge of Africa", were sure of being able to practice what had worked for them in a continent they still perceived as a homogeneous whole. The result had been a catastrophic nightmare from which Paris had a difficult time extricating itself. President Mitterrand was gone and his successor, whose instinctive Gaullist reaction had been to reach for the veteran Jacques Foccart, had to deal with an African situation Paris was trying to bring back to "normalcy". The personality of Jacques Chirac was ideal[8] for operating with *Françafrique*. In spite of his upper class education he was not a "Parisian" but a member of the provincial upper middle class, an important distinction in elite sub-identity. His direct ways with the African leaderships could co-exist with an apparent freedom of language no French president would have felt at ease using in the previous forty years. In a letter written in answer to the French Episcopate in January 2001 in which the French Bishops had asked him to be more distant and prudent with the authoritarian African leaders, he answered: "we have bled Africa dry during four and a half centuries. Then we looted its natural resources. And now to top it all we say that the Africans are good for nothing ... After getting rich at its expense, now we want to give lessons to Africa".[9] This was a typically bold *Françafrique* remark: using a rough and apt summing up of Europe's brutal handling of Africa since the sixteenth century, Chirac's conclusion led to an unexpected paradox: cold-shouldering African dictators today would be "giving Africa lessons". God forbid! To prevent such an infringement of the dictators' human rights Paris had recently nodded its approval to rigged elections in Cameroun (1997), in Togo (1998), in Gabon (1998) and in Djibouti (1999). Even more brutally, it had condoned the murder of a French judge in Djibouti who had overstepped the boundaries of the proper *Françafrique* code of behavior.[10]

The man's name was Bernard Borrel and his body had been found on October 19 1995 at the bottom of a ravine in Djibouti. His death was attributed to suicide in spite of the fact that in order to kill himself he would have had to douse himself with gasoline, set his own body on fire, crawl to the edge of the ravine and jump. What also became clear in the course of the judicial inquiry was that he had been hit from the back in a couple of places by some object which would have been capable of causing his death, quite distinctly from the bruises the rocks of the ravine had caused. Borrel had

THE BIG SLEEP (1995–2012)

been posted as a *Coopérant* (technical advisor) to the Djiboutian Ministry of Justice since 1994 and he had had access to some sensitive files in a country which besides being a valuable *Françafrique* preserve was also the focus of international interest.[11]

In Paris the death of Borrel was extremely sensitive and became a French *affaire* which was followed closely by Michel de Bonnecorse.[12] Mrs Borrel lodged a complaint against various Djiboutian institutions and personalities, including the then head of the Secret Service (SDS) Ismail Omar Guelleh who was asked to come to Paris and to testify in a French court of law. He was received privately by President Chirac who told him that he personally believed in the suicide theory! Chirac advised Ismail Omar Guelleh to lodge a complaint to the International Court of Justice (ICJ), which he did. The ICJ could then condemn France for refusing to transmit the file to The Hague under the pretext of the separation of powers. That way the case would be entirely judged in Djibouti. This led of course to the end of the story.[13] The case of the judge who had committed suicide by dousing himself with gasoline and jumping off a cliff had reached a dead end. As for Ismail Omar Guelleh, he became President of Djibouti in 1999, a position he still holds at the time of writing after several successful "re-elections".

What was of interest in the Borrel *affaire* was the procedure by which the French Presidency had "solved" the problem. President Chirac had had to make use of an international institution because a medium size nation state such as France no longer had the capacity to impose its will in a transnational case.

Similarly the problem of carrying out the will of the government in a domestic context had become increasingly difficult. The Ministry of Cooperation—"rue Monsieur" to the cognoscenti—was in fact a "Ministry for Africa", much too open in its procedures for close examination, parliamentary or otherwise. By 1996 an internal audit showed that Public Aid disbursed by the Ministry of Cooperation had decreased by 11.5%. Increasingly Public Aid was going through the Ministry of Finance pipeline, where professional financiers could blend it in discrete channels that were more neutral than the folkloric way it had been so far handled by the Ministry of Cooperation. If we look at direct aid to Africa dealt with by the Ministry of Cooperation (there were of course other beneficiaries apart from those of the African continent) it now represented less than 50% of the total while it had peaked at 80% around 1980. The number of *coopérants* (field advisors), the foot soldiers of French cultural and technical influence in Africa, was shrinking. They went from over 10,000 in 1980 to a little more than 2,000 by the end of the 1990s. The "technicians" were circling the old financial structure of Africa-in-Paris and in February 1998 the *Caisse Française de Développement* was turned into an "Agency", which was considered to be the French equivalent of USAID.

THE BIG SLEEP (1995–2012)

The staff of the Ministry of Cooperation, who felt that they were heading towards the exit, issued a public statement saying that they were not responsible for the "mistakes and the general drift" of development aid to Africa. Their complaint was clearly linked to both the Rwandese catastrophe and the Elf scandal in that it mentioned "private networks" and "corrupt lobbies which proliferate both in the public financing and in the privatization of African companies". But the process of corruption, and even the outright manipulation of statistics began at the government level itself. Many of the computations that lead to internationally official figures were too often seen globally without deconstructing the figures that went into the global results. For example the money spent by Paris included the expenses made for the French Departments and Territories (DOM/TOM), which are administratively and internationally considered to be part of France itself.[14] Therefore counting the money spent in the DOM/TOM as international aid would be similar to doing so for UK expenditure in Jersey and Guernsey. DOM/TOM expenses represent 30 to 40% of "international aid". Another miscalculation of the latter is that it included the funds spent on asylum-seekers whose presence in France hardly counted as aid for the countries from which they fled. Some of these asylum-seekers paradoxically had fled from countries whose governments benefited from that very French foreign aid! Moreover export guarantees, including those to the countries that benefit from French foreign aid, were computed as part of French aid when they were disbursed. For example French export guarantees let us say to countries such as Congo Brazzaville or Cameroun—both notorious for not paying the invoices of French exporters—the French government would pay the unpaid bill and the amount would be credited as part of French aid to Brazzaville or to Yaounde. Another dubious arrangement was tied aid. This meant that the beneficiary country placed an order with a company from the donor country for the aid project. Knowing that such a system was reliable and submitted to hardly any close supervision, businesses in donor countries—France being the second largest aid donor after the US in terms of taking back with one hand what it had given with the other—usually over-invoiced after distributing largesse among the local political elite which had "selected" the company, it of course being the ultimate beneficiary.

The transition that was taking place was simply a technical evolution of the French *pré carré* (our backyard) by which internationally accepted accounting procedures and transparent administrative techniques were so much new décor, rather than representing any substantive improvement in such aid schemes. In 1999 the Ministry of Cooperation was finally simply closed down and its personnel redistributed to various branches

THE BIG SLEEP (1995–2012)

of the civil service. But there took place one of these anecdotes which in their stark simplicity summarize a whole era, a whole new setting. The Ministry of Cooperation had been established in the 1950s and housed in a beautiful eighteenth-century former convent, 20 rue Monsieur in the 7th arrondissement of Paris, one of the most prestigious parts of the French capital. In 2000 the sumptuous building and its gardens were sold to Russian investors who had bided their time and in 2012 the entire group of buildings and gardens was bought after years of diplomatic negotiations by the People's Republic of China. Beijing immediately launched a five year program of "modernization" and in April 2017, 20 Rue Monsieur, the former official economic home of the Ministry of Cooperation and officious hub of *Françafrique,* became the Chinese Embassy in Paris. The symbolic weight of that imperial transfer is left to the reader's imagination.

But meanwhile business as usual continued and that meant maintaining law and order, whatever the ambiguity attached to such words, on the part of the now definitely limping *Françafrique.* The clever administrative and accounting measures carried out in Paris were designed to maintain a proper facade (and to keep making a good amount of money) of French influence, notwithstanding the unending problem of security. Small emergencies continued to erupt, such as when General Gnassingbe Eyadema, a pillar of the

Françafrique edifice and President of Togo, found himself in trouble in late 2002. General Eyadema was a kind of *Françafrique* archetype. He lived decolonization in a particular way. Being the subject of a mandated territory[15] he had started his life by crossing into Dahomey (later Benin) to join the French army. He was sent first to Indochina and later to Algeria as a French soldier. On his return to Togo he tried to join the small Togolese army that had been created at independence but was turned down. He then took part in an uprising during which soldiers killed President Sylvanus Olympio, joined the army and became president after conducting a military coup of his own. He held on to his new position by hook or by crook[16] from the coup in 1967 till his death in 2005. But in 2002 he met a hurdle which only Paris could help him clear: he was diagnosed with cancer and wanted to modify the constitution to enable his thirty-five-year-old son to succeed him as president in spite of the fact that constitutionally the minimum age for the presidency was forty-five. This created an obstacle to the instauration of the hereditary monarchy he was dreaming of and in turn prompted a French intervention, but Eyadema lived another three years and it was only after a final 52% "re-election" in 2003 that he died in power in 2005. And when things got a bit more difficult, Parliament was used to ensure the "election" of the new president. The civil service smoothed out the process (the former president's son,

THE BIG SLEEP (1995–2012)

Faure Gnassingbe, got 60.15% of the vote according to the obedient Constitutional Court) but then the exasperated population took to the streets. Thirty-eight years of military power and a neo-colonial country where per capita income had declined steadily over those years. It was an unarmed uprising and 790 people were killed according to local sources—with the UN claiming only 400 to 500. For Togo the Big Sleep continues: there were three more presidential elections—in 2010, 2015 and 2020—and in the usual Togolese manner a fair number of corpses were dumped in the ocean, making counting the casualties somewhat difficult. Each election result was better than the last: 60.9% in 2010, 58.75% in 2015 and a triumphant 72.36% in 2020. But Togo remains a "danger zone" for *Françafrique*, given fifty-six years in power for the same family. As we will see in the next chapter when we look at the case of Gabon, a monarchy without a tradition is extremely difficult to keep stable in the long run.

Since the early 1990s a growing popular agitation had led to the setting up of "National Conferences" whose primary aim was to try to limit the unending mandates of the *Françafrique* presidents. The "National Conferences" often achieved their aims only to be defeated later by constitutional manipulations. We saw above how this was circumvented in Togo. In Cameroun, Paul Biya, in power since 1982, had no dynastic ambitions. He just wanted to "die in power" as one

Camerounian analyst said. In February 2008 the constitution was modified to allow for an unlimited number of presidential mandates. But this modification immediately triggered massive demonstrations around the slogan "Biya must go" (in English) which everybody recognized as the not-so-dead-body of the UPC flickering to life (see the previous chapter). The rioters prioritized ransacking French shops and businesses, although the rioting was country-wide and not only in Bamileke country, the former UPC stronghold. The repression was massive and a minimum of 140 people were killed. This did not prevent Biya from being reelected in October 2011 with 78% of the vote. He was seventy-eight. Within a few months fighting broke out in the Buea/Bamenda English-speaking part of western Cameroun. It was not only a symptom of the failed protests of 2008; it was also the re-apparition of a ghost that had never been dead, that of Ruben Um Nyobe. The fighting is still going on at the time of writing. But when President Macron visited Cameroun (July 2022) after his re-election, nothing concerning this problem was discussed, just as if the civil war did not exist.

Death (and history) are constant companions of the *Françafrique*. So death finally caught up with the man who had fathered the name and later was its kingpin and main symbol, Félix Houphouët-Boigny, who went to the grave in 1993. By the time of his demise, the Ivory Coast was a (modest) case of economic success, a commercial hub for the entire west African region, with trade connections far inland. But due to the impact of the La Baule speech or more probably due to Houphouët's remarkable political flair, the glorious veteran of post/neo colonial struggles decided to switch the Ivory Coast's political system from a single to a multi party system. This change had been an earthquake in most African countries in the 1990s before the rulers understood the new rules of the game and moved to develop authoritarian pseudo-democracies. Houphouët did not have time for "African democracy" (to which he would certainly have adapted) but he died as the changeover was in process. It took place just as the *Françafrique* "business as usual" which had creakingly adapted to the post-genocide Rwanda era had painfully reached cruising speed. But in many ways the Ivory Coast was the boat's economic engine. And it started to sputter.

Identity politics lead to a sporadic civil war in Ivory Coast

Anybody can be a member of a single party, it is only a question of political and personal loyalty to a monolithic system. But when the ground opens to any organization aspiring to rule the country, this calls for a problem of criteria defining what that organization is. And here enters what is the 600lbs gorilla sitting in most presidential palaces in Africa and about which nobody wants to speak: what are the borders in Africa and how is citizenship defined?

The mid-nineteenth century, when the European Powers began to upgrade their presence in Africa from trading stations to embryonic colonies, was when the colonial problem began to develop. The absence of durable nation-states with defined borders across Africa left the geographical situation diplomatically undefined at a time when intra-European imperialisms, semi dormant since the Treaty of Vienna in 1815, were revived. This was particularly the case after the German victory over France in 1871 which had brought in Berlin as the new arbiter of the post-Napoleonic era. Africa was a global exception, the largest "free" territory anywhere on earth and militarily the weakest. But Chancellor Bismarck, who was culturally a man of the early nineteenth century—he was 56 when his victory in the French war gave birth to the German Empire—was not particularly interested in these distant spaces. After the victory over France and the rise of Germany to a leading partition in the European "Concert of Nations", he long refused to interest himself in the latest fashion of acquiring colonies. However a number of the Bismarckian elite began to experience what the Germans called the *Tosrschlusspanik* (the panic of the closing door): Germany had come late on the European scene, as Africa was being discreetly partitioned between France and Great Britain,[17] letting Germany (and the new Italian state) stand gawping at the side of the road, at a time when a colonial empire was the equivalent of a UN Security Council seat today. Many in Germany began to think that their brand-new country ought to play a key role in Africa even if very few members of the national elite cared in any way about the dark continent. In 1882 the *Deutscher Kolonialverein* (German Society for Colonization) had been founded and joined the colonial lobbying, finally dragging a reluctant Bismarck into calling for a world conference of "civilized nations" to address the subject (November 1884).

Initially the topic of the conference was far from the one to which it led in practice: it was supposed to legislate on the question of the territories King Leopold of Belgium claimed in Central Africa and on the freedom of navigation on the Congo River. All the "Great Powers" assembled in Berlin for that official purpose but since Belgium was far from being a key member of the conference, the assembly soon turned to sketching out the territorial dismemberment of the African continent. The conference lasted four months (till February 1885) and in the diplomatic history of the world, it is probably one of those which has had the biggest and the most durable impact of all times (Tordesillas had long been forgotten!). Some small adjustments were made later and a big reset occurred after 1918 when Germany lost all its colonies. But the results are still with us today and they imply a very approximate view of the borders which were negotiated very far away from the people they concerned and with none of their participation. The problem was compounded because the Europeans had only a limited knowledge of the geography and even less knowledge (and interest) in the tribal realities that underpinned the "borders" artificially drawn by foreign powers. Those borders were essentially the results of the power relations between the Europeans themselves without regard to the improbable nations that were one day to be born out of these colonial arrangements. In 1885 a map of independent Africa belonged to a kind of Alice in Wonderland world. For the Europeans, in the perspective of the time, this was nothing to be concerned about.

Let us now jump to post-colonial times. On August 26 1995 Henri Konan Bédié introduced the concept of "Ivority" in the definition of the eligibility of a person for the Presidency of the Republic. Like so many of the decisions concerning citizenship and politics in "independent Africa" this "new concept" was in fact a tactical move dictated by immediate circumstances. Konan Bédié had been President of the National Assembly at the death of Houphouët-Boigny and as such he had inherited the presidency in 1993 without needing to hold any election. His main rival was Alassane Ouattara, a Dioula from the North who might not have been able to satisfy the "Ivority" requirement for candidacy, given his region of origin and a later very international career.[18] The following year he became president of the *Parti Démocratique de Côte d'Ivoire* (PDCI), the first step to becoming a real *Françafrique* presidential boss. On the surface at least it started fairly well with the 1995 election which he won with 96.44% of the vote. But this mandate was based more on being the heir of Houphouët-Boigny than on his own charisma and to a deft amount of poll-rigging. Later, when a large scandal erupted around the huge sums of money paid by the European Union to fund health programs in the Ivory Coast and which were allegedly stolen by the President, the regime wobbled. Additionally and above all, these stupendous results were the outcome not only of neat automatic rigging mechanisms but more than anything because all potential presidential candidates had agreed to boycott the polls because of the "Ivority" criteria which almost nobody found acceptable. More than many other countries in Africa, the Ivory Coast was a crossroads of marginal and "foreign" ethnic groups and hardly fertile ground for identity politics.

As for the French, who had a massive presence in the country but purely from the angle of a business cornucopia, they were out of their depth. On December 24 1999 President Konan Bédié was overthrown in a coup led by a former Chief of Staff of the Ivorian Army, General Robert Gueï, and Konan Bédié had to be airlifted from his presidential palace by a French Army helicopter, a shocking emergency symptomatic of the deep crisis into which *Françafrique* had descended. As for Gueï, he was born in the southwest region of Man, of the Géré tribe, a perfect example of the complex origins that made the "Ivority" rule a dangerous and unenforceable piece of legislation.[19] But Gueï had no solution to the ethnic dragon which had raised its head when Konan Bedié had introduced ethnicity as a pivotal factor in Ivorian politics, a country where non-citizens represented 26% of the population during his period in power. During the next few years of the Gueï *de facto* mandate the government played with the "Ivority" rule as with a live grenade, not knowing if it was going to use it to coerce the electorate or as a weapon against its challengers. For the elections planned for 2000, fourteen out of the nineteen candidates were rejected by the Supreme Court because of the blind application of the "Ivority" clause. But Gueï had instructed the Court to let through the Front Populaire Ivoirien (FPI) led by Laurent Gbagbo and the Rassemblement des Républicains (RDR) led by Alassane Ouattara. This meant a Bété from the South and a Dioula from the North and was apparently based on the hope of simplifying the ethnic conundrum which had blocked politics since Konan Bédié had forced his tribal decree on the political debating floor. Nevertheless the election led to ethnic clashes and Gbagbo was somehow proclaimed as president on October 26 2000. The

THE BIG SLEEP (1995–2012)

situation remained precariously balanced till September 19 2002 when multiple uprisings started in Abidjan itself, in Bouaké, the country's second city and capital of the central region and in Korhogo, third city of the country and capital of the North. President Gbagbo was conveniently abroad in Italy. Several political leaders were killed, including Robert Gueï himself. The whole political system of the Ivory Coast collapsed, causing a sporadic civil war which would last five years (2002–07), in which the French took part and which ended because of battle fatigue and the promotion of Alassane Ouattara as a conciliator and a lesser evil.

This was not another Rwanda, i.e. a complex unknown cultural world whose deep workings were foreign to *Françafrique*. Nor was this a head-on ethnic conflict with a long and brutal history. It was a collision course between the *Françafrique* Paris-led system and the reality of the continent. Houphouët-Boigny's long career went back to the French Fourth Republic and to the colonial era since 1946. He had been the original pillar of the *Françafrique* system and even the creator of its name, even if at the time it was in a completely different context than the one it acquired later. He was familiar with Paris and Paris was familiar with him. The unacknowledged "Empire" rested on one basic prop, the single party system and vertical authoritarian power chains. Democratic change, which the African populations were going to associate with the breaking down of France's grip on power, could not survive in the *Françafrique* system as it had been working hitherto. The *Françafrique* system was neither a real political system nor a gentlemen's club—it was a mutual support association of authoritarian leaders (mild or rough, depending on the circumstances) which incarnated at the head of the former French colonies the interests of France. The Ivory Coast had been the first *internal* upheaval of *Françafrique* (Rwanda had been external and even deliberately externalized) but in the Ivory Coast Alassane Ouattara had remained as a mild buffer—not as the saviour of the system because by then nobody could be anything other than its life-support machine. Whether he actually stays in power or loses it in the future remains an open question. Other long-standing *Françafrique* heads of state were either dead (Bongo) or politically largely spent (Sassou Nguesso). This made Alassane Ouattara the last smiling caretaker of what was now a slowly dying empire.

Trying to ride a wounded animal: Françafrique*'s attempted romance with Paul Kagame*

Rwanda had no French colonial tradition. It had been a last-minute patch added to the *Françafrique* quilt but one that prompted the ripping up of the entire ensemble. The Francophone African elites had felt a global solidarity that Paris had nurtured from the start and the Rwandese tragedy was privately seen by many of them in a very French way. Yes this was a terrible event but it was also seen as a systemic political catastrophe before being perceived as a humanitarian one. And there was no need to pander to the new regime since it was obviously an "Anglo-Saxon" creature. Nothing has been written about that and for two good reasons: the first is decency—or at least its pretense—and the second is practical expediency. Before being *genocidaire* the post-Habyarimana regime was first and foremost, vanquished. The private discussions in African Francophone political circles were verging on the unmentionable, but what was being lamented was how Mitterrand had bowed to the "Anglo-Saxon" camp. African solidarity did not easily cross the language barrier. But there was a crack: France had been caught red-handed in an exposed situation, not of collaborating with the genocide as some extreme critics of *Françafrique* ventured to write, but of being *on the wrong side.* It meant one thing: being protected by the French was no longer sufficient; you could be protected by *Françafrique* and be vanquished and overthrown anyway. Of course the apparent cause of your defeat was enormous, the crime of crimes. But everyone knew that even if the "Hutu Power" regime had fallen after committing a genocide, the genocide had not been the cause of its defeat. It was already falling apart *before* the genocide, meaning that being under France's protection was no longer the 100% fire insurance it used to be. Actually the breaking point, little noticed at the time, had been the Ivorian civil war: France's protective mantle could not prevent a civil war and once it had broken out it was unable to guarantee victory for those Paris supported.

Françafrique had been a transnational political creature and the Rwanda tragedy had been the blade that stabbed it. Jacques Chirac was obviously not aware of that open wound and carried on in the good old ways of the good old days. He overlooked the Ivorian civil war, apparently thinking Rwanda had been an exception where Mitterrand had stumbled but not the logical consequence of a basically flawed system.[20] President François Hollande intervened in Mali (2012) in the old *Françafrique* style without being fully aware of what he was doing. As was frequent in his presidency, things happened without the events being fully or clearly understood or calculated by the president himself. His refusal to run for a second term was probably the wisest decision he ever took. But starting in 2017, this left several gaping holes. And President Macron, whose view of Africa was charmingly naïve, was left with a cracked earthenware structure for which he needed something drastic, either a complete overhaul or the junk heap. He chose neither and simply went looking for new parts to be added to the old Rube Goldberg contraption. In the completely transforming political landscape of the early twenty-first century, President Macron went shopping for a technician to fix the apparatus, but as always trend conscious and self-contradictory,[21] he chose the best known African in the world, the Rwandese President Paul Kagame. Paul Kagame also happened to be the arch opponent of the damaged old French system.

The beginning of the French *rapprochement* with Rwanda's RPF, the former enemy, took at first a most non-military aspect, that of France's handling of the *Organisation Internationale de la Francophonie* (OIF) politics.[22] Since 2014 the Secretary General of OIF was a Haitian-born Canadian lady, or should we say perhaps *Québécois* lady, named Michaëlle Jean. A prestigious and clever member of the Haitian bourgeoisie (her family fled Haiti in 1968 to escape the dictatorship of François Duvalier) she married a white Frenchman[23] and entered Canadian politics and society at the top level through a remarkable career as a bilingual journalist and TV personality. In 2005 this itinerary culminated in her being appointed Governor General of Canada, a position of very little power but extreme prestige. She was the third woman and the first "black" person to be a Governor-General. Having reached a kind of aristocratic social ceiling in Canada she looked for an international position to continue her career beyond her adopted country. With the support of Abdou Diouf she was unanimously chosen as the new OIF Secretary General in Dakar in 2014. She was perceived as the stylish and clever "voice of Paris" at the head of the OIF, something completely typical for the *Francophonie* club since its outset. With the added "dash" of being female and "colored" she looked like a modish twenty-first-century-compatible notional addition to *Françafrique*.

But in 2017 Emmanuel Macron was elected to the French presidency. His relationship to Africa was ethereal, derived from having been despatched for an internship by his socially exclusive *Ecole Nationale d'Administration* (ENA) to Nigeria.[24] He came from a provincial middle class background with the technocratic credentials essential to achieve ENA membership. And being propelled from there into Africa, he was in the position of an *haute cuisine* chef who was sent to McDonald's to flip burgers. There he met a number of Nigerian technocrats and he thought that Abuja represented Africa. This was both logical and completely warped. Emmanuel Macron was an untypical animal in the French political landscape. He came to power to carry out reforms, any reforms, with the certainty of being always right about everything (hence his other nickname, "Jupiter"). He seemed to think there was a technical solution to every problem, an attitude which had already done a lot of damage to many aid programs in Africa. In the new president's office, there were still bloodstains on the Africa desk left from the 1994 horror and the recent decision by President François Hollande to send troops to Mali had given a dismal *déja vu* impression to the French public. "Not again!" was the popular feeling. Actually the *Barkhane* expedition had nothing to do with the French intervention in Rwanda in 1990, except that it was taking place in Africa. But for somebody with a hurried and inexperienced view of the continent such as Mr Macron, this was enough for him to eschew anything resembling what had been done by the incompetents who preceded him. He had found a "technical solution" to what "old Africa hands" would have thought peripheral: OIF contacts were made with Kagame who cautiously proposed the possible candidacy of his Minister of Foreign Affairs, Louise Mushikiwabo. Given the nationality of Michaëlle Jean, further contacts were made with Justin Trudeau, and apparently the Canadian Prime Minister had no objections.

So in October 2018, at the Yerevan Conference,[25] Louise Mushikiwabo steamrolled the attempted extension of Michaëlle Jean's term and Paul Kagame now sat indirectly at the head of the world *Francophonie* organization. Done. Jupiter had put Africa in its pocket. Or had he? There were criticisms, some personal and irrelevant—Louise Mushikiwabo was married to an American—but also some more rational: in 2003 President Kagame had replaced French with English as the European language of choice for Rwandese schools and Rwanda had joined the Commonwealth. For old *Françafrique* diehards, this was hard to swallow. But President Macron did not seem to care even though Ms Mushikiwabo took a broom to the OIF staff positions.

All Department Directors were replaced through a simple letter—even those who were close to retirement. Money was used loosely, with certain staff members spending lavishly, to the point that the French government asked for an audit from KPMG, a neutral Anglo-Dutch consulting firm. KPMG concluded that "OIF had become a structure pyramidal and also informal in its management", something Africans are unfortunately quite familiar with in their own administrations. But President Macron had already moved on to some other "reform" and President Kagame, who pays far more attention to detail, diplomatic or otherwise, had added another string to his fiddle. It was not the only one. There was Africa, after all.

There Paul Kagame had embarked on a new business: to become the continent's overall force for security, ready to face off either the jihadist guerrillas that were beginning to proliferate in the Sahel[26] or perhaps the Russian Wagner group which had begun a different form of implantation. Mozambique had been his training ground. Mozambique and Angola had been the major Cold War areas of confrontation with a civil war between pro-Russian and South African-linked guerilla groups (1977–92)[27] but the conflict which had later drawn in the Rwandese in Mozambique was quite distinct. It had started in March 2021 with a jihadist attack in the North where a mixture of local Muslims (they were part of minority tribes) was joined by an international adjunction of Islamists from the Congo, Kenya and from as far away as Somalia, all having regrouped in nearby Tanzania which they used as a rear base. The post-Cold War poorly-equipped Mozambican army was in no shape to repel the attacks. The Russian Wagner militiamen tried to do so and were defeated. All this was taking place in a province (Cabo Delgado) where a consortium of fossil fuel companies headed by the French oil giant Total was prospecting an estimated $30 billion natural gas deposit, one of the biggest in the world. Due to the fighting all the LNG prospectors had halted their operations. The new streamlined Rwanda-friendly *Françafrique* was contacted by Total and the results were impressive. It took the Rwandese expeditionary force less than eighteen months to push the jihadi force back into Tanzania. There were long discussions with Total and its associates (Chinese, Italian, US and Indian) and a pause was agreed. The exploration work might restart in 2024. President Macron expressed his discreet satisfaction.[28]

Another deployment of the Rwandese was also linked with the presence of the Russians that became rather abruptly noticed through the murder in CAR in July 2018 of three of their journalists. The reason for their presence was unexpected but logical: they were trying to piece together a study of the presence of mercenaries from the Wagner Group, at the time a little-known shadowy presence, which had fought freelance alongside the Russian forces in the Syrian civil war. The three Russian journalists had heard about the (small) Wagner deployment in Africa and were trying to learn more about it. Wagner was indeed present in a mode typical of the reason for creating it, that is to operate secretly on behalf of Moscow's interests. The journalists were killed, directly or indirectly by Wagnerites. But this time the Rwandese did not displace them; rather they joined forces in a strange parallel alliance unofficially going through the UN.[29]

It was in late 2017 that Yevgeny Prigozhin, probably on the orders of Vladimir Putin, chose to extend his Middle East operations to Africa. His choice was strategically perfect: the CAR was the weakest point in the whole continent where a religious and ethnic civil war had broken out in December 2012 after years of confusion alternating with dictatorial government—"the Empire" of Jean-Bedel Bokassa proclaimed in 1977, the French Army retaking direct control of CAR in September 1979, the Bozize coup in 2003 and finally the civil war in 2012. In the colonial era the then-named Ubangui-Chari (and by extension the whole of former *Afrique Equatoriale Française* or AEF) was nicknamed by the civil servants in the Ministry of Colonies as "the Cinderella of the Empire" and by the rougher-speaking colonial troops "the ***hole of Africa." Now the weakest point of what had been the Empire had become the weakest point of *Françafrique* since 1960. It is interesting to note that Prigozhin always felt the *Françafrique* had turned the former French colonies into the soft underbelly of the continent at the expense of the West while both the French themselves (through pride and ignorance) and their American allies (through ignorance and laziness) felt that during the Cold War the French were in a position to "keep order" in Black Africa. It was a catastrophe waiting to happen and Prigozhin was right. Now the catastrophe had happened and it was not the Russians who had caused it. They just took advantage of it.[30]

There was no real trigger point in the CAR. The territory was not only AEF but the worst part of AEF. It had always functioned poorly and when a new factor was added—a Muslim rebellion even though there were only 10% Muslims in the country—this was the straw that broke the camel's back. Since its army was of such low quality the Muslims of the Seleka group managed to occupy Bangui in March 2013. They behaved with extreme brutality during the six months they were in power (March–September 2013) and this led to a Christian reaction of genocidal proportions (the formation of the anti-Balaka movement) which was condemned by the UN and which led in turn to the creation (in 2014) of a 17,000 man MINUSCA UN Army.[31] The "religious war" in the CAR was not on the general jihadi model because Seleka had no links with Arab fundamentalist Islamist organizations and it was more a fight where the northwestern tribes (who had been Islamized by contact with the Sudan) fought the central and southern tribes which were Christian and had been a little bit better treated during colonial times. The problem was more economic neglect and the non-existence of the state than a religious conflict.[32] The French left in 2016 and Faustin-Archange Touadéra (elected by a marginal majority in 2015) chose to call in the Russians.[33] They conducted operations with appalling violence and in June 2021 MINUSCA announced it would no longer collaborate with them against the rebels.[34] Wagner dug in and soon became the dominant political-military force in CAR. Now, after Prigozhin's assassination, the Russians who have remained on the spot are fighting both the CPC and Seleka on several fronts and the Bangui office has become the Russian militia's "central command" (inasmuch as there is one) for Africa.

In fact the "decentralization" of Wagner or of its successive militia brands is one of the main problems of Russia's intervention. There is no contemporary equivalent of the Comintern, particularly in political terms. The deciding factor is all too often money and strategic commercial opportunities. Thus the murder of nine Chinese workers on March 19 2023 at a gold mine near Bambari was initially attributed to Bozize's CPC and caused friction between the Russians and the Chinese in the CAR.[35] The Americans consider the

THE BIG SLEEP (1995–2012)

Wagner Office in Bangui to be run irrationally and were putting a certain amount of pressure, directly and through the French, to get Touadéra to kick out Wagner and replace them with Rwandese forces.[36] But things didn't seem to go the way the Americans would have liked in order to destabilize Wagner in Bangui. Wagner flew several planeloads of militiamen with their equipment to the CAR to ensure that the July 30 "Referendum on Terms Extension" for President Touadéra went the way the Russians wanted.[37] The rebellions (CPC and Seleka) are not over but today the main job of Wagner in CAR is military assistance to Hemedti in Darfur[38] and also to help him in the financial and accounting work for the gold mines it controls.

But what about *Françafrique* in this confused mishmash? Basically it was wobbling because its link with official French policy had been ruptured in December 2016 when François Hollande refused to put Operation Sangaris (the French deployment force) back on the road. Hollande had just terminated the four year long and frustratingly unsuccessful military expedition France had deployed in the CAR. Even the most convinced supporters of *Françafrique* were tired of wading in the Central African swamp. The mess was beyond frustration, the rewards, even symbolic, were limited and when President Macron was elected the following year he brought in a new (simplified) vision of

Africa, one that differed from that of the colonial era bureaucrats and advisors. I mentioned earlier the removal of OIF senior staff because (a) it was something *Françafrique* veterans would have opposed had they been able; (b) there were no important business contracts at stake; and (c) the French army, already deeply enmeshed in its recent deployment in Mali, felt uneasy about extending more men and material into a renewal of the CAR commitment, which was already a lost cause. If Paul Kagame was able and willing to go in deeper and confront the Russians there, this was exactly the kind of situation Macron had befriended him for.

Libya: One intervention too many
In the first chapter of this book we followed the birth of *Françafrique* but we never defined it (was it ever possible to do so?) and nor did we set out the rules governing its activities. This is quite logical since *Françafrique* never existed legally (it was a perfect illustration of the English saying: "The proof of the pudding is in the eating") and any document underpinning it, like a charter of rights or obligations for *Françafrique* "members", would have been an aberration. The existence of the beast was acknowledged in political speeches and declarations but it was always accompanied with remarks about its demise and declarations about positive changes for which the speaker claimed credit and about which he announced seductive reforms (here we need another

THE BIG SLEEP (1995–2012)

popular saying, French this time: "The more it changes, the more it remains the same"). But there were unspoken rules directing its functioning. We can summarize them roughly thus:

1. French interests come first and our action is here to serve them;
2. We are the last rung of a tradition's long ladder of which we are proud;
3. We operate by ourselves. Any ally or helper is subordinate to our wishes;
4. We work in our former colonies with whom we share experience and friendship and whom we can force to obey us in case they break ranks;
5. We obey no one. We can and will work our way around disagreeing partners.

These principles are not ranked in terms of importance. The feeling was: we are freebooters.[39] We do what we think is good for *la patrie* and personally what is beneficial for us. The problem was that none of these rules applied to the French intervention in Libya. How did it happen?

On December 18 2010 a young man by the name of Muhammad Buazizi immolated himself in the small town of Sidi Buzid in Tunisia. He was a street fruit and vegetable vendor and a police officer had overturned his cart because he was doing business without a vendor's permit. To make matters worse the police officer was a woman who spat on him. Hence his gesture of despair. Limited spark, enormous consequences. His death initiated all across the Arab world a huge social and political upheaval commonly known as "The Arab Spring".

How did *Françafrique* enter this definitely non-French geopolitical space? Obviously sideways. Large disturbances which eventually forced President Zin El-Abdin Ben Ali to flee erupted in Tunisia. Similar demonstrations began rapidly to affect neighboring countries. The speed at which the social wildfire of the Arab Spring was spreading was truly amazing and it suddenly brought to life how much the Arab world was both deeply unstable and part of a single universe which was cracking at the seams, no matter the nature of the regimes.[40] And that included Libya. But Libya was a special case: ruled by an unusual regime since the 1969 coup which had brought Colonel Muhammar Gaddafi to power, it was neither an Islamist regime nor a simple military dictatorship. It was presented as a *Jamahiriyyah* (state of the masses), a kind of "decentralized revolutionary anarchist dictatorship", a unique type of creature that political science textbooks balked at defining. In fact this was the carapace hiding a centralised dictatorship. Since its beginnings in the 1970s Gaddafi's *Jamahiriyyah* had drifted from bad to worse. Its political choices had been an apparently limitless string of gross abuses: killings of opponents residing overseas, supplying weapons to the Provisional Irish Republican Army, blowing up American and French airliners, helping the US Black Panthers and Nation of Islam while supporting the overthrow of the American government.[41] This "revolutionary policy" was insane but it was buttressed by enormous financial resources derived from oil. Washington had bombed Tripoli in April 1986 in a clumsy attempt at killing Gaddafi. This bombing raid did not have the hoped for result in the short term but it seemed to have brought the whimsical dictator eventually to a degree of reflection when he began to realise the probable impact of the USSR's collapse in 1991. During the Cold War the USSR had been Gaddafi's main source of support. But by 2003 he finally dropped his nuclear research program, a move he tried to parley later into some kind of *rapprochement* with the US. In February 2011 an uprising against his regime in Benghazi had started, this being the Libyan dimension of the Arab Spring. Which is where *Françafrique* showed up. But was it still *Françafrique* or was it something different that was mistaken as being *Françafrique* simply because it was French? In many ways it was a hybrid movement. On March 17 2011 the UN had voted Resolution 1973 which aimed at stopping Gaddafi from indiscriminately crushing the population that had joined the Benghazi uprising. Two days later the French attacked the columns converging on Benghazi, bombing them while they were short of reaching the town. These attacks were taken over by NATO aircraft in compliance with Resolution 1973 and they were continued until Gaddafi was finally killed by insurgents in October 2011.

So: *Françafrique* or not *Françafrique?* Well, both at the same time and actually fifty-fifty. If we go back to the *Françafrique* unspoken rules we mentioned above, nothing fits. And not simply because the French forces which were involved were regulars. We have seen how French regular forces had often been involved in *Françafrique* operations before. But the framework was different:

1. French interests were not first and foremost;
2. There was no call to patriotism nor to any French tradition;
3. France operated together with other countries whose interests/aims/means were equal to France's;
4. Libya was not a former French colony;
5. The French coordinated with their Allies but this was definitely not a "one country show".

So then why hang this "Harmattan Operation" in the same window as other *Françafrique* interventions in Africa? Because of the force of habit and because of the people involved. By "involved" we mean the decision-making process which led to France voting for resolution 1973. The people who were behind the process at the organizational level were the usual *Françafrique* specialists although at the decision-making and political level it was completely different, in fact the complete opposite of the usual *Françafrique* actors. The people who used their influence to convince President Nicolas Sarkozy to support UN Resolution 1973 were intellectuals,[42] not a crowd usually associated with the workings of *Françafrique*. Here we have to mention a contentious matter: on March 21 2018, former President Sarkozy was charged by a Paris Court "for corruption, illegal financing of an electoral campaign and concealment of Libyan public funds". I offer no opinion on this legal case which is still under investigation.[43] The Libyan question is not the only problem former President Sarkozy has had with the financing of his 2007 election.[44] But the key person to dig more into this is Beshir Saleh Beshir, a former aide to Muhammar Gaddafi who was in charge of "anything French" in the dictator's cabinet, particularly concerning Francophone Africa. Beshir was interviewed in Johannesburg by highly experienced French journalists and this is exactly where all the submerged *Françafrique* stuff bubbled to the surface.[45] Names came up: the go-between "businessman" Alexandre Djouhri,[46] Jean-Yves Ollivier, the intermediary hiding behind his own shadow[47] and Claude Guéant, Sarkozy's very special advisor. Here we are swimming in a *Françafrique* Sargasso Sea which fully justifies including this sub-section in a book on *Françafrique*. What does Beshir

Saleh have to say about the charges against former President Sarkozy:

> I don't know much about this Franco-French stuff. I just know that Sarkozy did not care about my people and was thinking only about two things: getting re-elected and selling Rafales [a French combat plane] ... Gaddafi said he had financed Sarkozy and Sarkozy said he was not financed. I think I believe more Gaddafi than I believe Sarkozy.

To assess this remark we must remember Beshir Saleh was "Mr France" in a completely informal and "no-holds barred" dictatorial system. To conclude and give a whiff of the atmosphere interlinking the *Françafrique* role in the French intervention in the Libyan civil war we must mention Mr Boris Boillon, a former diplomat close to Muhammar Gaddafi and to former President Sarkozy, a former ambassador to Tunisia, who played a role in the French deployment in Libya and perhaps had been a facilitator when President Sarkozy had received Gaddafi in December 2007. He was caught by the police at the Gare du Nord in Paris on July 31 2013. Boillon was carrying €350,000 and $40,000 in undeclared cash as he was about to board a train to Brussels. He said this was his private money and he had no idea about the French laws concerning the carrying of cash. The bills had sequential serial numbers and had obviously never been used. The court who later sentenced him for this financial offence found him guilty but he got off with a light sentence. *Françafrique* or not *Françafrique*? This damning name was not mentioned during the trial. Did Mr Boillon know what it was? Since he was silent on the matter, who can say?

But in any case this was both a *Françafrique* operation (who was there?) and not a "typical" *Françafrique* operation. How do you rate the degree of involvement of something that does not exist into something that is extremely real and implies thousands of deaths? Great Britain shared the Libyan adventure (in a minor way) with the French. It would be interesting to know in greater detail about the British decision-making process to coordinate/follow the French one. *Françafrique* was involved with the intervention in Libya; but since there is no *Britafrica,* how did it work in London? In any case, this last venture of *Françafrique* was its last coordinated and centralized operation, too coordinated and too centralized perhaps. Here, from the shadows, *Françafrique* had one last hurrah. This was no longer the hybrid entity which had been born in 1960; it was an official humanitarian and virtuous move, something which would have puzzled Jacques Foccart had he still been alive. There was also a divergence between the networks. We already mentioned the "intellectual" atmosphere of the pressure points on Sarkozy. Another difference was the extreme ignorance of the people who intervened. In Paris, matters concerning the Arab world and Black Africa overlapped to some degree but were not the same. The people who pleaded with President Sarkozy were, to a large degree, ignorant of both. Their motives were moral and spectacular, not geopolitical. It was *politique spectacle* in the spirit of the new times. Money played a role, not in secret but almost in the open. A marginal Lebanese business operator by the name of Ziad Takieddine accused former President Sarkozy of having received money from Gaddafi to help him finance his 2007 election. Then suddenly as he was about to take the witness stand in the fourth Sarkozy court appearance on October 16 2020, Takieddine declared that what he had said about the French President having received money from Libya for his electoral expenses was false. For old *Françafrique* hands this was routine. The "thing" might be dying, but it was dying the way it had always lived. All except for the show business dimension. Libya had been one intervention too far, well beyond the traditional French comfort zone. Since 1960, *Françafrique* had been a Franco-French procedure but in Libya it had had to suddenly adapt to the wider world. It tried but it did not adapt. CAR and the Russian intervention there had been a forerunner of things to come. Libya—and its domestic bounce back—was a clearer sign that the machine had run its course. *Françafrique* was ill-equipped to overstep its traditional boundaries. The times had changed and the appearance of a new set of circumstances ruptured an already obsolescent system. France in Africa woke up painfully to a new world where the sins of the old days were suddenly up for a cash settlement? The shockwaves took some time to ripple out but once they did there was no stopping them.

5

FRANÇAFRIQUE IS NOT DEAD, IT IS MERELY FADING AWAY (2012–21)

Françafrique had never been an ideological construction. An indirect result of France's ambiguous Second World War history, it has been a makeshift product capable of keeping France's UN Security Council seat safe from Anglo-Saxon prying after a long series of colonial defeats and concomitant shrinking influence. In the anything goes confusion of the Cold War *mêlée* De Gaulle, with the technical help of Jacques Foccart, had put together a contraption with no serious basis other than it could be used in different situations. Springing from its Cameroon base, the machine worked fairly well, with many hiccups, till 1994, hence thirty-four years of acceptable near misses, a better option than African messes handcrafted by the Americans.[1] And then suddenly the Rwanda catastrophe. The African Cold War (or African Cold War lookalikes) had always been *practical* activities, never ideological ones. In Rwanda, *Françafrique* stumbled blindly into historical horror. In Libya, to which it was even less structurally adapted, *Françafrique* went into freefall, once again—as in Rwanda—because it was incapable of understanding the consequences of its actions. Nor was Libya, in a manner different from Rwanda, a philosophical abyss either; it was a simple geopolitical error. France had wanted to play in the adult league—billions of dollars, worldwide economic impact, junking a nuclear program, a move which jarred Vladimir Putin's primitive sensitivity—it all created a destructive, boomerang effect. Of course given the nature of *Françafrique*, it needed a specific transfer point between France's action in Libya and its consequences, blowing on the simmering embers of a conflict and transforming it into a major continental catastrophe.

Ghaddafi dies, his Tuareg Praetorian Guard drifts southwards and boosts the Sahelian unrest

What are the broad outlines of the Sahel, then and now?[2] Essentially the Sahel has always been and remains today the fatherless child of African geopolitics. It is a region of overlap between the Arabs of North Africa and the Black Africans of the deeper continent, sandwiching the native Tuaregs in between. It had long been an area of conflict, for both historical and climatological reasons. During the colonial period it was those "African sands" Bismarck thought could be left to France for scratching since the scratching had started as early as 1830. It ended up turning those sands into a legal extension of the "Mother Country" during the 1950s, partly to compensate for its European frustrations. The Algerian war (1956–62) and the political carousel of Muhammar Ghaddafi in Chad transformed the region into a ticking time bomb for the French. The Americans were safely far away and could handle a blown-up aircraft here or a bombed discotheque there, reciprocating offhandedly with inefficient bombing (April 1986). For the French who were next door and had remained deeply enmeshed with Maghrebi immigration problems, this was a key domestic headache. Overthrowing Ghaddafi, with whom the French were intertwined at the highest level, seemed superficially like a good idea. The so far reliable yet spluttering *Françafrique* was there for the job so it was put to work but the results were dismal: the engine had been jerry-built as a Cold War situational plug, never fine-tuned for use in the globalized world. The Sahel would be too much to handle all at once and it was not immediately seen as a possible consequence of fiddling with Ghaddafi. His crazy balancing influence was seen by Paris as crazy indeed but not as a balancing factor. On the contrary it was seen as a destabilising factor. Behind him, the Sahel was in fact an unknown quantity. The Sahel reality broadly covers, in terms of the independent "states" that followed in the wake of decolonization, Southern Libya (Fezzan), Southern Algeria, Eastern Mauritania, Northern Chad, most of Niger, Northern Nigeria, Northern Mali, Western Sudan to which should be added the Northern fringes of Cameroun, Togo, the Ivory Coast and Benin. An enormous if lightly populated land area (perhaps around a hundred million people covering roughly a quarter of the African continent), with sharply different populations superficially mixed but tending to coexist in human territorial patches rather than intermingling deeply with each other. Their coexistence had fluctuated between conflict and peace, depending on wider global dynamics—the Roman conquest of the Mediterranean shore which affected the inland trade, the Arab invasions from the East which at their peak pushed all their way up into Southern Europe, the Trans-Saharan slave raids and the Gold Trade with a pull factor from the North, the rough but stabilising Ottoman conquest which came through Egypt and last but not least, colonization from Europe. Most of the Sahel was left to France, given the third international ranking of French imperialism in nineteenth-century Europe, after the United Kingdom and the newborn "German Empire". The late conquest of Darfur by the British during the First World War was due to the tactical circumstances of the time rather than to strategic global interests while the late Italian occupation in 1911 of a poorly defined territory between Egypt and the French Maghrib had no durable impact on the Sahel. There was such a lack of colonial interest in the Sahel that when London around 1915 began to fear a Turkish intrusion in the soft interstitial territory of Darfur during the Great War, both Paris and Rome politely refused to intervene. London had to do so because there were no other takers. The main event of colonial times, unacknowledged by the colonizers at the time, was the penetration southwards of the Sanussi Tariqa (the Islamic Brotherhood) which drilled from the Maghreb into the Sahel, propagating Islamization either by converting the adepts of African tribal cults or by knocking about already established older *Turuq* (the plural of *Tariqa*) such as the Quadiriyya or the Tijjaniyya. The result was a superficially Frenchified world of diverse ethnicities brought together by geography, past history and a roughly-hewn Islam. The French fought the natives to prevent them from falling into the hands of rival colonizers rather than because of any direct colonial interest. These territories, administratively divided between the bureaucratic rivalries in Paris, were the poor children of colonization, neglected because of their lack of intrinsic value and their absence of strategic interest. They had some gold, many mangy camels. In the late 1950s and early 1960s, when decolonization was becoming mandatory for France, a delegation of Tuaregs met with General De Gaulle in Paris, asking him to create a state distinct both from *Maghrib* and from Black Africa. The general, who was struggling to extricate himself from the war in Algeria, knew that he would have to grant independence to the FLN, just as oil was being found in the Sahara, complicating an already complicated situation. So he spurned the opportunity to create a further difficulty by sponsoring a new Tuareg state and it was the attempt to finally create it[3] which prompted President François Hollande to intervene in Mali in 2013.

Ghaddafi was never "President" of Libya; he was the "Brotherly Leader and Guide of the Revolution", a title as grand and confused as the land he came to rule. "Libya" did not exist before the Italians forced it into life after 1911. They were not even convinced of the coherence of their conquest and reorganized it administratively several times. Between the Italian defeat in 1943 and 1951, "Libya" was an occupied enemy territory and since there were not enough educated people to organise elections, in 1951 the Allies chose a Sheikh of the al-Sanussi lineage and made him "King". He had no genuine influence on his sand-blown domain and was easily overthrown in 1969 by a young Colonel, Muhammar Ghaddafi, who presided over a metamorphic regime, improvising on the various Arab political possibilities of his time (1969–2011) till he was killed in the throes of the Arab Spring. His personal bodyguards were chosen from among the Tuareg who constituted a small and loyal minority in the southern Fezzan region of Libya and who stood by the dictator till the end. But after the Guide's death they drifted southwards with their guns[4] and resurrected the dream of a state of their own, in a region that was far from being at peace.

The main influence on the Sahel came from the north, from the fallout of the post-colonial Algerian civil war (1992–2002) to which Europe had paid so little attention.[5] After holding out for ten years, the Islamist radicals had lost the national war and created an insurgent guerilla group (*Groupe Salafiste de la Prédication et du Combat* or GSPC) which recruited in Southwestern Algeria but also outside the Algerian borders, in Eastern Mauritania and Northern Mali. It supported a radical Islamist program but raised money through non-Muslim sources: kidnapping hostages and delivering drugs coming from Colombia and Mexico through Guinea Bissau, which they sold on to the Italian mafia as the final customer.

There had been five Tuareg revolts in the 1990s in Mali[6] and a veteran of those, Iyad Ag Ghali, had created in 2007 the *Mouvement National pour la Liberation de l'Azawad* (MNLA). This was a truly Tuareg nationalist organization, albeit one that lacked a financial basis. So Iyad Ag Ghali joined al-Qaeda to get access to Arab funds and subcontracted some of his men to bolster Ghaddafi's guard for the same reason. By the time Ghaddafi was killed and his Tuareg soldiers started to head south, a *de facto* collaboration between al-Qaeda and the Islamic State (ISIS) threatened Northern Mali where a Pan-African Islamist movement (*Mouvement pour l'Unicité et le Djihad en Afrique de l'Ouest* or MUJAO) had grown and allied itself to the MNLA. Together they created an Islamist front (al-Qaeda in the Islamic Maghreb or AQIM). Complicated? Yes, indeed, but rather simple on the ground where the global Islamist forces took Kidal and Kuna, besieged Gao and Timbuktu and threatened Bamako. In a panic, President Ismail Boubakar Keita asked the French for help and within days a French expeditionary force landed in Mali. It was an official manifestation of *Françafrique,* a step up to the national respectability which had long been considered as missing in its operations. There was no money to be made in Mali and no strategic interests either. But it was a test of French international capacity, a measure of its military weight and political will, all in the name of a popular cause and with the support of the local population, a support which materialized in the "African" south of the country but not in its Arab/Tuareg North. Such "details" were neglected in the name of unanimity. It was an effort at replaying Rwanda, but upwards and forward, in the right glorious direction. President François Hollande flew to Bamako and was welcomed with a restrained show of gratitude due to the cultural differences between the culturally strange "Islamist" invaders and the mainstream Muslim victims they threatened. This was mistakenly taken for genuine "global" popular support. The Americans breathed a sigh of relief because in Mali the West seemed to enjoy genuine backing from a Muslim population, any Muslim population. The Malian Army had suffered severe losses at the hands of the Tuareg rebels who would definitely not have been welcome had they reached Bamako. The old system kept repeating itself without any special effort at changing the social and economic substratum which was the real cause of the insurrection. Far from improving, the "Islamist" uprising kept oozing out from its starting point and affected a growing part of Sahel, transferring itself from a specific *Tuareg* impact point to broader "African" populations.

The Jihadi oil slick starts spreading out of Mali

Mali was a special case in the global Sahel crisis because it represented a simplified entry point. The French troops performed well but the war went badly because the civilian population irrationally expected a boon of prosperity associated with the presence of the French Army, a kind of soft recolonization where the benevolent French would free the population from its French-protected elites. This was a bad case of mistaken geopolitical perception. The French were there to *protect* the elites they sponsored from an "Islamist" rebellion that was trying to maneuver itself into a position as global freedom fighters, albeit using rough means. Unavoidably, the coordination with the French expeditionary corps was poor (the French force numbered 5,000 men plus some 1,500 Chadian auxiliaries who were very effective fighters) and in 2020 a large number of Malian army POWs were slaughtered in cold blood by AQIM in the North.[7] There was widespread shock among the civilian population, with widows and mourning mothers demonstrating in public on the old Argentinian model of *las mujeres de la Plaza de Mayo*. This led to a military coup and the creation of the *Conseil National du Salut Populaire* (CNSP). In typical international diplomatic confusion, ECOWAS (the mammoth Economic Community of Western African States) demanded that the President Ibrahim Boubacar Keita be freed and re-established in his official position (August 2020), a demand which the Malian Junta laughed off. By October relations with ECOWAS had degenerated to the point where Colonel Assimi Goïta, head of the Malian state, kicked out the ECOWAS envoy and did not accept a replacement. The Pentagon grumbled when Prime Minister Choguel Kokalla Maïga signed an agreement with the Wagner Group in October 2021, providing for the sending of 1,000 mercenaries and $10.8 in military aid from Russia.[8] In December 2021 President Emmanuel Macron, who was scheduled to visit Bamako, cancelled his visit. His personality was such that he was unwilling to face difficult debates, particularly with Africans whose motivations remained obscure to him given his ignorance of the Sahel's historical and cultural background.[9] ECOWAS extended economic sanctions to Mali (January 2022) and in response the Malian authorities asked Denmark to withdraw the one hundred or so Special Forces (February 2022) which it had sent to reinforce MINUSMA under the spurious pretext that Copenhagen had "not asked for a special permit"! In fact this hostility to the Danes (who had never had anything to do with the Sahel in their history) was a symbolic rejection of the West, i.e. "France", and of its historical involvement in the locality. Paris, culturally blind as usual but shorn of its veteran "field Africanists" (now retired) who might have been able to handle this, thought the "local population" (which one, given it was so small?) was feckless given its supposedly triumphant welcome to François Hollande in 2013. That same month the French Ambassador was expelled for "interference in [Malian] internal affairs" and the Barkhane expeditionary force was asked to leave after ten years of blind good services. The West African Economic Monetary Union (WAEMU) cancelled the ECOWAS sanctions, without anybody clearly understanding how this should work.[10] This is when the Wagner boys started to arrive, trying to plug the military gap in the North as the Azawad forces attacked, soundly defeating the Malian army. The Wagners heard from an informant that AQIM was planning to hold a meeting in a village called Moura in the North and they occupied the place, backed by combat helicopters which started to strafe the small town (it was a market day) indiscriminately. And then on March 27 to 31, Wagner and the Malian Army began shooting civilian detainees in groups of ten or more, killing an unknown number that the UN later estimated at about 300.[11] The Junta admitted to the killings (which they numbered at 260) but said they were all rebel fighters, which did not make any sense. There were in fact a few (unarmed) AQIM fighters in the population going to market and visiting friends and relatives, but many victims were women and there were nine very small children (I talked indirectly through Peuhl friends with people who took part in the massive burial). MINUSMA, the UN Force for Mali, had a base in Mopti (about 50 km away) and did absolutely nothing in spite of being contacted by villagers fleeing Moura. The UN tried to set up an inquiry but Bamako and Moscow's representatives in New York blocked the creation of the commission in April.

Bamako was the first case of a *Françafrique* member falling into the arms of the Russians. Why the Russians? Because *Françafrique* had been a Cold War tool and therefore my enemy's enemy had to be my friend. To be honest there were no other takers either and the Sahel countries were hardly self-supporting.

In June the Mali junta launched a series of arrests of high-ranking members of the fallen civilian regime, particularly in relation to aircraft purchases by Ibrahim Keita, son of the deposed president, regarding a contract to supply Brazilian ground attack planes to the Malian Air Force.[12] On August 15 2022, the Barkhane Force finally departed from Mali, with little to show for nine years of effort and the losses incurred. The welcome of 2013 had worn off. In an improvised way France moved its troops to Niger, a choice which was to lead to further complications a year later.

The Wagner Group did not carry out their anti-terrorist operations with much efficiency and on July 22 2022 the AQIM forces attacked camp Kati.[13] The fighting crept closer and closer to Bamako. On April 18 2023 in a large ambush, the Chief of Staff of FAMa was killed, together with several Wagner soldiers. A new element was the presence of Black African soldiers in AQIM which up to then had been a very "white" (Berber and Tuareg) force. On June 16 the Junta demanded the departure of MINUSMA. It was useless militarily but important as a diplomatic symbol. On July 10 the Junta kidnapped and detained 46 unarmed Ivorian soldiers as they were disembarking at Bamako airport to reinforce MINUSMA. They were accused of "interference in the internal affairs of Mali".[14] In fact the poor hapless soldiers were diplomatic hostages for the break Bamako was trying to engineer with "the West" as an artificial bogey. In the array of new political concepts slowly emerging at the time this can be seen as the inception date for the concept of a "Global South". MINUSMA was falling apart as the British, German, Swedish, Ivorian and Benin contingents announced their intention to leave while no other countries volunteered to replace them. MINUSMA was on its way to oblivion. Mali had switched from being a single penetrating point from another conflict (Libya) to being the heart of a spreading transnational movement aspiring to "liberate" about three million square kilometers along loosely reinvented "Islamic" lines. *Françafrique* was completely out of its depth.

The Tuareg Azawad movement had been the Islamist reincarnation of a regional aspiration. When intervening in Mali, *Françafrique* was geared to fighting what it had always fought: a localised crisis with a clearly defined geographical center. The only global dimension it had struggled against was anticolonial left-supported movements. These were foreign-sponsored and without roots in historical Africa. The difficulty of Azawad was that, although Tuareg, it was dressed in the new garb of global Islamism. Soon the jihadi transnational impetus emanating from the Middle East began overflowing from its starting point because, contrary to the anti-colonialist movements, it could reach into the depths of local Islam to combine all grievances—social, historical, political and regional—into one greater wave of resentment. The main front of jihad has progressively transferred itself from Mosul to a moving, amoeba-like,

African slick spreading simultaneously eastwards, southwards and northwards from northern Mali. *Françafrique* was no longer fit for purpose in this new environment since paradoxically it faced the hostility not only of the jihadists themselves but of their enemies as well. Violence exploded in a way *Françafrique* had never predicted: it came from its former allies: in Mali itself, during the first six months of 2022 more people were killed by the government forces than by the Islamist guerrillas.[15] Burkina Faso's president Roch-Marc Kabore admitted that some of his citizens may feel safer living among terrorists than with their own country's security forces.[16] Regardless of its political choices, the government in Bamako was perceived as a projection of Paris. In fact greater and greater areas of the Sahel turned into hell as the two main Islamist movements—*Jamat al-Nusra al-Islam wa'l Muslimin* (JNIM, the African franchise of al-Qaeda) and the Islamic State in the Greater Sahara (a branch of the Islamic State)—started to fight each other as well due to their respective transnational alliances.[17]

Burkina Faso starts a coup cascade

As we saw earlier[18] Burkina Faso had been in October 1987 the theater of a Shakespearean tragedy where President Thomas Sankara was killed on the orders of his close friend and political advisor Blaise Compaoré. Compaoré ruled for twenty-seven years as the darling of the *Françafrique* establishment, before being overthrown in October 2014 by an exasperated civil society as he was attempting a to get a mandate for a fifth "reelection". He fled to the Ivory Coast where he was granted political asylum, leaving behind him a traumatized country. Many African heads of state are ephemeral, many others overstay their welcome but Sankara had been unique. He had been slowly enshrined in the collective memory of Burkina Faso as an exception: a president who not only genuinely cared for his electorate but lived within his ideal and had died for it. The gross mandates of Blaise Compaoré that followed added to Sankara's saintly image and there were few Francophone countries in Africa where the hatred of *Françafrique* was so strong. The slow-motion Islamist slide from Mali towards neighboring Burkina started in 2015, affecting a country where clear visions of power, both positive and negative, were stronger than usual in Africa. When Emmanuel Macron went to Ouagadougou after being elected to his first term in office, his behavior showed how out of touch he was with the local reality.[19] The man who might have gone to fix the air-conditioning was overthrown by a military coup in January 2022 when the level of Islamist attacks reached a peak. The cause of that first peak was complex: 60% of the Burkina population is Muslim but it was far from welcoming to the Islamists. Militias were organized at the grassroots level but they soon started to fight each other depending on their socio-ecological background: Fulani cattle nomads versus Mossi sedentary peasants versus traditionalist Dozo hunters. Meanwhile the jihadis made further progress. In September 2022 a new Army coup overthrew the Army regime. Not knowing what was happening, large crowds attacked the French embassy, thinking this was a French-sponsored counter coup. For once *Françafrique* had nothing to do with it. But the new coup leader, Captain Ibrahim Traore, had a plan: try to resurrect the ghost of Thomas Sankara. Facing a movement appealing to popular emotions he reached for the only available alternative, the image of the long dead nationalist hero. Be "anti-imperialist", shun the French and opt for nationalist, anti-tribalist ideals. But he forgot the fact that Sankara promoted such values but without entering the Cold War arena. On January 2 2023 the new Burkina Faso military junta asked France to recall its ambassador without giving any reason. This followed a strictly secret trip of Burkinabe Prime Minister Kyelem Apollinaire de Tambèla to Moscow at the head of an eleven-member delegation including four military officers and four ministers. Intermediaries (and transport) were provided by the Malian military government. The objectives of the Burkinabes were simple: get military help. Consequences: very little of what the Burkinabe wanted and what the Malians had (almost) promised, i.e. military hardware, materialized. The Burkinabe delegation landed in Moscow in the midst of the ongoing hot war with Ukraine and rejected some of the conditions the Russians insisted on. On January 25 the French ambassador returned to Paris and the French Government announced that its troops would go home within a month. A discreet Wagner delegation arrived in Ougadougou where they received a mixed welcome, many officers opposing the development of the Russian contact. Since 2015 some 2,000 civilians had been killed and 1.4 million displaced.[20] In February 2023 for the first time a large number of Burkina soldiers (about sixty) were killed in an ambush and Captain Traore, the head of the junta, decided on a large-scale mobilization of any paramilitary forces he could scrape together—forest guards, prison wardens, even some firemen—to create a new "volunteer" corps to fight the jihadis. The results were mixed:

- The army cooperated with this new volunteer corps (*Volontaires pour la Défense de la Patrie* or VDP) but did not issue operational directions to it.[21]
- The training was slow and the discipline poor. The equipment was lacking (one gun for seven men on average).
- Many of the volunteers (some were women with children, others were too old) could not be incorporated. The operational capacity was set at 50,000 men.

- The movement of national upsurge was genuine but the danger remained that these units could be drawn into violent quarrels that had nothing to do with the anti-jihadi counterinsurgency.
- The worst took place in April when a mixture of VDP and regular army wiped out the village of Karma (in Northern Burkina), killing at least 300 people. The persecutions were both systematic (most people killed by the Army/VDP were Peuhl (Fulani)) and chaotic: those killed in Karma were Mossi, the largest tribe in Burkina and none were jihadi. A few days before the army had suffered a heavy defeat in the nearby town of Aorema and sought revenge by simply killing civilians in the area, accusing them of "jihadism".[22]

To add a sinister note to this tragedy, former President Blaise Compaoré, who had been sulking in the Ivory Coast since the coup that had overthrown him, suddenly turned up in Ouagadougou. He had been tried *in absentia* for the murder of Sankara and pronounced guilty. His aim was obviously to try to take advantage of the troubles then developing but in spite of the trial, he was not arrested and retained his freedom of movement. The tragedy then turned into an unsavory farce when the old tyrant "apologized to the people of Burkina for the pain he had caused" without saying what "pain" he was talking about! The country was being torn apart by insurgency, and Compaoré was suddenly coming out of the shadows to apologise for an unnamed "pain" everybody knew about, to which he had massively contributed and which he refused to acknowledge in what could be called "cold reality". He neglected to address what was then happening, preferring to nurse the "pain" and "grief" of the bygone but unforgotten years. After this indecent "apology", he flew back to exile, having added insult to injury and exacerbated the confusion.

Far from delving into this painful past but prey to a short-term fear, the international community became very worried about the Russian connection but made little contribution to the global crisis. The Russians had nothing to do with the jihadi catastrophe.[23] The international plan to support Burkina only received 42% of promised funding in 2022 and the plan for 2023 received a mere 18%. It is difficult to believe that the $877m of humanitarian aid announced in April 2023 would trigger a more convincing result. IDPs now numbered two million people and the jihadis controlled between 40% and 60% of Burkina Faso. Some specialists suggested that the Islamist groups now fighting in the Sahel could one day take part in some governments.[24] This appeared far-fetched, particularly in Burkina Faso where Islamist violence seemed to have reached a point of no return. The Russians eventually turned up,[25] ostensibly to help in the country's defence, but actually to set up a Praetorian guard for Captain Traore.

Niger, Françafrique*'s diplomatic Waterloo, collapses without a military defeat*

In spite of the local context the July 26 2023 coup in Niger was not directly caused by the jihadi problem nor by Wagner. It started with what could be called a typical problem of succession even though it was taking place more than two years after President Mohamed Bazoum had been elected. Let us bring some background into focus: "Niger" was the perfect example of what France had taken for granted in Africa, demanding services which were forgotten the next day. For a long time Niger did not even exist administratively. Made up of various territories picked up from the old Kanem-Bornu empire, it was dumped into the lap of *Afrique Occidentale Française* (AOF), the "good part" of the French African empire but with the actual status and use of an AEF appendage, comprising pieces of Upper Volta, Mali and Chad that were thrown together. Very little administrative time was spent there, infrastructure was neglected, programs were conceived of as emergency stop-gaps and as soon as "independence" was granted "the feeling in France was that of a total lack of interest and the post-independence generation told us: 'you have colonized us for sixty years and you know nothing about us'".[26] The country was still-born, having tottered through seven coups since independence. Centered economically around the Imouraren uranium mines it was seen as existing for French interests only. When the mines were temporarily closed by Areva (the French firm running them) it was explained that this was due to a drop in uranium prices and that they would reopen when the prices rose again and made the metal profitable again for the company. The workforce was "temporarily laid off", without unemployment compensation and told to fend for itself. Thousands of people were affected and fell into destitution because Areva was the main, indeed almost the only link between the Niger economy and the outside world.

After years of trying, a credible transethnic and catchall democratic party (*Parti National pour la Démocratie et le Socialisme,* PNDS) had finally been established and managed to get its leader Mahmadou Issoufou legally elected president. At the end of its mandate, Mahmadou Issoufou organized a caucus which chose the next PNDS candidate, Mohamed Bazoum, who in turn won the election. This was the first case ever of a democratic transition in Niger.

Part of the problem was in the ethnic origin of the President who was from a Libyan Arab clan (Ouled Souleïman). His family had immigrated from Libya and Bazoum did not enjoy a deep enough civil society support base since the Arabs represented only 1% of Niger's population. Former President Mahamadou

Issoufou—a Hausa, the largest Niger tribe—was his mentor but he was too inflexible and tried to keep control of everything. After leaving the presidency he had carefully placed his men in a series of key positions. His son for example was minister for Petroleum and Energy[27] while the presidential guard remained headed by General Abdourahman Tiani, a Hausa. President Bazoum tried to force him to resign, Tiani refused and instead executed a coup. Tiani's problem was to convince the regular army to follow his lead. After he had succeeded it was to convince/force the deposed president to sign a letter of resignation, a difficult task since Bazoum is strongheaded and kept Twittering that he refused to junk the slim margin of democracy achieved by his election. So the coup could not be "completed". This was a local micro geopolitical problem. The conflict around the leadership of the presidential guard was whipped up by segments of the old Hausa elite who mobilized the latent frustration of the youth to tell the French to go to hell. The problem was that after over sixty years of *Françafrique* wheeling and dealing this was probably the only feeling shared by all classes of society, ethnic origins notwithstanding.

There were two possibilities in such a situation: either the old *Françafrique* network could be used in the usual way and the reluctant general would have been brought into line, or else a small warning light would have come on and the consciousness that the old system had reached its limit and that a large overhaul was needed before a truly participative new agreement was ushered in. A dose of the old medicine might have been in order to convince Issifou that a page was being turned. Instead President Macron, whose understanding of both history and Africa is usually subsumed in quick "fixit" technological (and symbolical) maneuvers immediately panicked into evacuating French civilians (July 31), thereby switching the burden of a solution to the army. Yes, there were jihadi problems in Southwestern Niger. But they were limited and the difficulty was focused on the tri-border contact zone with Burkina and Mali, where the situation was perilous. Bazoum and his government had accepted without complaint Macron's request to host the French troops evacuating Mali when Barkhane folded. But without any compensation or support mechanism in Niger, this turned what should have been simply a technical measure into a show of defeat and of an instrumentalization of the host country. The African vision of the situation was not anti-French at first and there was no problem in letting in the French army soldiers evacuating Mali. But without an integrated approach, it soon turned into an open sore.

On August 18 the African Union had rejected a three year transition program offered by the coup leaders as a timetable for re-establishing an electoral system. Former president Issoufou, considered to be the informal head of the large Hausa tribe, was weighing his options. Eleven members of ECOWAS (out of fifteen) had declared their readiness to opt for a military operation to bring the coup-makers into line and President Macron took refuge behind this organizational offer which would have been in fact extremely difficult to carry out. At the worst moment possible, President Bazoum, who was worried about Hausa support for his pro-French stance, had asked for a preventive deployment of troops. On August 26, when the coup began, the then Prime Minister Massaoudou had made an emergency request for these troops. Paris answered by asking for written authorization. Foccard must have turned in his grave! It was way too much of a demand and it was issued far too late.

Even though Russian flags were deployed after the coup, they were not displayed by the army but by civilian elements of the M62 "Movement". It seems Wagner had no role in this but stood ready to reap the benefits. The jihadi pressure has been on since 2010. It had been used by General Tiani as an excuse for his coup, a difficult excuse to accept since he was personally in charge of anti-jihadi operations and his main concern was keeping his job. Bazoum had tried to operate against the jihadis but he chose to make deals with secondary Al-Qaeda leaders who did little to help because it was the Islamic State which was the most efficient jihadi movement through its presence in the tri-border area of Burkina, Mali and Niger. The deals Bazoum struck with al-Qaeda's local leadership were not very efficient and they fell through the moment the president was detained. If the anti-jihadi operations were a problem for the French, they were too for the US in case it decided to deploy the anti-jihadi special forces they had deployed in its two bases.[28] The Americans preferred to play their own game and on August 7 sent the interim Under Secretary of State for African Affairs, Victoria Nuland, to Niamey. In March 2023, when Secretary of State Blinken had come to Niger, he had talked about the country being "a key partner for democratic transition in Africa". De facto the US accepted the coup, hoping it would fade into the background of the then frantic world situation.

There was an increase in Islamist attacks, coming mostly from Burkina, during August. This was the key moment to try to save a genuine anti-insurgency program by asking for Bazoum, who had fired Salifou Modi, an efficient Zarma, one of the few ethnically neutral actors previously in charge of anti-Jihadi operations, to be reinstated and tell the Hausa that national interest must supplant tribal considerations in a moment of stress. When on August 23 the French ambassador was asked to leave, Macron initially refused, only to cave in on September 25, accepting at the same time the withdrawal of French troops. Meanwhile the Americans had discreetly moved their entire force to the northern base of Agadez, closer to the fighting. Petty quarrels had proved the death-knell of the anti-jihadi program because every group had looked first for its own interests and nobody had represented those of Niger as a nation-to-be.

After a series of forceful declarations, President Bola Tinubu, who had followed the situation and promised Macron that he would sponsor an unwieldy ECOWAS intervention, understood that the French had lost their golden touch and were now the whipping boy. There was no point in ECOWAS risking a major conflagration to back up a fragile and improvised French intervention. Tinubu, being a Yoruba, preferred to short-circuit the large and clumsy ECOWAS machinery. Instead he chose to ask Sa'adu Abubakar, the respected Hausa Sultan of Sokoto, to go to Niamey and negotiate with General Tiani ... and former President Issifou! The fire could be contained but not put out so the putschists—Malian, Burkinabe and Nigerien—put together a quick-fit diplomatic front to stop French protests and keep open a usable channel with the international community. Contrary to journalistic interpretation, this was not a Russian plot but a simple form of local opportunism and of tribal damage control.

On September 27 President Bola Tinubu put on another hat and sent his (i.e. Nigerian) National Security Advisor Nuhu Ribadu to Paris to discuss more precisely both Boko Haram and the Niamey difficulties.[29] Paris had stumbled at every turn and its influence had evaporated. Not a shot had been fired but the wastepaper baskets were overflowing.

As a kind of ironic post-script, on December 4 2023, General Tiani welcomed the Russian Vice-Minister for Defence, Colonel-General Yunus-bek Evkurov, who signed a protocol of Cooperation with the Niger Military Committee. The same day Niamey broke contact with Brussels. What was amusing was that Evkourov was a Russian version of what *Françafrique* had been: a "neo-colonial" type, with a mixed politico-military hybrid dimension. He is an Ingush Muslim who used to be the Head of State of the Ingush Republic and was nearly killed in a bomb attack linked to Chechen-Ingush politics in June 2009. Before landing in Niamey he had made two quick stopovers in Bamako and Ouagadougou. In 2018 he had been the founder in Libya of the Africa Korps which had inherited Wagner's Africa Estate after Prigozhin's assassination. Putin at first tried to recruit former Wagnerites at $3,100 a month, a fortune in Russian terms; but there were very few volunteers hence the creation of Afrika Korps, initially seen as an official alternative to Wagner.[30] As *Françafrique* started on its downward path, other alternatives to deal with the continent had an eerie resemblance to what others, including the French, had devised in their time. Was it Africa's fate to be subcontracted to *ad hoc* all-purpose handlers?

FRANÇAFRIQUE IS NOT DEAD

Odd man out: The Coup in Gabon

In the night of August 29 to 30 2023 a group of soldiers announced they had cancelled the election in which Gabonese President Ali Bongo had just been "reelected". This "coup" was in fact not a coup against a legal government but a therapeutic intervention against a dictatorship backed by the French for the last three-quarters of a century. The "coup makers" had nothing to do with the two bogey groups that are always brought up to "explain" the recent rash of African coups in Francophone countries, the Jihadiyya Islamists or the Russians, in their Wagner form or some other identity.

There are fewer than 10% Muslims in Gabon and half of them are petty-bourgeois migrants who came from all over Francophone West and Central Africa while others are Lebanese. They have no political or armed movements and they are mostly involved in small or medium-size businesses. Catholicism is the dominant religion.

As for the Russians, they never had anything to do with Gabon and never tried to influence or interfere with the political process. After the coup a civil service delegation went to the Russian embassy (with no military personnel among them) and asked the ambassador: "We just carried out a coup against Bongo and his friends. The French will not help us. We heard that in some other countries you helped the people supporting democracy. Can you protect us?" They carried a few hastily sewn Russian flags and did not appear to have any sense of humour. What was the actual situation these lost souls were facing? The French-supported "Bongo dynasty" had been in power since 1967 and Omar Bongo's son Ali had held the reins since his father's death in 2009. He suffered a stroke in 2018 and was hospitalised in Saudi Arabia for fifteen months. The family system was in place (his French wife was in control with different people in key positions) but Ali was the only person who had the hand over the family fortune he had inherited from his father, roughly one billion Euros. The government was on auto pilot for all the time of his hospitalization and the joke on the streets had been that since the regime had been privatised a long time ago, then the real head of state should have been the health minister. After this episode Ali Bongo could hardly walk. The last time he had come to Paris he had stumbled on the stairs at the Elysée Palace and had avoided falling down only by grabbing President Macron's jacket. There were two planes side by side on the tarmac at Libreville Airport, ready to go: the President's official plane and the President's ambulance plane with a flight plan ready for London (Ali was afraid of the French who were everywhere in the government, the security services, the army, the banks, the big companies). There was no independent political life. The dictatorship has been shaven smooth and for thirty years was a one-party system. Later it had become a multi-party system in which the opposition never won even 1% of the vote. In the first and only hotly contested election (2016) the opposition leader was Jean Ping, a very popular and powerful opposition figure, a former Secretary-General of the African Union who never had a job in Gabon's government and did not depend on the government in any way. Ping won, the polls were rigged, popular anger was massive and the crowds converged on Ping's headquarters. The security services used a helicopter to bomb the complex, setting it on fire. The French Minister of Defence was present and in good *Françafrique* tradition refrained from raising any objection. The government admitted to three casualties while the minimum must have been at least sixty. Ping, who is a dual Chinese-Gabonese citizen, supported the 2023 coup which he had not engineered. The leader of the coup, General Brice Oligui Nguema, was himself a M'Teke, that is Bongo's tribe. But there are fifty-two ethnic groups in Gabon for a population of 2.4 million which makes tribalism largely irrelevant in the country. But the hatred of the regime seemed almost universal and the popular support for the coup was massive. Apart from the initial amusing visit to the Russian Embassy, the Russian presence has not been mentioned. There had been extreme tension during and in the immediate aftermath of the election. The army had been put on special alert and special instructions given. The troops carried them out but with a purpose opposite to that of their instructions. This was because Oligui Nguema was a secondary—but not irrelevant—insider of the regime who after being sidelined as a military attaché to Brazzaville had been able to organize the coup as an inside job. In the last few days running up to the election, the government panicked. First it refused any international observers, especially from the UN which had condemned the massacre which had put an end to the 2016 elections. Then it cut off the internet. Then it switched off the connection to French television channels (which everybody with a TV set watches in Gabon). And finally it refused any contact with the press, whether national, international or French. So when the coup finally came it felt a bit like a public safety administrative decision. There was no violence.

As we saw in Chapter Two, the place of Gabon in *Françafrique* had been special; it was actually its real birthplace. The first president of independent Gabon, Léon M'ba, had been overthrown by a coup in 1964. De Gaulle had sent in the French army, shot the mutineers and brought M'ba back to power. Later M'ba being old and sick had been succeeded by a Vice-President chosen in agreement with the French. In 1967 when M'ba died this Vice-President, Albert-Bernard Bongo, became President. This was the creation of a dynasty which seems to have finally ended only on August 30 2023. *Françafrique* had considered Libreville as its capital. During the post 1960 period the newly "independent"

African states voted as a bloc in the UN managed by Paris and Libreville performed an almost official vice-regal role. So the 2023 coup was a fundamental shock, along with the disappearance of a cash box. Omar Bongo summarized the situation when he said, "Africa without France is like a car without a driver but France without Africa is like a car without fuel". It seemed in the heyday of the "dynasty" that Bongo could do as he pleased vis-à-vis France. De Gaulle himself was a devout Catholic but he tolerated considerable leeway on the part of his African vassal.

As previously discussed, Bongo was born without a clear religion but had converted spectacularly to Catholicism to obtain an audience from the Pope and reinforce his authority in a country where Catholicism was the majority faith (he got his audience). But a few years later he had a problem with oil producing countries (OPEP) so in September 1973 he converted to Islam and became Omar Bongo. He soon became a key person to manage problems between oil-producing Arab countries and Africa.

The influence of Bongo in French politics was enormous. Bongo had 53 children from thirty different women. As time went on, he "placed" them in comfortable and well-paid jobs. The whole government system progressively became an extension of the Bongo family. The man extended his hand into French affairs, and this not only to kill people he did not like (besides

Robert Luong he had several opponents killed, often by French assassins) but to obtain from Paris the firing of French civil servants he disliked. For example Bongo did not like the attitude of Jean-Pierre Cot, the Minister of Cooperation, whose influence led him to dismantle the gangster networks of his predecessor Jacques Foccard. Bongo complained and Cot was forced to resign.[31] Jean-Pierre Cot had sworn to dismantle *Françafrique* and Bongo was the very embodiment of that "organization". He was also the clearly recognized Godfather of the mafia in charge of defending the privileges of the group, both against African disobedience and French encroachments. After J.P. Cot was dismissed in 1982,[32] he was replaced by Christian Nucci who was very polite and deferred to the *Françafrique* model. Meanwhile huge sums of money were gobbled up in Gabon by the presidential mafia and today half the population still lives beneath the poverty line.

Bongo's relationship with a series of French Presidents was central to his power and he got total support from Mitterrand who in 1990 sent troops to put him back on the presidential seat after he had been temporarily deposed. In May 1990 his political opponent Joseph Redjembe had died in suspicious circumstances which prompted riots threatening the 12,000 French nationals living in Gabon. The Port Gentil disturbances led to the destruction of French property and French troops came again to "reestablish order". After Mitterrand left power

Bongo was on close terms with Jacques Chirac and later helped the election campaign of Nicolas Sarkozy.[33]

As for the 2023 coup, there was no violence, direct or symbolic, except for the brief bout of shooting in the night of August 29 which was due to presidential guards who had not been briefed correctly and who shot at other presidential guards. It was brief and nobody was hurt. The streets were awash with joy and those people who were arrested (hundreds and the arrests still went on for days after the coup) were grabbed more by unarmed private citizens than by the police or the Army. It was a sort of revolution minus the violence. There were few firearms in evidence, Libreville is a very small town and everybody knew where the regime's beneficiaries lived. Groups went and forced the Bongo entourage out. They might have been manhandled or insulted but there were no lynchings. People shouted and argued in the following style: "aren't you ashamed of what you have done? We are poor and you live like lords. Now this will be finished." Among the people arrested was Marie-Madeleine Mborantsuo, President of the Electoral Commission, a.k.a. "The Tower of Pisa" (because she always leaned towards whatever power was the strongest), the fabulously rich Nur-ed-Din Bongo Valentin, son of the president born in March 1992, and who was being lined up to become the next president,[34] and his mother Sylvia, a French citizen of Italian and French origin, born in Paris and considered to be the power behind the throne as well as very wealthy in her own right.

There were of course problems issuing from this too-good-to-be-true coup d'etat. First with the French: Olivier Véran, the French Government spokesman issued a statement on August 30, saying that Paris was opposed to the putsch and "was waiting for the return of the situation along democratic lines". This was an amusing paradox because the so-called "democratic process" was in fact a rigged election organized to perpetuate a dictatorship which had lasted three quarters of a century. The French press depicted the actual nature of the election and the declaration of Mr Véran added to the ridicule because apart from his position as "government spokesman" he was also "Minister in Charge of Democratic Renewal". The coup gave him a nice opportunity to have discharged his ministerial duties since Ali Bongo was not in the position of President Bazoum in Niger,[35] i.e. an elected president. The appeal of "returning to democratic rights" was quietly dropped.

Then there was the apparent winner of the election, Albert Ondo Ossa. A 69-year-old economist who had created the A23 platform, a loose coalition of 23 small opposition parties which he managed by a miracle of clever diplomacy to regroup into a bloc that backed him as the one and only opposition candidate. At the time it was easy: people were competing for the unpleasant position of being beaten, arrested and/or kicked out of their jobs. Such competition was extremely limited. But after the coup the situation looked quite different. There had never been a moment of political life and freedom in Gabon, no knowledge of functioning within a democratic framework and politics was a winner takes all system. Now there was a completely unexpected victor. Mr Ondo Ossa was one of these professional opponents the Bongo clan kept on hand. His "victory" would be quietly forgotten.

What of the military victor, General Brice Oligui Nguema, head of the Presidential Guard and till then a minor member of the Bongo clan, who turned his weapons against his former masters. What was his ultimate aim? Right now he was the most popular man in Gabon. He could not walk in the street because people insisted on carrying him in triumph on their shoulders. He did not carry a gun. But he was a distant cousin of Ali Bongo and a M'Teke, one of Bongo's tribe. When he selected his cabinet he appointed a few members of the clan as ministers, telling them: "I would rather have you inside under my eyes than outside and trying to get back in". He started a measured and careful house cleaning. But the crowds were vociferously anti-Bongo: would they accept a superficial dusting of the presidential palace? This was a soft landing for *Françafrique* whose future in its homeland is now controversial but potentially heavy with adjustments that might prompt further tension if they cut to the bone or disappointing if they are considered to be too little too late.

As for the international community, it kept a low profile. The US declared, after hesitating, that yes, this was a coup, but imposed no sanctions. General Oligui Nguema visited in succession, Chad, the Central African Republic, Equatorial Guinea and the Brazzaville Congo. These were low profile visits to variously hostile countries. These trips culminated in December 2023 in a trip to Cameroun where the regional organization, the Central Africa Economic and Monetary Community (CEMAC) which had taken sanctions against the coup under the aegis of veteran *Françafrique* leader Paul Biya, discreetly relented and did not implement the sanctions even while it did not abrogate them. The matter was quietly put aside.

Was *Françafrique* dead? Not really, but it was brought low. Its beneficiaries were disappearing but there was still one bastion that could fight: Chad.

The Chadian last redoubt

On Monday April 19 2021 "Marshall" Idriss Deby Itno fell in combat facing the rebels of the *Front pour l'Alternance et la Concorde au Tchad* (FACT). Or did he? The Commission of Inquiry into the death of the President held a session, several months after the event, at Koro Toro, an isolated fort in the desert, in a closed session and wrote a report whose contents were never published or commented upon. Then who killed Idriss Deby? Probably members of his own tribe, the Zaghawa, who had such a monopoly on power that they could afford the luxury of internal dissension.[36] Some months after the President's disappearance a housecleaning operation laid off about two hundred of the six hundred generals from the plethoric Chadian officer corps; ninety percent of those dismissed were Zaghawa and Idriss Deby had just been reelected for a fifth mandate in a typical *Françafrique* "democratic" contest. Since his French sponsored raid on Ndjamena in December 1990 he had been the perfect embodiment of the Francophone African leader. He was so sure of himself that he took his tribe for granted and as one of his officers told me "it was his own army that killed him". We will see in the next chapter how further events reinforced this (so far) unproved assessment of Idris Deby's killing.[37] On April 23 President Macron was in Ndjamena to give his blessing to the accession to power of the purely military and unconstitutional Transition Council. The Council was presided over by Mahamat Idriss Deby, the late president's son. Macron was the only head of state present and patted the young man's hand in a gesture that looked more filial than diplomatic. The *Conseil Militaire de Transition* picked a seventy member Dialogue Organising Committee. Most of the members were Goran from the North who were close to the late president. "Transition" and "Dialogue" felt like empty sloganeering, without any real content. To make this clear the "Dialogue" which should have opened on May 10 was stopped a week before its proposed start and postponed "to a later date". Then on October 20 2022, Mahamat Idriss Deby announced that the transition which should have lasted eighteen months was going to be extended without discussion for another twenty-four months. This was considered to be too much and the country and its paper-thin government exploded in armed demonstrations in the main towns (Moundou, Abeche, Bongor, Koumra) and of course in Ndjamena itself. "About fifty" demonstrators were killed and three hundred wounded.[38] The Foreign Affairs Ministry in Paris issued a statement saying that "France had no role in these events which concern strictly Chadian internal politics". Of course. Five days later the Economic Community of Central African States (ECCAF) appointed Congolese President Felix Tshisekedi as a facilitator to help solve the crisis. This was in fact a hurried gesture by Tshisekedi (who presided over ECCAF) to make it look as if the listless organization actually existed and also to keep the African Union from getting too close to what was happening. FACT, the insurgent movement that was supposed to have killed Deby, was not "Islamist" in any way; it was just an opposition armed group based in Libya where the absence of government facilitated its activities. It was the

US which supplied the missing part for a typical anti-*Françafrique* plot when Washington issued a statement saying that Wagner "was working with Chadian rebels to destabilize the government and kill its president, a key counterterrorism ally of the West".[39] As often happens in similar circumstances, this was a fabrication which had the advantage of putting all the bad guys under the same banner even if this "evil unity" (Putin supporting the *jihadis?*) was somewhat hard to believe. Paris was in such a desperate African situation that even this charitable and unlikely US fabrication was welcome.

Then given the situation in the Sahel and given the fact that the multinational European force *Takuba* (supposed to be deployed in Mali) had died before it was born something happened that seemed borrowed from the repertory of Opera Buffa*:* on November 6 2023 the Hungarian Parliament voted for the establishment of a 200 strong military contingent to be deployed in Chad. This was declared to be "a reinforcement of military-diplomatic relations between Chad and Hungary", which indeed was probable since there had never been any. Two weeks later the newly minted Chadian Minister of Defence, one of the ruling party's MPs, flew to Budapest to invite a delegation of the Hungarian Government to Ndjamena to inaugurate the brand-new embassy. The whole movement had taken place at the request of Mahamat Idriss Deby who seemed to be trying to show that even without inviting the Russian

Great Satan he could provide a cut-rate version of the play by inviting emissaries of Victor Orban. *Françafrique* had been born in the fracas of weapons; it was now on the way to gasping its last in a diplomatic farce where the French would be shown that there were alternatives to their presence.[40] Chad being the last credible *Françafrique* partner still in business, a touch of blackmail could be forgiven. A Hungarian deployment in Chad seems like a belated continuation of Viktor Orban's blocking of Brussels' attempted budget for helping Ukraine. Was it planned after consultation with Vladimir Putin? This is a possibility, not a certainty. But the atmosphere would be the same: a tragedy played by *Commedia dell'Arte* actors. Seven months later no Hungarian troops had been seen in Chad.

Oozing towards the coast: Will there be a last stand?

There were two dimensions in the global Sahel conflict where *Françafrique* was pitched against a vast politico-ideological project emanating from the Arab Middle East and the agents of that project on the ground in Africa. In a certain way this went back to the origins of the *Françafrique* concept: fighting a large force originating from outside. But there was a huge difference: anti-colonialism incarnated itself in local forces close to the Communist International and therefore operated in a cultural sphere where it could exist only through "bourgeois" nationalist parties. These agents of "anti-France" had very shallow roots in local African cultures, as exemplified by the evolution of the RDA.[41] Not so with the jihadis. But there the "movement" was also dependent on the presence of Islam (and of what kind of Islam) as it was present in various African environments. There was of course no "center" to the growing Islamist activity in the Sahel where Mali became the geographical hornet's nest from which the movement irradiated, along lines of Islamic presence. In Ivory Coast for example, the Muslim fighters coming in from the North from Burkina Faso through the Bukami area had the problem of being among Kulango and Lobi tribesmen who were often still animists. Therefore the jihadis "imported" Peuhl/Fulani fighters (and to a lesser degree Mossi) who were Muslims from Burkina to act as their fighting force. How should we then rephrase that social placement from the Maoist point of view of guerillas being like fish in a river? Was this a religious war? Not really. Islam should not be considered as a religion in this African context but rather as a culture. A way of eating, of working, of running a family. Does that then mean that the progression of Muslim insurgents would stop when potential insurgents were not Muslims and thus put an end to the spread of rebellious movements? Not really either. Because there is a third dimension, the French colonial dimension. And that is more relevant. The regions where conflicts have known their largest growth had been the neglected parts of the French colonial Empire. And Muslim insurgent activities are still today linked with the neglected (or most exploited) corners of the French Empire, the Central African Republic being the worst example, even though the Muslim communities there are not key to the conflicts. The drive to the coast by the rebel forces of the interior is mostly a fear expressed by former colonial powers who see this trend as a vast geopolitical threat, something culturally menacing and inimical to their interests. The point is rather the social situation of the inhabitants and how it fits in the global picture. Tensions that have nothing to do with Islam can flare up such as those that arose around the move by Alassane Ouattara to run again for the presidency in August 2020. And the main tensions came from among the Bete—and Bete-related populations—in the Ivory Coast while the Bete are not Muslims but were the supporters of Ouattara's political rival Laurent Ggbagbo. The same is true if we look at Togo where the jihadi affected areas are in the North, contiguous with Burkina Faso, while all the political agitation is mostly in the Christian South and closely related with constitutional problems linked to the reinforcement of the typical *Françafrique* regime. Some West African regimes had briefly banded together to stop what could be seen as a push to the coast, a kind of Africa-originating *Takuba*.[42] One instance occurred in February 2022 when troops from Niger, Nigeria and

Cameroun wiped out many jihadis—about a hundred—in the Boko Haram-infested zone around Lake Chad. This was an operation of the Multinational Joint Task Force which had been created as a specific anti-Boko Haram unit. But when *Barkhane* was disbanded the only country that seems to have understood that there was no Islamist "rush to the sea" is the Ivory Coast which has simply chosen to look at where the Islamist radicals actually operate. And the answer was clear: it was in the country's poorest areas. So Abidjan is trying to fight them not with guns but by training for the youth and with zero rate loans for them to set up small businesses after they finish their training. Roads and electrification are another means of calming the situation. The results are not massive, but the jihadis seem to have stopped progressing in these areas. This is obviously not enough but it is a step in the right direction, the complete opposite of the military only *Barkahne* approach. At the other end we can find Benin which seems to mostly consider that fighting the Peuhl/Fulani with the help of both the Rwandese and the Russians will help. In the last year the guerrilla attacks have multiplied by a factor of ten and devastated tourism by the simple expedient of setting up ambushes in the national parks. So we are left with a littered and messy landscape, the progressive fading away of *Françafrique,* evident not only in the varied coups of the 2010s but also in the evacuation of *Barkahne.*

Folding up *Barkahne* was not a radical cut off point. It was an attempt at damage control, at accommodating (without admitting it) the growth of the anti-French feeling of the younger African generations who do not feel the fear/respect of their elders and had veered towards open hostility. An occasion also for a diplomatic readjustment and for some budget savings as military danger was rising in Europe and the French Ministry of Defence was asked by President Macron to start a rearmament program to contain the Russians. *Françafrique* was largely obsolete in its traditional form. But although *Françafrique* was not dead, it was on life support. The ogre of the French African contextual system was by then on its last legs, wading through a terrain littered with debris, surviving porticoes, venomous snakes and half-starving insurgents.

6

WHAT IS LEFT AFTER DISMANTLING, SPREADING ONESELF THIN, PICKING UP THE PIECES AND HOPING TO PLUG THE GAPS? (2021–24)

There has been no global collapse of *Françafrique* but rather a transmogrification which has turned a complex and contradictory structure into something smaller but perhaps even more difficult to understand with the present day complexities of the international landscape. *Françafrique* had been multifaceted but its base had first and foremost been military so it was the dismantling of Operation Barkhane in Mali between August 15 and November 9 2022 which acted as the catalyst of destruction. *Françafrique* never had a birthdate, so it was logical it would not have a burial date either. It was a complex piece of semi-soft machinery running low on economic fuel, in an environment of growing public hostility and towards the end "led" (if the word was still appropriate) by incompetent chief engineers, President François Hollande and President Emmanuel Macron. First and foremost its real power base, whose brutality had long managed to make up for its fragility, had eroded beyond any perceivable twilight zone. *Realpolitik* had imposed the predominance of the reality principle and "*La gloire*" was finished.

Francophone Guinea: The muted last hurrah of Françafrique

Francophone Guinea was the first of the long series of coups that marked Francophone Africa during the 2020s. But could it be chalked up to the first sign that Paris and its African protege were losing control of the situation? Not really. Why? Because Guinea had always been the odd man out in the Francophone family, the only one to reject in 1958 the new "*Communauté*" De Gaulle was offering to the French Empire in lieu of a decolonization process. And it still has a special relationship with Paris. De Gaulle himself was in a delicate position when he came to Brazzaville and gave his famous speech on August 28 1958 when he said that a referendum would soon be offered to the French public—including in the colonies—where the future of France would be decided.[1] Why did he choose Brazzaville? Because of the lingering memory of his 1944 speech where the hint of a possible autonomy for the colonies had indirectly been floated. The 1958 speech was a continuation of the 1944 one, equally clever, equally fundamental and equally hypocritical. In August 1958 De Gaulle was a *de facto* head of state, popularly legitimate but not formally legal, and he was trying to get the support of the colonies—one of which, Algeria, was in the midst of a war of independence. In 1944 the purpose had been to mobilise the Empire to support the Free French movement against Vichy; in 1958 the hope was to get the support of Francophone Africa against the Great Powers (especially the Anglo-Saxons) and the underlying aim was not military but diplomatic, to carry in the United Nations assembly a weight greater than that of France alone.[2]

Guinea later paid a high price for its "independence" when its nationalist leader Sekou Toure became a dictator who ruled with brutality until his death in 1984.[3]

So did Paris organize in some way the September 5 2021 coup against President Alpha Conde when he followed Sékou Touré's duplicitous path? Definitely not since by then *Françafrique* did not have the energy let alone the political will of its younger years. But it was nevertheless a success because in the last years of his rule Sékou Touré had mellowed and understood that with *Françafrique* the former colonial master could become a tolerant ally. He became a friend of Omar Bongo, reconciled with Félix Houphouët-Boigny and even invited Jacques Foccart to Conakry for talks to smooth out the bilateral differences left by recent history. But the years that followed Sékou Touré's death had not been a democratic success. A sequence of faceless and hardly competent army strongmen had ruled Guinea till 2010 and Alpha Condé, the first elected head of state, used his newly acquired status to modify the constitution and give himself a third mandate.[4] He was 83 when he was overthrown and he is still discreetly alive. His successor, Colonel Mamady Doumbouya, had the profile of an ideal *Françafrique* head of state: he was a French Foreign Legion veteran, very Francophile (he had married a white female *Gendarme*), and he was very watchful of possible jihadi activities; so far there are none as Colonel Dombouya has arranged with the French forces stationed in Dakar for unscheduled patrols on the northern border with Mali where trouble could possibly emanate from.[5] Colonel Dombouya has told Paris that he has no intention, in spite of his good relations with Colonel Assimi Goïta, to join the *Alliance des Etats du Sahel*.

Is not Africa a magic place where ordinary logic doesn't apply? For the time being there is not enough electricity in Guinea to power an aluminum plant. Could the Russians organize an industrial coup similar to building the Aswan Dam in 1960? Cooperation with France seems unthinkable. Meanwhile Colonel Dombouya has made himself General and his promises for elections seem to have become more and more imprecise. He is asking for a further postponement (February 2024). In the meantime the international airport in Conakry has been renamed "Sékou Touré Airport", a change which had a somewhat shocking effect on the population. The military junta was looking for a "national hero" but the choice was unfortunate because the misery ushered in during the 1960s by the latter was still clearly remembered as there were surviving witnesses. There have also been a spate of arrests and demonstrations against the military commission that have led to several deaths and the Guinea strongman has named a new Prime Minister from among the opposition. But the man has changed sides several times and been condemned in absentia for an assassination attempt against Alpha Condé. Has this kind of detail ever been a problem for *Françafrique* at the peak of its power? It was not and probably still isn't, even in its present damaged state.

Gabon: The discreet low-key putsch settles in

The coup in Guinea had been the first of a series and—so far—Gabon has been the last in the sequence. But there has been little in common between the moderate cleaning operation in Gabon and the succession of operatic Sahelian coups that the international media has tended to depict. As we mentioned above:

- The coup in Gabon was highly popular. At present, ten months after General Oligui Nguema took power, he is still called "le libérateur" in the streets of Libreville. And anti-French slogans—which in the Gabon case would be somewhat justified—are absent.
- This *"liberation"* is of course the removal of the Bongo mafia which had ruled the country since 1967.[6] Yet there have not been any anti-French popular demonstrations such as those that occurred in Bamako, Niamey or Ouagadougou.
- The military government is handling the situation with a complete absence of militant rhetoric of any kind.
- The tour of five African states by General Oligui Nguema in December 2023 has led to the discreet suspension of various sanctions.
- There is no evidence of a Russian intervention at any level of government or the army.
- There has been no violence, nor any arrests or media restrictions. All the (limited) number of people presently detained are well-known for their involvement in the fifty-six-year-long corrupt Bongo tyranny and the demands of the street are not for less but for more arrests since many notoriously guilty persons are still free.
- France, the former evil genius of the tyranny, has been discreetly placated in exchange for its neutrality.

Negotiations with Paris for the positions and roles of the French advisors and technicians presently in Gabon are still underway, not aiming for vengeance or financial blackmail, but more from a perspective of damage control.[7]

- During April and May 2024 Oligui Nguema called a national conference where the population was supposed to express what it wanted from the August 2023 coup. This "National Conference" was a highly controlled event where no organizations were put forward but the few that existed were allowed to speak freely. The term "National Conference" was not correct; it was in reality a "National Cleaning Up Forum" where the Gabonese publicly excoriated the Bongo regime. The fifty-six years of National Nausea ended in a symbolic release.

One element that facilitated the prudent moderation of General Oligui Nguema was the fact that in Paris President Macron had allowed for the development of the so-called "lawsuit about the *biens mal acquis*" (ill-acquired properties). Since his election in 2017 President Macron has bragged about "being neither left nor right" and has proceeded to do several things "en même temps" ("at the same time"). The result of this approach has often been a lackadaisical smattering of confused and contradictory policies; this is particularly evident in the case of African policies for which the

President has obviously little appetite. Gone are the days of De Gaulle or even Mitterrand or Chirac when—for often questionable reasons—African policies were a matter of serious attention. The Presidential Africa Unit on 2 Rue de l'Elysée still exists as a ghost of its former self and is now occupied by Jérémie Robert, the former French Consul in New York. When Robert was offered the job in late 2023, he refused it at first because he guessed this could be a programmed run for nothing. He had a good experience of Africa but of the "Wrong Africa" from a *Françafrique* point of view: Eastern non-Francophone former British (or assimilated) colonies. But he is a former school friend of the President, both of them having attended the prestigious École National d'Administration. This school *camaraderie* has been an important factor in the President's administrative appointments. Macron's view of Africa is obviously vague and conceptual and all he seemed to have wanted was an easy rapport with this formerly symbolic but now practically dead administrative unit. Jérémie Robert understood the problem, weighed his own interests and finally accepted the job. The results are tenuous.

But as far as Gabon was concerned the situation has been put in the limelight by the legal action against the *biens mal acquis* or BMA (ill-acquired assets). This is a procedure which was started in March 2007 by two Africa-oriented French NGOs, Sherpa and Survie. It targeted Denis Sassou Nguesso,[8] Omar Bongo,[9] Blaise

Compaoré,[10] Eduardo Dos Santos[11] and Theodoro Obiang,[12] with charges of theft of public funds. The procedure was far from smooth, with spasmodic attempts from "unknown sources" at judicial and reputational counter-measures. The half judicial half conspiratorial moves were aimed at Monsieur William Bourdon, the key lawyer behind the BMA process, and ranged from anonymous threats to demands by Equatorial Guinea to the International Court of Justice that the charges against the country be dismissed by France (they were not). This finally led to the confiscation of significant Guinean assets (belonging to Obiang's son) located in France. Loïc Le Floch-Prigent, the former Elf CEO, who had been condemned in 2003 for his financial juggling,[13] was brought in 2020 as a witness into a collateral of the BMA procedure.[14] Since he was no longer personally under suspicion (he had served his jail time) Le Floch-Prigent could afford to be candid.

> In Gabon Omar Bongo always wanted to have a formal bogus opposition and he wanted to be the one controlling it. The "opposition" members were chosen by Elf Gabon which paid their salaries ... all the expenses of the Presidents of the African countries and of their staff when they came to France were paid directly by Elf. It was always paid directly and only in cash.[15]

In a BMA-related court case, Pascaline Bongo, the late Gabonese dictator's daughter, dismissed the arguments of the court. She was accused of using her position not only as the daughter of the dictator but as his chief of staff for fifteen years and his Foreign Minister as well. But there was no trace of questionable financial movements that the French courts could prove, even if witnesses could mention that her nickname when she worked for her president-father was "Mrs 5%". Nicknames are no proof of guilt but the fact that even some of the French, long-time supporters of the Bongo regime, felt emboldened to turn against it helped soothe Franco-Gabonese relations because it went down well at the popular level. For the first time in over half a century the Gabonese people had the impression that they existed. President Macron decided to bypass the AU sanctions that were unavoidable and to let bygones be bygones. A new ambassador was accredited to Paris but when Ms Victorine Tchicot, head of General Oligui Nguema's personal staff, became the boss of Gabon's National Investment Strategic Fund,[16] this was perhaps a little too cosy. She had been Omar Bongo's personal secretary and this embodied a degree of proximity between the old regime and the new one that went perhaps beyond simple diplomatic good manners. Oligui Nguema's visit to Paris in early June 2024 has been ambiguously seen: for those who understood what he was trying to do, it was the last turning of a page before trying to write a new chapter. For those that still thought they were reading an old book, Oligui Nguema was in Paris to get the usual imprimatur a new *Françafrique* boss should get before starting to write his own authoritarian manual. We will see what interpretation was the right one but many signs point at a transformation rather than at a continuity.

The Alliance des Etats du Sahel (AES): An attempt to streamline the confusion

The creation of the formal AES Alliance on September 16 2023 was the first clearly dateable nail in *Françafrique*'s coffin. How did it come about? By bringing together the three most anti-French regimes in the Sahelian region—Mali, Burkina Faso and Niger— brought together by a combination of stress, expediency and friendly Russian prodding. We already mapped out the first elements of this new fragile structure in Chapter Five. Let us now look at how things went from improvised and tentative to hastily slapped together and mock-official.

First there was the need to plug a hole in the leaking dyke of anti-jihadisn. The French-led G5 Sahel alliance[17] had been created in 2014 and had fought listlessly the various strands of Muslim fundamentalist guerillas in the Sahel for nine Paris-manipulated years. The hope was to manage to involve the European Union in a global security effort benefitting the Sahel countries. In

December 2023 they finally threw in the sponge after the first three African countries broke with France, which led the two surviving allies of Paris—Chad and Mauritania—to give up. European countries—Denmark, Germany and Sweden—which had planned to help moved out if they already had troops in Africa (as was the case of Germany) and immediately started to withdraw. Two months later Mali, Burkina Faso and Niger decided to quit the ECOWAS regional force as well after it had walked out of the Niger crisis with a figurative black eye and also repeatedly failed to hold its ground at home in Borno and Zamfara states. Mali, Burkina and Niger, Muslim-majority states all fighting insurgent radical Islamist insurrections, perceived ECOWAS not as a protective bulwark but as a pro-Western alliance which they saw as being manipulated by France.

Worse still, the regional alliance was not only considered as a Trojan horse for Western interests but it was also despised for its impotence. After the Russians had participated in massacres in Mali,[18] both ECOWAS and the UN had wanted to clarify the situation. The regime in Bamako not only refused but it cancelled its defence agreements with France (May 2022). Nothing happened. In July 2022 ECOWAS lifted its sanctions on Mali in exchange for promises of elections in February 2024. Those were forgotten and the elections never took place. The role of the Russians is often mentioned and usually exaggerated because it is picturesque[19] and an identifiable reborn feature of the Cold War. But they are in place more to take advantage of the regional mess than of initiating it. The great majority of these problems are emanating from the Francophone countries.[20]

What is often overlooked is the deepening penetration of Iranian diplomacy and secret services in the Sahel region. In September 2022, after a meeting between Iranian President Ebrahim Raïssi and Burkina Minister of Foreign Affairs Olivia Rouamba, Tehran reopened its embassy, closed since 2001, and the following month inaugurated a mixed Burkinabe/Iranian Commission for Economic Cooperation in spite of its limited scope. In November 2023 the Nigerian Minister for Foreign Affairs Bakary Yaou Sangaré issued a common declaration with Iran about "our common resistance to European hegemony politics". These small bastions of *Françafrique* had become advanced positions of "anti-imperialism", all the way to the most outrageous propaganda-bloated statements such as when the Dogon militia—supporting the Malian government—accused Paris of aiding militarily the fundamentalist guerrillas. This drift towards militant anti-French positions was not the product of any kind of Africa-wide conspiracy. In fact it was more a situation where the French, who had managed their brutal *Françafrique* project in a very arrogant and unilateral way, found themselves caught in a dead-end street.[21] The myriad problems of a difficult continent, often regional, tribal, fragmentary and inherited from old colonial neglect, ended up in the Gallic lap. As the French withdrew or were kicked out, the switch to the Russians—or to their Iranian proxies—was more a plea from the African side which desperately needed international support and knew that it would come neither from China nor from Washington. The *Alliance des Etats du Sahel* was a cohort of the poor and the powerless, under siege by desperate rebels and with limited means to protect the money and the power that they had earlier received from France. Moreover this occurred at a moment when the international system had entered after February 2022 its deepest crisis since 1945. In Mali, which confronted the worst situation of the three countries, the fighting that took place was at times triangular, with the Army fighting the African jihadists fighting the Tuaregs. Some of the reactions, such as when the Malian authorities took as hostages the Ivorian soldiers sent to help them (July 10 2022), were deeply irrational, verging on desperate. It was definitely not something ordered by the Russians and its "anti-imperialist" value was hard to fathom. Facing the AES France was alone and had no means (or will) to fight. This left the Americans facing the Russians in a kind of tropical parody of the war in Ukraine. In Mali the UN folded up its mission on December 31 2023 and abandoned the country to its fate. The least bad situation was in Niger where the Islamist attacks were limited and contained to the Southwest, in the tri-border area.

The worst situation was in Burkina Faso where the fighting had seeped down to the lowest, most intimate and most domestic levels of society. This had started with an attempt by Captain Traoré at taking the war to th level of a national cause by boosting popular participation through investing, financially and humanly, in the *Volontaires De la Patrie* (VDP or Fatherland Volunteers) program.[22] Since many of the jihadis were ethnic Fulani (Peuhl) the "patriotic" program led, to a large degree, to a war against the Fulani, and indirectly to a push of those same Fulani into the arms of IS Sahel or JNMIS, the two Muslim radical groups struggling both with the government and against each other for control of Burkina Faso. The Fulani took this step partly as a means of finding shelter against the targeted attacks of the regular Army. This led to a civil war in the deepest sense of the word such as on February 26 2024 where fifteen Catholic worshippers were killed in a church in the village of Essakane while on the same day twenty-four Muslims were killed at a mosque in the small town of Natiaboani. Both groups were killed by Islamic State guerrillas, the Catholics because they were Christians and the Muslims because they were "bad Muslims" who had not joined the radical insurgents. The French troops had evacuated Burkina in

January 2023 and the Burkina government accused Paris of helping the Islamic movements in retaliation, which nobody believed, even in the country itself. But *Françafrique* had completely lost its protective capacity.

In Mali, Colonel Assimi Goïta declared publicly (on December 7 2023) that the AES should, in due course, become a Federation and he (discreetly) sent an emissary to Moscow to sound out the Russians on such a development. Moscow's answer was diplomatic but non-committal.[23] It was hard to discern why the Russians were not really interested in the proposal, at least for the time being, but it seems to have been due to a mixture of causes ranging from a fear of antagonising the Americans further before the November electoral deadline to doubts about the solidity of the Federal project being presented by AES and from a mixture of puzzlement about the situation on the ground to limitations of the financial commitments Russia was prepared to make. To smooth out the situation vis-à-vis the unofficial (but real) AES, Moscow sent more weapons to both Bamako and Ouagadougou but without making any promises. This was at a time when 62% of the people living in the "AES" countries considered Russia to be the foreign actor they trusted the most versus 10% opting for the US, 5% France and 1% the United Kingdom.[24] The 5% trust in France as a referent country spoke for a dwindling nostalgia in a former *Françafrique* area of influence.

WHAT IS LEFT AFTER DISMANTLING

Then, what about Chad? In the political hodgepodge *Françafrique* was sinking into, Chad was the last surviving element of the former system in the Sahel.[25] Mahamat Deby flew suddenly to Moscow where he met Vladimir Putin who congratulated him on his new constitution and wished him "good elections which will take place at the appropriate level".[26] Many observers of the *Françafrique* scene commented *sotto voce:* "Here goes the last one! Deby in Moscow! The end is near!" In fact it was a final manifestation of the *Françafrique* way of doing things: on February 28 2024 Yahia Dillo Djerou was killed a few hours after attacking (unsuccessfully) the central office of the Internal Security Agency in N'Djamena. Yahia Dillo was a nephew of Idris Deby who had led a rebellion against him in 2021. His uncle had tried to arrest him and the commando raid against his house had failed but killed both his mother and his son. To appease him Deby made him a minister. But after the death of Idris[27] Yahia Dillo announced that he would run against his cousin in the next election. When the election preparations were reported, he carried out his unplanned mini-insurrection. After its failure he ran back to his party's office where he was killed[28] and the next day the party's office was razed to the ground with a bulldozer. President Macron, who had rushed to N'Djamena to comfort Mahamat Deby at the time of his father's contentious death, made no comment. The last bastion of *Françafrique* had not betrayed the French connection to go over to the Russians. Simply, Mahamat Deby who is wise in the ways of that peculiar world and who knew the French were at a low ebb of popularity, just went to Moscow to burnish his credentials. Putin obliged, Mahamat flew back to Chad, his cousin was impatient and poorly organized, he tried to grab power with insufficient means at his disposal and he was summarily executed. It was a typical Zaghawa episode in sorting out the state control of Chad. *Françafrique*'s last bastion had stood firm with the usual means and checking in with Putin had been a simple precaution before things got serious. But it is telling that the imprint of the French no longer sufficed. The Russian symbolical *imprimatur* was needed before a rival could be eliminated. *Françafrique* had not disappeared but its capacity for projection had shrunk.

The pieces left behind

There are three fallback tactical positions in the *Françafrique* debacle:

1. Business as usual
2. Frenzy
3. Some kind of hope

Let us start with position number one :

- *Ivory Coast:* On March 22 2024 President Alassane Ouattara was invited for dinner at the Elysée Palace

in order to confirm the focus of the only African Francophone regime which could reasonably look forward to a reasonable future.
- *Benin* is a sliver of a state but with a 6.5% rate of economic growth and no foreseeable political problems, President Patrice Talon has so far stuck to his business-as-usual attitude.[29]
- *Togo* has remained a *Françafrique* old style run-of-the-mill case so far, with a dynastic president automatically re-elected four times since he replaced his father on the throne in 2005. A sign of the times, a spooked Faure Gnassingbe is trying to promote a new reform-proof constitution where the president would be "elected" by his bogus parliament. What passes for an opposition screamed bloody murder. How this "reform" (now adopted) will survive will be a test of the capacity of this isolated bastion of *Françafrique* to carry on its own form of rusty business as usual.
- *Chad,* as we saw, is the last surviving bastion of *Françafrique* military might.[30] After being forced out of Mali, Burkina Faso and Niger in 2022–23, it is only in Chad that Paris can still deploy an army whose movements are entirely under its own independent control. At present France is "preparing" the next Chadian presidential election together with Mahamat Idris Deby after the convenient killing of the young president's cousin

and political enemy, Yahia Dillo. Paris is dealing directly with the Zaghawa tribal dictatorship which has ruled Chad since 1990. But this last island of *Françafrique* military power is structurally fragile.

- *Cameroun* is the catastrophe waiting to happen. One quarter of its population lives under the minimum annual survival threshold of $650, the North is regularly raided by fighters from Boko Haram and the West is prey to the revolt of the English-speaking Bamileke secessionists who would like to have their own independent state or, failing that, to join Nigeria. The Camerounian president is ninety-one, he has been in power for forty years and is a bit under the weather. There is fighting on the road to Bamenda, forty kilometers from the capital Yaounde towards the Anglophone part of the country. The army has the capacity to hold the capital but not to control the three western provinces.

- A special mention should be made of *Djibouti*, which has been *Françafrique* since it became independent in 1977. It remains *Françafrique* in its political style—President Ismail Omar Guelleh has been in power since 1999 and it is home to 1,500 French soldiers—but it is today a neutral space, a *worldafrique*, with military bases from half a dozen countries—including China and the US—on a territorial area of 23,000 km^2 (half the size of Switzerland). The President is seventy-six and was "re-elected" in 2021 with 95.58% of the vote. The territory is split between the Somalis—themselves split between six sub-clans—and the Afar. The past belongs to France and the future is split between Beijing and Washington.

So let us move now to our second category, the frantic reaction. As we saw earlier, in 2022 the folding up of the Operation Barkhane expeditionary corps in Mali—and the sending home of the 2,500 Chadian soldiers who were there in support of the French troops—marked the end of *Françafrique*'s last war. Mali kicked the French out, Burkina Faso did the same, Paris switched them to Niger, Niger had a coup and also kicked the French out. All these had been allies of the French and they were now furiously lashing out at France. President Macron decided on a radical disengagement measure: withdrawing more troops from the four bases—Dakar, Libreville and Abidjan, perhaps from Djibouti as well—where they were still stationed. The Americans had hoped to stay in Niger even after the French left by keeping a low profile. But in February they were told that they had to exit Agadez from where they had been monitoring their drones. The only sanctions they could think up were to stop the delivery of armoured vehicles to the Nigerian Army, leaving the jihadi radicals as the only beneficiaries of the whole switch. Eventually in mid-May, after more talks with the military junta, the

Pentagon reluctantly agreed to leave by September 15. All over the Sahel the collapse of *Françafrique* was having two consequences: boosting the position of jihadist rebels in all "AES" countries and facilitating the arrival of Russian Private Military Companies (PMCs) which were only "private" in theory. The superficial media take on this was: the French are out and the Russians are in. Africa was in fact abandoned to its fate since the Russians approached it only as a deliberate "annoyance to the West" which Vladimir Putin considers as a global enemy. The Putin regime will make some money out of it, mostly after gaining control of scattered artisanal mining sites, offering their PMCs as an anti-jihadi after-sales service. So far the results have not been very successful. "Wagner" remains as a myth but its successors have had little real impact.[31] The various PMCs which replaced it are not very efficient, operate sporadically out of their mining sanctuaries and beg Moscow for equipment. The Ukrainians try to counterpunch them, without much more efficiency.[32] There is no "*Russafrica*", except in the Western imagination. Mali and Burkina Faso are in serious trouble as the French are pulling out and nobody is replacing them. Will Russia launch itself into a full geopolitical influence plan if it prevails in Ukraine, after attaining either conquest or even a diplomatic settlement? Hard to say but unlikely at first glance. Russia causes a disproportionate degree of fear which is rooted in its nuclear capacity coupled with an erratic leadership. The erratic leadership could be a problem[33] but the nuclear capacity is definitely not a part of the African picture.

This leaves us with the third category of response, the appropriate one. There were only two cases, in radically different situations, but both have raised a tempestuous wave of local support whose disappointment would be tragic: Gabon and Senegal. We discussed earlier the "useful coup d'état" in Gabon. At the time of writing,[34] temporary president Brice Oligui Nguema has engaged in a month-long "national psychodrama". Its strongest outcome? The collation of 38,000 papers outlining the "dysfunctions"—the term is weak—of the Gabonese state. Its weak point? The assembly responsible for the national transition has no capacity to enforce any conclusions it comes up with. Its probable outcome? General Oligui Nguema will stand as a presidential candidate in an election he cannot lose. What matters will be what the probable winner will do with his victory. The other reasonable option, in Senegal, went through an election even though at the last moment President Macky Sall tried to postpone it. Bassirou Diomaye Faye went in a matter of weeks from being detained[35] to being elected President of Senegal with 54% of the vote in the first electoral round. Several of the measures that figured in the party program were immediately deleted[36] and the winners of the polls immediately made declarations of appeasement directed at France. The troop removal demand was dropped while the CFA Franc action was switched from withdrawal to reform. What was obvious was that popular feeling on the street was intensely hostile to France.[37] President Macron sent a conciliatory message to the new President. Normalization, at least in the short term, is on the way. In his first speech after coming to power President Bassirou Diomaye Faye announced that he was going to ask for an audit of the oil and mining sector. This has to do with the Sangomar oilfield development[38] which was the discreet main issue at stake in the Senegal elections.

Françafrique has already largely faded away. It was not neocolonialism; it was an archeo-post-colonialism, a specific product of French history in the 1950s, fathered by General De Gaulle himself and bequeathed to his successors through the permanent efforts of the French political elites to justify France's seat in the UN Security Council. *Francophonie* still has an official existence, but *Françafrique* has slowly lost its long-term tangible if unofficial status. It was a *de facto* reality, never a *de jure* one. No need for a military band to play at the funeral. But the disappearance of that devilish angel of mercy has left a large political hole in the African continent. A secondary center. A focus, not a beacon. Replaced by what? Definitely not by Moscow which has perhaps the will but definitely not the means. Nor by the impotent UN finally withdrawing from the Congo after twenty-five useless years. China perhaps? Unlikely. The Chinese attempt at world hegemony will go along the more traditional "Belt and Road" corridor, not through "the Dark Continent". Where and what then, in the new globalized world which is among the final consequences of decolonization? Africa will most likely have to look at itself and embark on its own internal decolonization, obviously a long-term phenomenon.

Full circle: In which France has to face decolonizing itself

As we mentioned in Chapter One[39] France has made enormous exceptions in its decolonization process. Of France's landmass (apart from Corsica which is considered a "metropole" in spite of being insular simply because it is in Europe) 18% is overseas. But practically all these territories, apart from French Guiana, are islands, all with varied histories but where only a minority of the population is of French origin even if all those born in these "confettis of Empire" carry a French passport when they travel abroad.

(a) The Comoros

Of all these "confettis", one has recently leapt to the forefront of France's structural social problems: the island of Mayotte. It is not mentioned by Jean-Claude Guillebaud in his seminal work on the remaining pieces of the French Empire because it was not officially "a part of France" at the time of publication. Why? Because

Mayotte, a French colony since 1841, not only was not decolonized when the rest of the Comoros archipelago became independent in 1975 but became a French *Département* (i.e. an integral part of Metropolitan France) in 2009! This matters because Mayotte is 8,000 km away from France but only 70 km from Anjouan.[40] The total population of the Comoros is 850,000 (with a growth rate of 1.9% a year). In Mayotte, the population is 321,000 but with a growth rate of 3.8% a year. Per capita income in the Comoros is $1,610. Per capita income in Mayotte is estimated at $4,000. In Mayotte 42% of the population is foreign-born but with only 6% of French-born people, the rest being mostly Comorian. Through finessing identity papers, residents of Mayotte have had a fair chance of somehow getting to France (where per capita income was $51,600 in 2021). As a result Mayotte is a rich world siphon smack in the middle of one of the poorest regions of Africa and *kwassa-kwassa*[41] full of pregnant women arrive day after day from Anjouan to Mayotte. Many of the children born in Mayotte from Comorian women will not make it to France and many will be abandoned to the mercy of Mahorais.[42] Roaming gangs of very young children have become a plague in Mayotte and the Mahorais Swahili are fed up. They have organized a social movement which blocks roads and demonstrates around the clock against illegal immigration (50% of the population) and the collapse of social services. In addition, due to climate change, the archipelago is a victim of drought which the Paris government has neglected to address. Daily life is falling apart and those with enough money take their young children to La Réunion, 1,430 km away, a two-and-a-half hour flight. La Réunion is another piece of "French confetti" but with a more balanced social and economic situation which allows Mahorais children to be educated in the French language, in a safe and sound environment. Of the babies born in Mayotte, 60% are not French and are left by their Comorian mothers to the hopeful care of French relatives or family friends. This has nothing to do with race and the main victims are Black Mahorais who now live in the poorest of all French *départements*.

How did this picturesque tropical island turn into such a hell? By being the victim of history and a bizarre *Françafrique* distortion. Mayotte was bought by King Louis-Philippe of France from Sultan Andriantsouli on April 25 1841. France had lost its main territory in the Pacific—the most important being *L'île de France*, today's Mauritius—during the Napoleonic Wars. France was then painfully hobbling around on its broken imperial legs (Algiers had been occupied in 1830) and felt it needed a base in the Indian Ocean. The Sultan of the Comoros was a Malagasy conqueror who had occupied the archipelago but who had problems with his rebellious Swahili subjects, against whom he sought European protection. But soon after the French bought

Mayotte, Louis-Philippe was overthrown by the Republican revolution of 1848 in France which abolished slavery. At the stroke of a pen in Paris, all the Swahili slaves in French Mayotte became free while the rest of the archipelago, which was formally "free", kept its slave-owning status.[43] This instantly created a link between the island's peaceful masters and the French, who loved to be loved for their role in lighting the world with their shining freedom.[44] France decided on a quaint process of decolonization for its Comoros territory: on December 22 1974 a "consultation" (the word "referendum" was never used) was held in the four islands as to whether the population wanted independence. The polls took place in a rather quaint way: in Mayotte, the majority was in favor of voting "no;" the politicians did not dare to go into the three other islands because they knew their position was unpopular in Grande Comore, in Anjouan and in Mohéli. The support of non-Mahorais Comorians was expressed in a highly original way by the so-called "*chatouilleuses*" (women who tickle). These were groups of laughing nationalist women who assaulted the (male) Mahorais politicians and tickled them not to death but to falling on the ground where the lady "tickleresses" kept tickling them to prevent them from talking. No Mahorais politician so amusingly harassed was able to organize in any of the other three islands before the polls. The result of the "consultation" gave a large majority in favor of independence (99%) in the three nationalist islands while Mayotte voted to remain French (63.22%). The French took it as a tribute to their reasonable policies—which it was not, it was simply the result of very special historical circumstances—but then what happened in the "independent" Comoros?

France by organising its "consultation" had violated the UN/OAU rule that decolonized territories should keep their former colonial boundaries. By accepting the separation of Mayotte, Paris had not respected that rule. Ahmed Abdallah, first president of the Comoros, condemned France and declared the unilateral independence of the country—including Mayotte—in January 1975 with UN support. In August that year he was overthrown by a three-tiered coup d'état. The new President Said Mohamed Jaffar was a conservative aristocrat; but behind him stood a young pro-Chinese Marxist revolutionary, Ali Soilih; and behind both stood the French mercenary Bob Denard, a veteran of Katanga who had fought in Yemen for the pro-Saudi royalists and whose gun was for hire. By his own boasting, he was a *Françafrique* freelancer. It was Denard—who was at the time busy in Chad—who brought the muscle in time for the coup. Said Mohamed Jaffar resigned in 1976 and Ali Soilihi stepped up to power. He ran a Maoist government both with what was beneficial in such circumstances—measures to cut the power of rich landowners, more freedom for women, ground level democratic initiatives—and with what was much less good, particularly the creation of a militia supposed to be the Comoro Red Guards, on the Chinese model. These were a bunch of thugs who raped and killed at random, not on Soilih's orders but because he had quickly lost control of them. Meanwhile Denard had moved to South Africa where he was training militias to fight in Mozambique and Angola on behalf of the South African apartheid regime. He met Ahmed Abdallah who had fled to Johannesburg after Denard had overthrown him. Over drinks they worked out what was going on in the Comoros, concluding that they could try another coup to reinstate the former president in power, this time with the support of apartheid South Africa. On May 13 1978 Denard landed in Greater Comoro with forty-three French mercenaries, overthrew Ali Solih and brought back Ahmed Abdallah. Ali Solih was killed a few days later (May 29).[45] Bob Denard converted to Islam to blend better in the local landscape and set up shop in Greater Comoro. He put together a 600-strong Private Guard (but did not disband the Comorian army, an oversight he lived to regret), and got the apartheid regime to pay their salaries. He relaunched his program to put together mercenaries to fight FRELIMO in Mozambique and the MPLA in Angola and in his free time did the odd job for the French Secret Service. *Françafrique* now had its own state and it kept running it for the next eleven years without any interference from the international community. Denard never meddled with Mayotte which remained de facto a French colony while the international community considered it as part of an independent country. But as the British say, eventually every man meets his Waterloo. For Denard it was his negligence of the Comorian army which was underpaid in comparison to his private militia by a factor of roughly six to one. The Comorians prepared a coup to kick the French out, Denard found out about the plot and rushed to Ahmed Abdallah's office with two men. He dictated a decree to Ahmed Abdallah that dissolved the Comorian army and Abdallah signed it but objected to the wisdom of actually implementing it. There was a quarrel and the President and his bodyguard were both mown down by AK-47 fire. By whom? Probably not by the cleaning lady. After four different trials—all in France, with charges brought by Ahmed Abdallah's family—a French court finally exonerated Denard (May 1999) and he walked away free while pining for his island paradise. He had returned to South Africa but the collapse of the apartheid regime had put him out of a job. So he tried for one last time and during the night of 27–28 September 1995 he landed in the Comoros with a small all-French commando unit, overthrowing President Said Mohamed Djohar who had been elected after Denard had left in 1989. Given his previous record, he was careful not to kill anybody. But the times had changed and Denard had become more a liability than an asset for the spooks in Paris. He lasted for about a week and then the French sent Special Forces from their base in Djibouti who corralled the old mercenary and took him away without a fight.[46]

Now let us compare the French conservative stance of help for the non-independence of Mayotte in 1975 and for eleven years (1978–89) the tacit support of the *Françafrique* quasi-state in "independent" Comoros. The picture is somewhat contradictory. Grabbing Denard and throwing him out in 1995 did not add up to coherent whole. Exonerating him from perhaps having killed President Ahmed Abdallah blurred the picture further. Taking one island out of the four others in the archipelago and turning it, 8,000 km away, into a piece of genuine metropolitan France and hoping against hope that somehow the magic alchemy of Gallic civilization would work a miracle, was just a little bit crazier. The final touch of madness was added by Gérald Darmanin, President Macron's Minister for Internal Affairs, on February 12 2024 when he returned from a trip to Mayotte where he had witnessed a society completely out of control. He came back with one conclusion: Paris had to modify the Constitution of the French Fifth Republic exempting Mayotte from *Jus Soli*, the principle basing French nationality on the very ground of France. The poor man seemed to think that this would be the solution to the mayhem in Mayotte. In spite of being a Minister for Internal Affairs he would have needed a refresher course in constitutional law: the *Jus Soli* of France is a symbol which means, since we are in France, something much more potent than reality.

In our country the Jus Soli is conditional: you are not born a Frenchman unless one of your parents at least had been born on French soil, which results in a "double Jus Soli". If neither of your parents was born on French soil, you have to wait till you are thirteen to obtain French nationality. For people born in Mayotte a law voted in 2018 requires for one of the child's parents to have been living legally on French territory for at least three months before the child's thirteenth birthday. This has caused a big drop in naturalization applications although it has not stopped pregnant women from coming to Mayotte and many young Comorians from coming to the island. What brings them to Mayotte is the level of per capita income of this "European" département which is much higher than the income of any given country in the region.[47]

But the French extreme right, which seems more aware of the ins and outs of the legal status of French nationality than the Minister himself, noisily supported his idea, hoping that a project of constitutional modification could lead to a referendum where the general question of immigration into France could be the subject of plebiscite.[48] So the distant consequences of a *Françafrique* mess have led to the possibility of having to modify the constitution in ways that are still unknown. But modifying the constitution will not make Mayotte less of a provocative oddity or less of a magnet for the poor of East Africa. France is stuck with Mayotte and there are no solutions, only adaptations. On February 14 2024, a new *Préfet* was picked to head Mayotte, the 101st département of France and the poorest. The Ministry of Interior announced that "he would go to Mayotte as soon as the roadblocks are removed" and that a new Mayotte Emergency Law would be discussed by the French Parliament on May 22 2024 (it was not). The independent Comoro Union declared it had no intention to help manage the immigration flux into Mayotte and that it reiterated its demand that France should abide by the UN resolutions and let Mayotte join the three independent islands. At the same time Mayotte's MP in the Paris Parliament alleged that "the corrupt Moroni government is organizing human trafficking from the African continent into Mayotte". Given the degree of corruption and electoral manipulation that was evident during the recent polls in the independent archipelago state (February 2024) she was probably right. There are now tented camps in Mayotte populated by Somalis, by Rwandese, by Congolese refugees and others, dumped there from Moroni and largely abandoned in the debris-cluttered entry hall of prosperous France. The Mayotte native population is stuck with a double citizenship,

French and Comorian, usually with no passport. Their future is opaque.

(b) New Caledonia

This is the tail of the tail or perhaps *Die unendliche Geschichte* (the never-ending (hi) story) of *Françafrique*, i.e. of French colonialism up to and beyond Africa. "New Caledonia" is not in Africa but it has been shaped and later run by the *Françafrique* informal lobby in Paris. It is an informal member of those confetti pieces which, in spite of being former colonies is now a *Collectivité d'Outre-Mer à Statut Particulier*, a politically correct name for the small archipelago which was occupied by France in 1853. This part of France is 16,700 km from the "mother country" and it is still at the time of writing (mid 2024) in the throes of a decolonization struggle rooted in the very harsh way these territories were colonized. First and perhaps worst, the small archipelago was a biological isolate and the simple intrusion of humans with a different germ population caused massive deaths among the indigenous peoples.[49] The *Code de l'Indigénat* (Native Code 1874, modified in 1881) was a legislative body which parked the Caledonian Kanaks into a series of Native American style reservations. There was no education, no modernization and fierce military control.[50] The native pre-colonial population, estimated at around 60,000, had fallen to 27,000 by 1921. At the 1931 Colonial Exhibition in Paris, the Kanaks were displayed locked up in iron cages, something which would have been unthinkable for black Africans. In March 1942 the islands, whose Governor had rejected the authority of Vichy, were opened to the US Army which landed several thousand soldiers embarking on the Pacific counteroffensive against Japan. The New Caledonian reserves were dismantled and the Kanaks saw Black American soldiers driving trucks and shouldering guns. In 1945 the US Army left the archipelago and the French Gaullist government inherited a territory which was a socially boiling vat where even the whites were sharply divided between French colonial families and the other half of the European population which was of *bagnards* (deportee) origins. In the 1970s, as the Kanak independence movement began to get off the ground, the French Prime Minister Pierre Messmer issued an official document pushing the metropolitan population to send colonists to Caledonia. During the next ten years Paris supported a "second colonization" of the islands and by 1980 there were 55,000 Kanaks facing 50,000 whites and 26,000 "others". It was these "others" which turned the cooking vat into a pressure cooker which is still letting off steam to this day. Who were they? A multicultural population which came mostly from the Wallis and Futuna archipelago, another piece of French imperial confetti.[51] But that particular confetti is pro-French and pro-colonial, which has turned its population into a fifth column for the Kanak independence movement. The Caledonian independence movement started in 1984, way behind anything in Africa. It quickly led to what is still remembered by the Caldoche population[52] as "*les évènements*" (the events) when the Kanaks and the Caldoches clashed sporadically for four years (1984–88). This left ninety people dead on both sides, a shaken economy and a durable backlog of hatreds which were added to the collective memories of the colonial past. Some of the episodes (hostage-taking, summary executions) were grim and it took a new "Agreement" negotiated in Paris in 1988 and revised in 1998 to suspend the situation rather than solve it. The apple of discord is still the electoral body and the problem is still that of the "others", i.e. of those who are neither Caldoches nor Kanaks. It is the electoral status of those 25,000 "aliens" which is threatening to revive another round of *evènements*. Noumea blew up during the night of May 13–14 2024 and it is still simmering at the time of writing after seven people were killed and hundreds wounded. The streets were littered with burnt-out cars and half-dismantled barricades. This is because the so-called "broadening of the electoral body" was perceived as a direct threat by the Kanak independentist movement since most of these new voters were anti-independence.[53] There have been over 2,000 troops deployed in the territory since the new electoral law was voted by the Parliament in Paris. After a quick dash to Noumea President Macron brandished the threat of a "national referendum" which would put the future of New Caledonia into the hands of an indifferent French public, something whose consequences are hard to guess. Especially since this forgotten colony is tossed by forces way outstripping its local problems. First, President Macron is on his last constitutional run and many in France are preparing for 2027 when he will bow out. Second, French political opinion is increasingly fearful/hopeful of a victory for the extreme right *Rassemblement National* (RN), whose former neo-fascist colors have been whitewashed over time and which has drawn to its ranks all manner of frustrated victims of globalized liberal capitalism. To make matters worse the cutting edge of the Kanak nationalist movement has recently fallen into the hands of ... Azerbaijan. This geopolitical paradox is a product of the Ukraine War. Azerbaijan won its recent conflict with Armenia and France has tried to help the Armenians, provoking the ire of Baku. As a result President Putin used Baku to try to get back at President Macron whose position concerning Ukraine is not to Moscow's taste. We are apparently very far from *Françafrique* unless we consider that the hybrid creature was born out of a Paris playing card. Messing with exotic diplomacy is a two-way street and the next corner might turn out not to be where it was expected. Could New

Caledonia be a fuse to light the RN's electoral bomb? That is now a distinct possibility.

So in this first quarter of the twenty-first century the French government is still playing the decolonization game in a strange parody of the time *Françafrique* was born in the 1960s. The difference is that at the time of its birth, "the colonies" were at the heart of a situation where France was playing out its destiny in a regime that was the product of a colonial coup. Today, in spite of French media hype—finally something else in the news other than the Ukraine conflict and its sickening smell of World War Three—it is not even a distant remembrance of things past but simply a tiring problem much less exciting than that of Palestine.

CONCLUSION

Karl Marx wrote that history does, at times, repeat itself. But that if the first time is often a tragedy, the repeat episode tends to be a farce.

General De Gaulle, in tragic times, conjured up what came to be known colloquially as *Françafrique* in order to support the myth of France's *grandeur* and to benefit from greater global influence through the command of an African vote bank. He half-succeeded. Now, eighty-four years later, this mixture of myth, diplomacy, defiance, blood, money and high jinks is dying. *Françafrique* has played its role, both tragic and farcical and in order to survive a little bit longer it has been grabbing at any branch overhanging the river of time. As we saw the latest brittle twig was the proposal to excise the *jus soli* from the French Constitution. An approximate English translation of *jus soli* would be "right of the soil", i.e. the fact that birth on a certain territory gives a person a privileged access to the citizenship of that land. For the French the personal aspect of the issue is often hidden but discreetly influential. Gérald Darmanin, the French Interior Minister who is trying to promote his "solution" to the Mayotte problem, comes from a family of immigrants mixing Maltese and Algerian origins. His grandfather was born Mussa Ouakid in Algeria and, as a French Army warrant officer, had fought with the *Resistance* FFI (close to the Communist Party) for the freedom of France in the Second World War and later *against* Algerian independence with the *Harkis* (usually organized by extreme right-wing French officers just returned from Indochina). The man is the physical and psychological embodiment of the vicissitudes and contradictions that governed the *Françafrique* universe during those past eighty-four years. I learnt of the gentleman's real name when he was called in public by his Muslim name "Musa" by Abd-el-Majid Tebboune, President of the Algerian Republic. What was the reason for this sudden calling up of a "French Minister" through his distant native Algerian origins? The minister had issued a decree limiting the number of visas Paris would be prepared to give citizens of Algeria. So Abd-el-Majid Tebboune was calling Musa to the public's attention. Some people in the French body politic immediately picked it up with a mixture of rage, passion and bad faith not seen since the Algerian War and which it is difficult for other Europeans not so intimately enmeshed with a colonial past to understand. The French Extreme Right is preparing (with a modicum of

CONCLUSION

ordinary French neutral support) to withstand what it calls "the great replacement", namely the alleged invasion of France by hordes of Muslims. For the fringe elements fighting for this it would be the beginning of a race war on the coattails of a hoped for victory of Marine Le Pen in the 2027 elections. And this in turn would be a revenge for what is seen by the Right as the "Algerian defeat" and shame of 1962. At its birth *Françafrique* was seen by some of its movers and shakers as the revenge of the 1940 defeat followed by another one in Dien-Bien-Phu, a way to use the "traitor" De Gaulle for a nationalist revival which he had betrayed by his false promise of June 4 1958 in Algiers. "Moussa" was born in 1982, twelve years after the death of the General. He belongs to a political party which is a watered down version of the former genuine Gaullist distilled spirit. It both embodies and ends *Françafrique,* the "thing" De Gaulle brought to life. For many people in contemporary France, none of this means very much anymore. But one-issue activists are using the present frantic international climate to dig up old corpses and zombify them back into life.

Miss France for the year 2000 is called Sonia Rolland. Ms Rolland was born in Kigali, Rwanda in 1981 of a French father and a Rwandese Tutsi mother. On May 30 2023 she was charged with "corruption" by a Paris Court for allegedly having accepted the gift of a luxury flat in the posh 16th arrondissement of Paris from the Bongo family. The present had been made by Omar Bongo's widow whom Ms Rolland had simply advised on how to create a Miss Gabon beauty contest. A typical *Françafrique* event, in *Françafrique* terms. First of all the "salary" for the services rendered was out of proportion with what the services had been;[1] second, the nature of the services rendered was definitely beyond politics. They could perhaps have been construed—by stretching them—as "cultural". Third, no contract had been signed and the amount to be paid for services rendered had never been defined. The charges against Ms Rolland were just an appendix of the legal action against the widow of the dictator. The real dirt was swept under the carpet, the massacres in Togo or Chad, the economic exploitation of the Ivory Coast, the millions stolen from Gabon or the Brazzaville Congo, the ongoing civil war in Cameroun had all fallen by the wayside. In the UN many Francophone African delegations had begun to "vote wrong", i.e. in line not with Paris, but according to their own interests or whims. But in any case, did the UN have any influence left over the affairs of the real world? On September 4 2023 Catherine Colona, the French Minister of Foreign Affairs, declared to *Le Monde* that "the idea of Françafrique has been dead for a long time". But the agony was still being played out in full view of everybody, everywhere, in the UN General Assembly in New York, in France where President Macron was replacing the "Franco African summits" of yesteryear with chummy little civil society get-togethers where African boys and girls would chat and drink Coca-Cola together, without any impact on the massive problems of the continent, in African where military equipment was being hauled aboard, in Niamey where the Embassy had been closed until further notice.

Françafrique in some ways had been a love affair. And given the nature of love in *Françafrique*, it was logical that the tail end of that love would end up caught in court. But now the animal was moulting and love was definitely no longer on the cards. Mr Bolloré was discreetly and efficiently selling off billions of euros of transport assets and systems in Africa.[2] Not with a bang but with a financial whistle. And in case the reader wonders: no, Ms Rolland did not marry "Musa" Darmanin. After all this was *Françafrique* and not a Hollywood movie. Let's play the *Marseillaise* and see what we can do with Mayotte, the pint-size leftover of former glories. And what the others can do with their assorted orphan assets.

It was now every man for himself and the scattered nature of the reactions to *Françafrique*'s gradual demise were topical: nobody had an "African policy" any longer—France least of all—and local pressures and circumstances defied any global assessment. How the situation developed was predicated on regional—and national?—contexts. Since *Françafrique* had been a French phenomenon—apart from Biafra it never overstepped the old colonial/linguistic boundaries—only Francophone countries had to be considered when trying to understand the post-*Françafrique* transformation. As we saw, *Françafrique* was the product of post-1940 French history. It was tragic and ridiculous at the same time, an organic product of French destiny. When, as is my own case, "your Africa" is Kampala, Nairobi, Khartoum and Addis Ababa, your fellow French wonder where you have been and even those who are familiar with Dakar and Abidjan wonder why you have gone prostituting yourself in places "ruled" (?) by "*Les Angliches*" (French for "the limeys"). *Françafrique* is not European, it is French, and more anti-British than anti-African. When I mention that my research is more often published in English than in French there is an irritated shrug of the shoulders because it means that I do not know Africa, the Africa that matters, where real Africans (who obviously love the French) live. *Françafrique* is still a ghost in the French military mind and those who are ready to go fight in Mali are often those who resist the idea of fighting in Ukraine.

I will leave the end of this conclusion to a former high-ranking member of the French Secret service, the DGSE, now retired:

> At the institutional level France does not exist anymore. In terms of force its threats are desultory and in terms of attractiveness its capacities are too weak. In Africa or in the Middle East a French

CONCLUSION

Embassy carries the weight of Denmark or even Lichtenstein. In 2022 France offered Lebanon solar panels saying that it would be ecology that would save the country. The Lebanese refrained from laughing. We used to be aggressive, today we are irrelevant. Even in countries where the economy is in ruins and the politics vitrified.

The one thing that remains is the intimacy: from a minister (Darmanin) to a beauty queen (Sonia Rolland), *Françafrique* has remained a French tribe. The man chosen to be the Olympic torch-bearer for the Paris Games in 2024 was Oumar Dieme, a former colonial Senegalese soldier who fought in Indochina in the 1950s and turned down his pension in order to return to fight in Algeria in the 1960s. He lives half of the year in Senegal and half of the year in Paris. He is *Françafrique*. He is still fit. But he is ninety-one.

NOTES

1. GENEALOGY

1. Thomas Pakenham's *The Scramble for Africa,* London, Weidenfeld and Nicolson, 1991, probably presents the clearest and most dynamic picture of this late imperialist development. The case of India, which went smoothly from the first "imperial" type to the nineteenth-century "colonial" type is unique.
2. Savorgnan de Brazza was an Italian working for the French and John Rowlands, an illegitimate Welshman from straitened circumstances, became an American working for the King of Belgium who was German. Rowlands was so internationalized that he later changed his name to become Henry Morton Stanley, a newly minted British citizen after having been born British in the first place. Working for the King of Belgium (not for Belgium itself) he was the epitome of colonization, conquering a piece of the world for the private pleasures of an ill-tempered "Western" toy king.
3. David Todd, *Velvet Imperialism: French Informal Imperialism in the XIXth Century,* Oxford University Press, 2021.
4. In fact as a Black man Eboué was not even a "native" of Guyana but a descendant of slaves.
5. An administrative structure created in 1903 to bring together Gabon and the French Congo (Brazzaville).
6. Afrique Occidentale Française. France's African colonies were administered as two separate units, AOF and Afrique Equatoriale Française (AEF). AEF was the poor relative.
7. The *Code de l'Indigénat* (Native Code) was an outdated piece of legislation

that the French government had issued in 1830 with the conquest of Algeria to guarantee the freedom of native legislation against interference from French law. This so-called "protective law" had in fact created a kind of human and legal corral where the "natives" were "free" to live by their own laws i.e. not to benefit from the democratic human rights progressively conquered by the "true French" in the metropole. Most "natives" opposed this native code and its abolition in 1944 belonged to historical archeology and did not represent anything beyond a kind of symbolic freedom.

8. On December 1 1944 a group of some 1,600 African POWs recently liberated from German *Stalags* was fired upon at the Thiaroye camp near Dakar when they were demonstrating for their unpaid wages. The French government acknowledged the killing of thirty-five soldiers which was half the real number of the victims.

9. A French empire-wide African political party with limited representation in the French National Assembly. Small as it was, the RDA had a non-negligible role in the splintered and divided politics of the post 1944 regime where it could parley its limited support to build fragile coalitions.

10. His resignation was due to the return to power of the political parties whom he judged to have been responsible for all ills from the 1940 collapse, to the clumsy way the Indochinese war was being handled. De Gaulle's failure to push through a new more authoritarian constitution by way of a referendum led him to resign. Politically sidelined, it would take him eleven years to return to power, through another collapse, the military coup of the French Army in Algeria (May 13 1958). Throughout this time, including his period engaged in what he called "crossing the desert" (1953–58), he actively thought about the relationship between the Metropole and what was still for him "the Empire".

11. It was again a colonial crisis and in that same year (1898) Spain lost its international role while France accepted playing second fiddle to British international interests so as to keep a place among the Great Powers. This was exactly the opposite of Spain where the nineteenth century was marked by a series of increasingly confused domestic problems and civil conflicts where the country coiled upon itself as France was growing back into a major international position only to see this position brutally challenged again in June 1940. The whole of the future *Françafrique* is to be seen as part of a Gaullist attempt at repairing the international status of France and putting it back at the level of the USSR and USA through achieving nuclear autonomy and getting out of NATO.

12. And to think that it was Great Britain which in 1830 had insisted on boosting the "Belgian" runt of the Southern Netherlands to attain a neutral national status!
13. El Haj Omar (1795–1864) was a Peuhl from Senegal who became both a Tijani preacher and a warlord. He fought the French invasion and vanished mysteriously in Bandiagara where his body was never found.
14. The volatile juggle of cabinets between 1946 and 1958 meant that *all governments* were fragile and that UDSR was happy to accept as an ally an "African Party" whose tiny size could anyway make the difference between power or no power. Mitterrand was many times a Minister in both "left" and "right" cabinets and helped Houphouët-Boigny become a kind of *de facto* "representative of Africa" in the French Parliament. I invite English-speaking readers to look back to the British Parliament of the 1950s (and even more to the US Congress of that time!) where such a position as Houphouët's never existed.
15. Albert Cohen, *Belle du Seigneur,* Paris, Gallimard, 1968.
16. This Japanese move is understandable only in the pre-nuclear situation of the late Second World War. The notion that Japan could disappear as a military power and that its future would essentially be commercial is a post-Hiroshima concept.
17. Here again its blueprint is not in a scientific work but in the novel of Jean Lartéguy, *Les Centurions,* Paris, Presse de la Cité, 1960. Nationalist, revolutionary and vaguely Socialist but not Nazi (or even racist) because the French model was colonial, voluntarily pan-ethnic and in search of "good natives".
18. Except of course from this unique French practice of creating what Jean-Claude Guillebaud has called the post imperial paper toys (*Les confettis de l'empire,* Paris, Le Seuil, 1976). Overseas territories represent 18% of France's landmass but they are not colonies, they are an integral part of France even when they are located thousands of kilometers away from the "motherland" and when people of French metropolitan origin are a very small minority. This is a product of French philosophical imperialism, a definite component of *Françafrique.*
19. Two of the future Central African Republic states were ruled by former French Army officers—Jean-Bedel Bokassa and André Kolingba—who had fought in Indochina and later in Algeria. Former French Army soldiers such as Colonel Mamady Doumboya, today's President of Conakry Guinea, are still present all over the Francophone area.

20. Among the various organic components of *Françafrique*, money was often considered to be a key element. Even after that economic dimension withered away into practically nothing in the 1980s, memory of the lost commercial imperialism kept being proffered as the main *raison d'être* for that system.
21. Thomas Deltombe, Manuel Domergue, Jacob Tatsita: *Kamrun !: une guerre cachée aux origines de la Françafrique (1948–1971)* Paris, La Découverte, 2019, p. 44.
22. Guy Georgy, *Le petit soldat de l'Empire,* Paris, Flammarion 1992. Georgy had just arrived in Cameroun as a colonial agent and later became engaged against the rising Union des Populations du Cameroun (UPC) but in the name of an African-friendly Gaullist policy. His "anti-racist" manipulating policy made him one of the key creators of *Françafrique*.
23. Achille Mbembe, "Le conflit des symboles", *Le Monde Diplomatique,* April 1985.
24. He was a Bassa, i.e. a member of the second largest ethnic group in Cameroun. And he insisted on spelling the country's name as Kamerun, enough to send shivers down French spines.
25. *Eurafrique* belonged to the same vocabulary as "*la force noire*" (for a mythical "African Army" ready to rise up and hit the Germans), "*la ligne Maginot*" (for the supposedly "unbreachable" and "impenetrable" ensemble of fortifications the Germans could never penetrate), a fog of fabrications the French were desperately clinging to, in the hope of not having to look the oncoming disaster in the face.
26. Thomas Deltombe et al., op.cit., pp. 125–126 [translated by Gérard Prunier].
27. See R.T. Howard, *Power and Glory: France's Secret Wars with Britain and America (1945–2016)* London, Biteback Publishing, 2016, Ch 7.
28. Louis Ngongo: *Histoire des forces religieuses au Cameroun. De la première guerre mondiale à l'indépendance (1916–1955),* Paris, Karthala, 1982, p. 208.
29. Deltombe et al. op. cit ., p. 159.
30. Jérôme Tubiana, the French specialist of Chad, is perhaps the main—remarkable—exception.
31. I intend to do so in a future book about how the world at large sees Africa.
32. Why acrobat? Because in the 1940s and 1950s France was acting in Cameroun more on the sidelines than officially and had to deal with those natives who accepted the deal. Many were quite out of the ordinary.

33. At the time François Mitterrand was up to his neck in UDSR flimsy majority-building and far from thinking that he could one day lead the revitalized Socialists then still mired in SFIO politics.
34. Nyobe was not physically present with the insurgent group. It could even be said that the creation of the CNO had been an anti-Nyobe move. But the split between CNO and UPC proper soon melted away.
35. The American Viktor La Vina (*Le Cameroun du Mandat à l'indépendance*, Paris, 1970 [published in French]) gave a careful estimate of 2,000 killed. He considered it to be a minimum figure.
36. The word "Sinistre" was borrowed from a poorly understood French communiqué after the repression where the French authorities had talked about the recent events as "un sinistre", i.e. in French legal parlance "an accident".
37. For a book written at the time offering a contemporary vision of the day-to-day *coup d'état* that shied away from the unpleasant (German) word "putsch", see Merry and Serge Bromberger, "*Les 13 complots du 13 mai*", Paris, Arthème Fayard, 1959.
38. De Gaulle had made it clear to his supporters that he would not accept a presidency that resulted from a direct military coup. He wanted a process wrapped up in "legalism" and since his parting of ways with the Fourth Republic had been caused by a constitutional conflict, he wanted that "legalism" to be a transitory bridge leading to the introduction of something akin to the semi-authoritarian constitution he had tried to get approved in 1945.
39. See endnote 38 for a detailed description of that shark-infested swimming pool.
40. Gazogène (gasifier) was a system of generating gas from the distillation of wood. Such systems, which gave little power and were hard to work, were used during the Second World War in Occupied Europe because of the lack of petrol.
41. Future President François Mitterrand noticed the same shift in the wind and in 1942 resigned his post in Vichy to join the Free French in London.
42. One proviso of the reimbursement was there should be no legal mention of Foccart's activities between October 1942 and August 24 1943. All the relevant legal material from the period were in the Saint Malo archives that were destroyed in the 1944 fighting.
43. Most of the "no" vote came from French Guinea where Sekou Touré had led the local branch of RDA. More than one million Guineans had voted

"no" in the September 1958 referendum, Guinea being the only French territory to leave the French Union right from the start. Foccart had organized a coup to overthrow Sekou Touré but Soviet intelligence warned him in time and the French coup project was not activated.

44. Being a UN Mandate territory Cameroun had not taken part in the September 1958 referendum.
45. "The French like Mr Ahidjo and Mr Ahidjo likes the French" wrote the *New York Herald Tribune* on June 4 1959.
46. Constantin Melnik, from a Russian family which had emigrated to France, was a fanatic anti-communist and, like the radical officers, felt that in Africa he could fight "the Bolsheviks".
47. Jean-François Bayart, *L'Etat au Cameroun,* Paris, Presses de l'Ecole des Sciences Politiques, 1985, p. 76.

2. ROUGH AND READ

1. "Non-Arab" is more realistic than French because many of these "colons" were of Italian or Spanish heritage. "Colons" is also ambiguous because the social reality of the *pieds noirs* was extremely diverse and often quite far from the conventional picture of rich and dominant colonialists. Many "Blackfeet" were in fact proletarians. The mother of the Pied Noir Nobel Prize winner Albert Camus was a laundress.
2. Bangladesh later broke away from Pakistan in 1971.
3. Between the 1944 *Libération* and the May 13 1958 military coup which overthrew the Fourth Republic, there were twenty-two different governments. Their average lifespan was seven months and their succession was often limited to exhausting permutations of the same political actors. The weary repetition of scandals limited the whole thing to a ragged game while the perils of the colonial wars eventually rose to an unbearable level.
4. It comprised French Sudan (today's Mali) and Senegal. Created in January 1959 it returned to its component territories in September 1960, Sudan keeping the Mali tag while Senegal reverted to its original name.
5. Thomas Deltombe (op.cit.), p. 564. The gap shows that either figure is unreliable.
6. Michel Debré: *Gouverner* Paris, Albin Michel, 1988, Tome 3.
7. The killer was arrested many years later in Belgium and expelled to Switzerland which had issued an international arrest warrant for him. But the Swiss authorities eventually released him for lack of evidence.

Documents revealing the assassination order (and several others concerning anti-French Africans and some Europeans involved in anti-French activities), all given to Jacques Foccart, were retrieved from the archives and published in a book edited by Jeune Afrique, *Foccart parle*, Paris, Fayard, 1995.
8. Pronouncing his obituary French President Jacques Chirac said: "He was my personal friend".
9. He even had a (French) former Waffen SS officer, François Barazer de Lannurien, as a political advisor.
10. This was the name given to his Tempest fighter by Pierre Closterman, the Free French Ace of Aces (thirty-three German planes shot down between 1942 and 1945). The kind of bonhomie that went with the nickname is typical of the Gaullist atmosphere. In the 1950s Closterman rejoined combat to fly over Algeria, shooting at close range FNL guerilla fighters who were often mixed with civilians. A less heroic type of fighting and the kind of drift that was typical of the transformations that gave birth to the less heroic aspects of *Françafrique*.
11. Similar to those of his military superior, family friend and future enemy Philippe Pétain.
12. Robert "Bob" Denard (1927–2007) was a notorious soldier who served in French official forces till 1952. He then became a mercenary and served eighteen months in jail after being arrested for taking part in a murder plot supposed to kill Prime Minister Pierre Mendes-France. Between 1960 and 1963 he headed the "*Affreux*" (the horrible ones), the special mercenary unit of the Katangese regime. He later became the quasi-king of the Comoro Islands after shooting its president. He wrote in his memoirs: "I was the privateer of the Republic. I always served it without ever being given orders". A typical *Françafrique* remark.
13. The failure of France to keep Biafra alive is an example of how time was working against Paris while the "unnatural" Anglo-Soviet alliance to bring it down was a new demonstration of the paradoxical realpolitik the receding Cold War would later give way to.
14. M'ba was a favorite of De Gaulle who had to put down his pro-French enthusiasm. M'Ba had petitioned the French Government for annexation of Gabon to France's national territory, on the Algerian model and De Gaulle had to tell him that this was not a good thing in the atmosphere of the times.
15. For example when the Guyanese Robert Luong, a house painter working

on the presidential palace in Libreville, became Mrs Bongo's lover. The Gabonese President expelled him to France with orders never to see his wife again. The couple defied the orders, they met in France anyway and Mr Luong was shot in the street of a small provincial town in Languedoc by two white men who ran away and whose traces were never be found.

16. As he was heading for the hospital with advanced cancer he told a friend that he had chosen to try his luck in Spain because he did not trust the French, saying clearly: "There have been too many contentious things between us. They might take advantage of this opportunity and get rid of me". He died anyway but with no interference.

17. The Treasury being a kind of king's cashbox, it was managed as a king's cashbox, with generosity.

18. We must stick to the *Zeitgeist* of the chronology: the word "Islamist" was coined by François Burgat in various articles later published in *Comprendre l'Islam Politique* (Paris, La Découverte, 2016) but it was not even part of the intellectual landscape at the time. The bogey word was still "Communism", which has in its turn become today a dusty historical expression.

19. For a literary, elegant and subjective way of writing about this tragical issue, see Chinua Achebe: *There was a country: a personal history of Biafra*, London, 1971 (reprinted 2004), Penguin Books.

20. This was the period (1967–2002) during which some sort of British interventionism could be seen as a possible parallel with *Françafrique*. It brought sequences of intervention in Nigeria (1967–70), Uganda (1978) and Sierra Leone (2001–02). But what was the difference? These British actions were government choices, clear cut and separated, not a ball of interwoven sociological and economic choices similar to the French animal growling in the bush. These policies had neither durable "national" guidelines nor a long-term sociology. They were one-shot-at-a-time interventions without a coherent cultural background and extra-African historical reasons. As a result this did not give birth to a durable organizational British wolfpack.

21. Let us never forget that what was at stake in the *Françafrique* game was not the money, as superficial analysts put it (even though the money was there) but the very soul of "Frenchness", the way the French looked at themselves after the defeats of 1940 and Dien-Bien-Phu. The fact that De Gaulle was the Godfather of the whole operation with Jacques Foccart as a tame well-controlled Devil turned the whole thing into a psychological

mystery play. Gérard de Villiers (1929–2013), the far-right thriller writer who sold over 100 million copies of his geopolitical, sex-laden books (brutal but well-informed) was the flag-bearer of that world.

22. Wikipedia. Having tried to get more precise figures (in British archives) I was fobbed off with remarks such as: "Oh, this was a long time ago", "there are no official figures" and "ask the Nigerians".
23. The formula was coined by Chad specialist Marielle Debos in Thomas Borrell et al., *L'empire qui ne veut pas mourir: une histoire de la Françafrique*, Paris, Le Seuil, 2021.
24. The permanent trouble situation (at times called "war" before reverting to "civil trouble") lasted from 1965 to 1990.
25. See Marielle Delbos: *Le métier des Armes au Tchad*, Paris, Karthala, 2013, p. 23.
26. He was to stay three years at the side of the new leader—with a "Special Advisor" position—before discreetly retiring.
27. For legal reasons I cannot write more but it is extremely unlikely that Deby's death took place in a straightforward clash with the FACT rebels. See the pages on Chad in Chapter 6.
28. Chadian troops had fought side-by-side with French troops in Mali during Opération Barkhane and were renowned for their excellent combat record. They were almost entirely drawn from Zaghawa nomads.
29. Such a promise (or news of *Françafrique*'s demise) were to be repeated for the next forty years and are still today—when the complete death of the animal is only a matter of time—repeated mechanically by French politicians. Nobody takes it seriously now that the *real* death is both going to take place naturally and now that it does not matter seriously any more.
30. The FLNC (Front National de Libération Congolais) was in fact the remains of the defeated independent Katangese army. They had taken refuge in Soviet satellite Angola where the regime used them as a test to see how ready the West was for answering an impromptu military attack. And in case it would work, why not try to push it and overthrow Mobutu, America's man in Africa?
31. When the 30th anniversary of the battle was commemorated in 2008 in the presence of the former president Giscard d'Estaing, the French newspapers titled it "*a final victory for the French Army*", an ambiguous way of putting it.
32. As Katanga had been renamed to make even the name of the rebellious province disappear.

33. It is an interesting technical footnote that the air assault by the Belgian and French troops had to be carried out by US planes because the USAF was the only Western Air Force having the technical capacities to do the job.
34. Giscard had been a Minister of De Gaulle's but he had interpreted the quasi-revolutionary events of 1968 as a warning sign that Gaullism had to be overhauled. He was careful to show how distinct he was from historical Gaullism.
35. François-Xavier Verschave: *La Françafrique: le plus long scandale de la République,* Paris, Stock, 1998.
36. Africa Logistics, the Bolloré Group, scrutinized by the French Bank BNP in February 2012 devoted only 25% of its business to transport operations but these represented 80% of the company's profits (Olivier Blanmangin, "Vincent Bolloré: Affaires Africaines", p. 829, in Thomas Borrel: *L'empire qui ne veut pas mourir, op. cit.*)
37. René Journiac died in a plane crash in Cameroun in 1980 while he was head of the Elysée's Africa desk.
38. Dulcie September, a member of South Africa's ANC and *de facto* ambassador in Paris of the anti-apartheid movement, was shot dead by two French-controlled hired killers on March 29 1988. The assassins were French Foreign Legion veterans who were hired not by the French secret services but by private interests who were nevertheless close enough to the French authorities to ensure the gunmen got away, even though their names were known (private sources).
39. The huge uncertainty is due to both the indifference of the Western media and very imprecise African statistics. On this topic, extending way beyond Rwanda, see my *Les cadavres noirs,* Paris, Gallimard, 2021.

3. MITTERRAND'S NON-REFORMS

1. His much vaunted "reforms" dealt with nice but minor problems such as the decriminalization of homosexuality or shortening the President's mandate. This announced the cultural politics of the twenty-first century.
2. Only a second lieutenant, he had displayed brilliant military instincts in the short war with Mali in December 1985. He was also known for his extreme left-wing politics and had declared while in office: "without a political education, a soldier is just a potential criminal".

3. Given the relations between France and Libya at the time over Chad (see previous chapter), this was seen by Paris as a deliberate provocation.
4. The new name given to the country meant: "The country of honest men". Sankara quipped that this should be not a joke but a guiding principle in the future.
5. The government defined food independence by two full meals and ten litres of water per day per person.
6. Today's African Union.
7. *Discours d'Orientation Politique*, October 2 1983.
8. The ANC, which was legalized in 1990, was still at the time a clandestine organization.
9. Personal disclosure: I was at the time a member of the International Secretariat of the French Socialist Party, directing some Africa-related matters but usually not those concerning Francophone Africa.
10. During Mitterrand's electoral campaign the only one of his 110 proposals that concerned Africa was a promise to support Chadian independence. It was in fact an anti-Gaddafi measure given that the Libyan leader had declared his project of annexing Chad to Libya. No Africa-aimed social or economic measures featured in the manifesto.
11. Personal communication.
12. He had replaced Guy Penne as the head of the Presidential Unit for Africa in 1986. His nickname was "Daddy told me", an apt description of his diplomatic capabilities.
13. The resulting policy anarchy was well described by the geographer Sylvie Brunel: "La géopolitique lumineuse" *Conflits*. Spring 2016 (pp. 6–11).
14. For the decolonization of "Ruanda-Urundi" as it was then called, see René Lemarchand, London, Pall Mall Press, 1970.
15. Rwanda and Burundi are inhabited by culturally homogeneous populations socially and politically split into two caste-like groups, the Hutu and the Tutsi. The Tutsi had been the historical rulers even though they were a demographic minority. *Rubanda Nyamwinshi* means "the majority people" (i.e. the Hutu) who had assumed power in Rwanda by insurrection during the violent events of its 1959–64 decolonization.
16. Yoweri Museveni is a Muhima from the Banyankole tribe of Uganda that is, in cultural and ethnic terms, a close relative of the Tutsi of Rwanda. During the Ugandan civil war (1981–86) many Tutsi refugees joined Museveni's guerrillas, the National Resistance Army (NRA). After its

victory they became closely associated with the new Ugandan power structure.

17. Both Habyarimana and Museveni were in New York for a UN conference on refugees. The whole thing had a comedy aspect with the presidents phoning their respective countries to know what their armies were doing. Nobody seemed to fully realise what was enveloping them.

18. It was a bogus operation, complete with Rwandese Army soldiers mimicking an attack and shooting in the air. The French Embassy in Kigali never sent any confirmation of this "intensive fighting" which had not killed anybody.

19. President Mitterrand went on a visit to the Middle East but he had given orders for a French force to be dispatched to Rwanda to protect the Embassy and evacuate French nationals (Operation Noroit, October 4 1990). The attack on Kigali supposed to have happened on October 5 had been a fake encounter (see previous note) by which Habyarimana was hoping to prompt the French to scale up their limited force into a full engagement. Belgium, which had sent a similar deployment, soon withdrew when after a few days thousands of Tutsi were arbitrarily detained and hundreds killed. France stayed and Noroit was soon the object of archetypical "mission creep". Short of engaging in direct front line fighting, the force turned into an auxiliary of the Rwandese Army.

20. When Jean-Christophe Mitterrand was asked to appear before the Commission of Inquiry into the French involvement in Rwanda, he denied having said that and even tried to deny having ever having met me. See *Enquête sur la tragédie rwandaise.(1990–1994)* Under the Presidency of Paul Quiles, Paris, Publications de l'Assemblée Nationale, 3 vols, 1998.

21. French Commission of Inquiry, *op. cit.* vol. 3, p. 185.

22. The precise figure was impossible to compute, given the fact that French aid was both official and unofficial. Officially France was not at war in the war it was in. The degree of corruption on the Rwandese side was astounding, eventually forcing Habyarimana to fire his own Minister of Defence and replace him with James Gasana, his former Minister of Agriculture, whose reputation for honesty was well-known.

23. Quoted in David Servenay, 'Le génocide des Tutsi au Rwanda: le rôle accablant de la France, in Thomas Deltombe, *et al,* op.cit., p. 598.

24. My own position at the Socialist Party International Secretariat was not important enough to allow me to sound the alarm bells. In any case

Ambassador Martre's report fell on completely deaf ears. His use of the word "genocide" was probably considered exaggerated and undiplomatic.

25. For a contemporary assessment of the Bagogwe tragedy later seen as an early warning of the Rwandese genocide, see the report by Eric Gillet for the *Fédération Internationale des Droits de l'Homme* (Brussels 1991). I tried to raise the alarm in Paris through the French Socialist Party (then in power) but without any result.
26. I learned of the event firsthand and met the officer (name withheld upon request).
27. My superior, whom I bothered about Rwanda and who was extremely aware and open-minded.
28. I was in Uganda at the time. For the broader picture of Franco-Anglo-Saxon rivalry in the world at large, see R.T. Howard, *France's Secret Wars with Britain and America (1945–2016)*, London, Biteback, 2016.
29. See my Chapter 6 ("Chronicle of a massacre foretold") in *The Rwanda Crisis: History of a Genocide*, London, Hurst and Co., 1997.
30. Where in 1884–85 the various European "zones of influence" were parceled out between the European powers. Nyerere had a sharp and clear vision of African geopolitics in the *longue durée*.
31. The literature on the genocide is huge. I recommend the two best documentary works produced by teams of specialists: African Rights, *Rwanda: death, despair, defiance,* London, African Rights, September 1994 (742 pp.) and Human Rights Watch, *Leave None to Tell the Story,* New York, March 1999 (789 pp.). The first compendium is on the spot, full of interviews. The second one has had the benefit of five years of research and is cooler and more all-embracing. For an analytical and historical approach I will shamelessly recommend my own book: *The Rwanda Crisis: The History of a Genocide.* London, Hurst and New York, Columbia University Press 1995/97 (424 pp.).
32. See General Didier Tauzin: *Rwanda,* Paris, Editions Jacob Duvernet, 2011. In his book (pp. 115–148) the Colonel (at the time) presents his own recollections of these few days in June–July 1994. It seems the digging of trenches was not really part of his plans but the brush with the RPF is described in almost friendly terms.
33. Some managed to escape but Turquoise did not have anything to do with these persons even if it is possible that some French individuals managed to help former Génocidaires in the prevailing confusion.
34. The proof had been made visible in the Brazzaville Congo when President

Pascal Lissouba had tried in 1993 to sell some of the Congo oil territories to the US company Occidental Petroleum (Oxy). This triggered a civil war which caused Lissouba to go back on the Oxy deal and eventually to lose power.

35. *L'Express,* December 12, 1996.
36. One of them was Jean-Christophe Mitterrand, during his tenure as Director of the Presidency Africa Unit.
37. See my *The Rwanda Crisis: History of a Genocide, op. cit.*

4. THE BIG SLEEP (1995–2012)

1. July 22 1995 in Libreville. Quoted by Benoit Collombat in Thomas Borrell et al., *L'Empire qui ne veut pas mourir, op. cit.* (p. 611) [translated by Gérard Prunier].
2. The Ugandans entered the war with Mobutu but with war aims only indirectly related to the Kinshasa regime. Museveni's problem was Mobutu's alliance with the Khartoum government which aided the Southern Sudanese rebellion (SPLA) which was based in Uganda and fought across the border. The ADFL/Rwandese attack in November 1996 marked the beginning of what I later called (I think aptly) *Africa's World War:* London/Hurst and New York/Oxford University Press, 2009.
3. Well at least on the surface. It is not impossible that at a deeper level the mineral-rich Zaïre appeared as a kind of Eldorado from which the invaders could derive sizable benefits.
4. In 1971 the Congo (Kinshasa) had changed its name to Zaïre which it kept till May 1997 when Mobutu fell.
5. The Rwandese represented 80% of the boots on the ground. But the small presence of other armies had a great importance. Paris presented itself as a great colonial power siding in Africa with the forces of evil to combat the forces of progress. This image was short-lived but it had a considerable impact as we will see later.
6. See further down for the evolution of the CAR episode.
7. The French love to have a large and often nitpicking civil service. Recently (November 2023) the government created a bonus for the repair of second-hand clothing (!). But in order not to favor the import of Asian clothing it defined the limits of the place of manufacture by latitude and longitude for the clothing eligible for the bonus. Funny papers had a great time commenting the decree.

8. I knew him personally since the days when he had been my teacher at university after coming back from the Algerian war.
9. 21st Franco-African summit in Yaounde. Quoted by Benoit Collombat in Thomas Borrell *et al.*: *L'Empire qui ne veut pas mourir op. cit.* (pp. 630–631).
10. Djibouti is a little-known corner of the French Empire, so strategically important that it was the last French colonial possession to be decolonized (1977). For an overall glance at this small territory see Sonia Le Gouriellec, *Djibouti: la diplomatie de géant d'un petit état,* Villeneuve d'Ascq, 2020.
11. The French had kept a military force there but over time China had built in Djibouti what remains today its only military base abroad, next to a US base, while Japan, Spain and Germany had developed their own facilities.
12. De Bonnecorse was a veteran Chirac aide who had worked closely with him since the 1970s. In 1995 he was ambassador to Morocco. He later (2002) became the director of the Presidential Africa Unit. He was fully devoted to the President.
13. The willful blindness of the French government had limits. When Christian Lafaille wrote a book called *Aux portes de l'enfer: l'inavouable verité de l'Affaire Borrel (*Paris, Scali, 1995) in which he claimed that Borrel had committed suicide because he was a paedophile and was afraid of being exposed, Borrel's widow sued him for defamation and won. In a separate case the state gave €140,000 to the widowed family.
14. France is the only former colonial country which has "nationalized" some of its former colonies ... by turning them into France! They have been "departmentalized", turned into French Departments and Territories (DOM/TOM) with laws and an administration similar to those of the mother country even as far as French Guyana or the island of Mayotte in the Comoros (the rest of the archipelago is an "independent" country).
15. Togo, a former German colony, had been under a League of Nations mandate after 1918. This mandate was transferred to the UN after 1945. According to this status the denizen of a mandated territory did not have the right to join the army of the mandatory country.
16. Four rigged elections with limited repression.
17. And even by the creeping expansion of the only "old colonial" power in Africa, Portugal. Portugal was silently pushing its African bushwhackers, cousins of the Brazilian *cangaçeiros,* east from Angola and west from Mozambique, in the hope of linking them somewhere in the middle of the continent. This initiative failed.

18. The Dioula are a trading tribe. Children of the same two parents are often born in different territories. The new law demanded that the candidate's *parents* had both been born in the Ivory Coast. According to this law easily a third of the population could not have passed the "Ivoirity" test. Konan Bédié being Baoulé—an ethnic group sitting smack in the center of the Ivory Coast—had of course no problem with the "Ivoirity" test.
19. The Géré are a tribe which are close cousins of the Yacouba of Liberia. The mix is undistinguishable and even Wikipedia lists General Gueï as a Yacouba!
20. Personal communication from a personal friend of the president.
21. Among the nicknames attached to President Macron's personality is one of his favorite expressions: "*En même temps*" (at the same time). It is a well-earned nickname since he seems to have a permanent problem sticking to one topic, and, once he has done it, to adhere to it as a consistent choice.
22. Created in 1970 in Niamey (but based in Paris) it is a kind of French international club, in a manner akin to the British Commonwealth.
23. She was Creole upper class, a typical member of the group targeted by Duvalier who promoted "blackness" as a demagogic political positioning and largely marginalized people of mixed-race ancestry who had till then constituted Haiti's ruling elite.
24. Being a high-class intern in Abuja's bureaucracy was the opposite of a genuine "African" education.
25. Armenia had become an OIF member in 2012.
26. See Chapter 5 for more on this proliferation and for the *Françafrique* reaction to it.
27. The civil war stopped with the collapse of the Soviet Union on one side and the end of apartheid on the other.
28. He was right not to be triumphant because Total is involved in another giant project in East Africa, that of building one of the longest pipelines in the world to bring oil from the Lake Albert Basin all the way to the Indian Ocean. This technological juggernaut is likely to be a major ecological problem. So Total is fighting to impose this project against massive transnational ecological opposition while shunning any publicity concerning the region.
29. See further down for the MINUSCA UN presence in Central Africa.
30. The catastrophe called AEF had been a source of inspiration for a tragic area of French literature. See André Gide: *Voyage au Congo* (1927) and Louis-Ferdinand Céline: *Voyage au bout de la nuit.* (1932). For a scholarly

treatment, refer to Catherine Coquery-Vidrovitch: *Le Congo au temps des grandes compagnies concessionnaires (1898–1930)*, Paris, Mouton 1972. "Congo" was the name loosely applied to AEF's changing boundaries.
31. As usual the "UN Army" was militarily useless. But it offered the logistics of a humanitarian service which had been absent for the last hundred years, a foreign eye on this God-forsaken country and a minor deterrent to Seleka expanding its areas of control.
32. This weak state problem is general and this is more a peg on which to hang political frustrations than a real religious causality. The leader of Seleka (and briefly *de facto* President of CAR), Michel Djotodia, is a Christian.
33. Faustin-Archange Touadéra is a Mbanja, the third largest (9%) of the ten CAR tribes. The French had traditionally been the "protectors" of the weak CAR state, but with their departure tribal competition grew and as Touadéra did not trust the Rwandans who were the largest contributors to MINUSCA he called in Wagner.
34. By then these were no longer the Seleka Muslims, but rather the CPC (Coalition of Patriots for Change), a political grouping organized by former president François Bozizé (2003–13), a member of the majority Gbaya tribe.
35. After the December 2020 "elections" which Touadera "won" with 53% from a 35% turnout, former President Bozize, now the government's main adversary, took refuge in Chad. The CIA asked Paris to put pressure on Mahamat Deby and ask for his removal. He left for Guinea Bissau on March 6 2023 and he had nothing to do with the murder of the Chinese. The Wagner Mission in Bangui realised that the crime had been committed by their own local auxiliaries, what in the CAR are publicly referred to as "the Black Russians". A few days later Xi Jinping was in Moscow and asked Putin about the killings. He was particularly displeased because the victims were employees of Ms Zhao Baomei, a very well connected local businesswoman who also runs another mine in the same area at Chimbolo. She knew who did it and had the capacity to complain directly to the Chinese President. This caused a dent in Russian-Chinese relations in the CAR and showed how loose was Wagner's management (private source). This small footnote gives a micro-idea of the CAR's unbelievable complexities.
36. Rwanda has two kinds of troops in CAR: about 2,000 members of MINUSCA and another 1,000 through a direct bilateral agreement with Touadera. It is those that Washington would have liked to see expanded

to replace the Russians. (Private source and Crisis Group July 2023 Report: *Rwanda's Growing Role in the CAR*.)
37. The referendum was held on July 30 and its results benefited the Russian position.
38. With weapons. There are no Wagner or Wagner auxiliaries in the Sudan at the time of writing. Such a presence could nevertheless develop.
39. Bob Denard, the archetype of the *Françafrique* mercenary operator, had chosen as a nickname the term "the Republic's pirate" to define himself.
40. The ones which were most stable and best preserved were the monarchies such as Saudi Arabia, Jordan, Kuwait and the UAE. They were not old, but they had recreated neo-traditional forms of order in the wake of colonization.
41. Supporting these Black American revolutionary movements was not a sign of sympathy for Black causes in general. In Libya itself, racist riots had killed hundreds in late 2000 and many African foreign workers had been repatriated in an emergency by their countries of origin (mostly Nigeria and Ghana).
42. A highly diverse group that numbered the right wing Renaud Camus, the socialist Bernard-Henri Lévy and the centrist Pascal Bruckner. These were the beginnings of the politics of feeling (which were not the politics of *engagement*) and which were beginning to emerge at the time. In a kind of desperate effort, *Françafrique* was trying to adapt to the new *Zeitgeist*.
43. The final public trial should be held between January and April 2025. Former President Sarkozy is still under investigation for alleged financial charges concerning his 2007 presidential campaign and was recently (November 2023) in court about this matter which is still also pending at the time of writing.
44. In France expenses for an election are limited by law. Using Libyan money for his electoral campaign would have had two motivations: (1) get money; (2) bypass the expense ceiling for the election. Former President Sarkozy was charged with having spent €42.8 million when the legal ceiling was €22.5m.
45. See "Bechir Saleh: le Libyen qui en savait trop" (*Le Monde*, 30 September 2017) a remarkable and seminal two-page interview of Beshir Saleh which I can quote since it is now public knowledge. The two journalist-authors were Simon Piel and Joan Tilouine whom I know personally and who are among the few press professionals I trust on this type of material. *Françafrique* is dying but it is not yet dead and it can still bite.

46. See the book written about him by Simon Piel and Joan Tilouine: *L'affairiste*, Paris, Stock, 2019.
47. See Ollivier's clever autobiography, *Ni vu ni connu, ma vie de négociant en politique de Chirac et Foccart à Mandela,* Paris, Fayard, 2014, where what is not mentioned is often more important than what is printed.

5. *FRANÇAFRIQUE* IS NOT DEAD

1. For an (implicit) comparison see Madeleine Kalb, *The Congo Cables,* New York, MacMillan, 1982 about which a reviewer wrote "the best parts read like James Bond but the scary thing is that the story isn't fiction" (John Chancellor, NBC). This had been the main African problem of the early Cold War. The Americans "solved it" with much violence and little efficiency. The French usually had steadier hands.
2. Sahel means "the shore" in the vocabulary of medieval Arab geographers when they picture Africa. This is part of a descriptive view where the Sahara (a general word for "desert") is seen as "a sea" (of sand and rocks) which ends in a mixed area of dry vegetation inhabited by nomads of various ethnicities. "Solid" Africa, that of wild bush slowly turning into forests with areas more densely populated by sedentary peasants, starts south of the Sahel.
3. Its attempted birth came in 2012 under the name of *Azawad.* To adapt its profile to the spirit of the times, it was said to be the product of an "Islamist" insurgency. We will see later that the relaunching of the fighting in Mali in 2023 is linked to the resurgence of the Tuareg nationalist dream more than to any kind of Islamic religious insurgency.
4. In 2011 the UN estimated there were 15 to 20 million guns for a population of about 7 million Libyans.
5. The best references on this extremely bloody but little-known period (1992–2011) are Luis Martinez, *The Algerian Civil War*, London, Hurst, 2000; and Gilles Kepel, *Jihad*, Paris, Gallimard, 2002.
6. All supported by Ghaddafi who saw the Tuaregs as a crowbar he could use to split open the Muslim countries to his south which he considered to be his first obstacle on the way towards some form of a Caliphate. Ghaddafi was an opportunist ideological Muslim but not an Islamist; he was too keen on his own form of personalized power to accept the religious limitations of *Shari'a*.
7. The exact number was never known officially but the estimate is around

600 deaths. This aspect of internal civil war inside Mali was simply overlooked.
8. Choguel Maïga had lived for eleven years in the USSR and been trained in Kiev.
9. Macron is rather ignorant of African affairs and his Africa team, led at the time by Frank Pâris, was uninspiring.
10. In a state of utter financial and diplomatic confusion, ECOWAS cancelled the meeting it was supposed to hold in Accra to discuss the problem (July 2022).
11. My own sources say 420 but they are mostly Peuhl and since the Peuhl comprised 90% of the victims, their estimates might be biased.
12. He had been granted political asylum in the Ivory Coast but the former Minister of Defence in the civilian regime, Soumeylon Boubèye Maïga (who was innocent), died in prison after being detained in horrible circumstances. This was a case of the chickens coming home to roost. Time had elapsed, France had faltered in Rwanda and zig-zagged confusedly in Libya. The weight of the long-gone but not forgotten dismal AEF colonial history was finally crash-landing. The French never even understood what had hit them.
13. For foreigners this was just an attack among others. This was not the case in Mali. Camp Kati is the Fort Bragg of the FAMa, headquarters of the Army and today it is the personal residence of Colonel Assimi Goïta. It is strongly defended but was nevertheless under siege for several hours.
14. It took months to get them freed and ECOWAS which negotiated on their behalf was treated as an enemy by the Malian government. The feeling was a reminder of the Cold War atmosphere but without the energy. *Françafrique* was forced to the sidelines and began to look anachronistic.
15. *Deutsche Welle,* June 1 2022.
16. *The Economist,* July 11 2020.
17. Heni Nsaibia and Caleb Weiss, '*The end of the Sahelian anomaly*', *Combating Terrorism Center Magazine* (West Point) July 2020, Vol. 13, Issue no. 7.
18. See Chapter 3.
19. Having briefly lost sight of President Roch-Marcel Kaboré, Macron commented loudly that "he might have gone to fix the air conditioning" (which had broken down). There was no laughter in the audience.
20. Since then the death toll has leapt to 14,000 and keeps rising.
21. This call for volunteers had been made on October 24 2020, asking for

50,000 men. But nothing had happened till the coup when 90,000 people answered, thinking a new page had been turned.
22. Many of the killers were themselves Mossi and all were Muslims.
23. There were a few useless old Russian planes in the Burkina Air Force. The Russians were busy at home with internal fights and quarrels caused by the fallout from Prigozhin's assassination and contributed nothing to the actual fighting in Burkina.
24. See the interview with Luis Martinez in *Le Monde* (March 26–27 2023).
25. *Jeune Afrique* (November 11 2023).
26. Camille Lefebvre, *Des pays au Crépuscule. L'occupation coloniale au Sahara-Sahel,* Paris, Fayard, 2021.
27. But he was the person usually dealing with Areva.
28. The main purpose of the US presence was surveillance. The combat commandoes were there to protect the drone operators. The total number of their troops (1,500) was roughly equal to those deployed by the French.
29. Boko Haram forces had come from Nigeria into Niger and Nuhu Ribadu was in charge of explaining to the French Secret Service what it did not know about the articulation between the Nigerian movement and the two other components of the jihadi attacks. Most of the Islamist forces in Niger were foreign.
30. The name was later changed to African Legion in early 2024 when some of Putin's advisors on African affairs realized that the new Russian name immediately recalled the memory of the German unit of the same name which had become famous under General Rommel during the Second World War.
31. I was an unofficial member of J.P. Cot's East Africa team and was shown the door.
32. He is today a judge in an obscure organization in charge of the laws of the sea.
33. It is interesting to compare Bongo's clever indirect support for Sarkozy and the (limited) scandal caused by the alleged support from Ghaddafi. The scandal is linked with the identity of the sponsor, a friendly member of *Françafrique* in one case, an international terrorist on the other, and not with the act itself.
34. Given the extremely poor health of Ali Bongo, this could have happened at any time. But meanwhile he was charged with high treason.
35. Since Ali Bongo is a sick man, he was not even arrested, and was allowed to fly into exile. His wife, even though she is a French citizen, is in jail.

Paris did not extend even informal contacts to get her freed. His millionaire son is also under arrest.

36. The Zaghawa are a minority ethnic group representing about 2% of the Chadian population. They were the backbone of the December 1990 raid from the Sudan that grabbed power in Chad under French supervision.
37. His death was once said to have occurred while fighting the enemy and another time to have taken place while he was reviewing his troops.
38. The final number of victims was never publicly given. It was probably around one hundred.
39. *Wall Street Journal*. February 24 2023. This statement was shallow and unsupported by any evidence.
40. This military contingent has not yet been deployed at the time of writing (March 2024).
41. See Chapter 1.
42. *Takuba* (created in March 2020) was an effort at creating a multi-European military force to supplement the French *Barkhane* operation. It was dissolved at the same time as its larger sponsoring force was disbanded (July 1 2022).

6. WHAT IS LEFT AFTER DISMANTLING

1. The Referendum was going to be a vote on a new Constitution. The existing one chosen in 1945, and whose implementation had prompted De Gaulle's resignation in 1946 could be replaced by a new one and at the same time in the colonies the referendum could end the "Union Française" and replace it with the "Communauté Française", a new colonial pact in anything but name. By 1960 the "Communauté" had been hollowed out by the progressive independence of one territory after another. But the formal existence of the "Communauté" lasted till 1995 and *Françafrique* was the informal tool allowing an important Metropolitan grip to remain on Francophone Africa, lasting till the present, albeit in a much diminished form.
2. At this point let us remind the reader of the book by R.T. Howard: *Power and Glory: France's Secret Wars with Britain and America (1945–2016)*, op. cit. Implacably factual, it is also blessedly free from the rhetoric frequently favored on this delicate topic.
3. The (unproven) figure tentatively issued by Amnesty International for the

number of victims of the Sekou Touré dictatorship is 50,000. There are no official figures, not even French.
4. He had been reelected in 2015.
5. The situation was not really tense since the Malinke populations in northern Guinea—usually pro-Conakry—represented a bulwark against the mostly Peuhl (Fulani) groups that make up the majority of Black African jihadis in Mali.
6. Removal or at least disconnection. But the prudent steps of General Oligui Nguema have allowed for a somewhat exaggerated leniency.
7. This is possible because Gabon is rich, its population is small and the Bongo mafia was politically on its last legs at the time of the coup.
8. President of Brazzaville-Congo since 1979.
9. Died in 2009. The legal action was transferred towards his son Ali who had "inherited" the presidency.
10. Then President of Burkina Faso, overthrown in 2014 by a popular insurrection.
11. Died in 2022.
12. President of Equatorial Guinea since 1979.
13. See above.
14. A large percentage of the BMA money came from Elf (later Total) "contributions", particularly in the Brazzaville Congo, in Gabon, in Equatorial Guinea and in Angola.
15. Reported by *Mediapart* newsletter (September 30 2020).
16. With a financial capacity of about $800 million.
17. Regrouping forces from Burkina Faso, Mali, Niger, Chad and Mauritania.
18. The worst being in Moura in March 2022 where Russian troops and helicopters killed many peasants and nomads (about 500).
19. The pro-Putin placards and the Russian flags make nice pictures. They are usually spontaneous and reflect more an anti-French mood than a deliberate Moscow ploy.
20. For the time being Nigeria is keeping its north under control (with difficulty). As for the case of Sudan which was an Ottoman colony (as was Libya) we should remember that the history of that peculiar form of colonization is clearly distinct. It has at present completely collapsed in civil war (Sudan) or melted into an unacknowledged secession (Libya) which follows the boundaries of the two pre-1911 Turkish "*Villayet*".
21. On this topic see (in the bibliography) the special issue of the publication *Revue Internationale et Stratégique* coordinated by Caroline Roussy.

22. For an in-depth examination of the VDP program and of its impact, see Crisis Group, *Burkina Faso: Arming Civilians at the Cost of Social Cohesion?,* 40 pp., December 2023.
23. Private information.
24. A limited survey done by *The Economist* (August 12 2023). The near zero ranking of the UK was due to the fact that all these territories were former French colonies where Great Britain was a completely unknown quantity.
25. After Idriss Deby's death his instant president son promised elections after eighteen months. The period expired in October 2022 and it was summarily extended to November 2024.
26. Reuters dispatch. January 25 2024.
27. Who might very well have been killed by his nephew since two completely different versions of the president's death were circulated.
28. The photograph of his dead body revealed a single bullet hole in the forehead, a trace more of an execution than of a wound received in combat.
29. Some Russian militiamen have been invited, more as a diplomatic insurance policy than as a fighting force.
30. In articles on the French presence in Africa, journalists regularly mention "French troops" on the ground. They are present in four countries (Senegal, Gabon, Ivory Coast and Djibouti) with limited means and legally encumbered, making them cut-out forces.
31. The two main examples are the Russian deployments in Mali and Burkina Faso where the results are mixed.
32. There is some shadow boxing in Sudan but without the two sides having so far ever come in direct contact.
33. This was already the case with the Wagner projection even if it was reasonably structured.
34. June 2024.
35. He was the Secretary General of a political party (PASTEF) whose president was already in jail and which was later outlawed.
36. Among the most important ones was the demand that Paris would repatriate its troops and that Senegal would walk out of the CFA Franc agreement.
37. Since 2021 anti-government and anti-French demonstrations have led to at least fifteen deaths.
38. Sangomar is managed by Woodside Energy which has bought the fossil fuel branch of the Australian mining giant BHP. A major dent in the "Anglo-Saxonphobia" of *Françafrique*.

39. See Chapter 1, endnote 19.
40. The Comoro Archipelago comprises four islands: Mayotte, Anjouan, Great Comoros and Mohéli.
41. Inter-island roughly-built boats with an outboard motor. Boat capacity (average): 50 people. Boat loading (average): 120 people. Shipwrecks are common.
42. This is the name of native-born inhabitants of Mayotte, regardless of their skin color. Since Mayotte is legally speaking as French as Marseille or Strasbourg, there is an imported cadre of mostly native French civil servants sent from the metropole to this far off island. They become "Mahorais", even though their purchasing power is way above that of locally-born fellow Mahorais. Their spending pushes prices upwards.
43. The slaves in the Comoros were a mixed population of Swahili, West Africans, Indians and even poor indebted Chinese who had been sold by their creditors.
44. See the Statue of Liberty enlightening the world offered by France to the United States in 1876 and still standing at the entrance of New York harbor.
45. The killing was carried out by a French mercenary who stabbed the former president.
46. He died of natural causes in Metropolitan France in 2007, still a free man. The whole episode is described in Pascal Perri, *Comores: les nouveaux mercenaires,* Paris, L'Harmattan, 1994.
47. Patrick Weil: *A Mayotte un projet inutile et dangereux. Le Monde*, February 22 2024. The author of this article is a specialist on the history of French citizenship since 1789.
48. A new law on immigration had recently been tabled at the French Parliament. But since the Government had no majority in the Assembly, it had to be pushed through with Article 49.3 of the Constitution, the one General De Gaulle had insisted be included in the text to enable the Presidency to have full powers to bypass Parliament. In September 1958 when De Gaulle organized a referendum to approve the new Constitution, France was on the verge of civil war. Yet article 49.3. has never been removed from the Constitution and the extreme right is thinking about the coming presidential election where changing the rules of nationality has to be seen as a preparation for its possible victory.
49. It was the same cause of death that killed practically all of the Caribbean Indians upon the arrival of the Europeans.

50. The main French colonial activity in the nineteenth century was centered around a penal colony (*bagne*) where criminals were mixed with political opponents. After the 1871 revolutionary socialist insurrection, known as the Paris Commune, most of the revolutionaries who were not executed were later deported to New Caledonia, a measure which turned the whole colony into a penal territory.
51. The islands of Wallis and Futuna, colonized by the French in 1888, were turned into a *Territoire d'Outre-Mer* (Overseas Territory or TOM in Paris's administrative denomination) in 1961. Their population is ethnically and culturally different from the Kanaks and closer to that of Tahiti. But Tahiti was too far and too expensive—the cost of living was nearly that of Metropolitan France—for the Wallis and Futunians who preferred to find work in the Caledonian nickel mines.
52. *Caldoches* is a colloquial name for the white French population, similar to the *Pieds Noirs* (black feet) white Algerian-born population. Similar to those many are second or third generation, born in the colony.
53. These "others" owed their social status and paper-thin economic integration to colonization. Since 1945 the Kanaks had benefitted from much better education and there were now Kanak doctors, lawyers and IT technicians. The independentist movement contained many seriously educated supporters and the Kanaks felt they could handle the modern world. Not so for the Wallis and Futunians who were forgotten by Paris and whose educational attainment level was much lower.

CONCLUSION

1. A decent apartment in the 16th will cost more than one million Euros.
2. After Bolloré had bought SCAC in 1986 and Delmas & Vieljeux five years later he had become one of the giants of the transport business in Africa. But his cultural analysis sense was even better than his business acumen. African Logistics, his African transport arm, represented 25% of his assets but 80% of his group's profits in a world that was changing. On December 1 2022 he sold Africa Logistics to the Italo-Swiss company MSC for $5 billion and he walked away whistling. A year before he had sold Universal Music Group for $7 billion after collaborating in Taylor Swift's rise to billionaire status while Bolloré's old friend former Guinean President Alpha Condé was wasting away in a tiny jail cell at 82. *Françafrique* had been a spear and a shield but it was now a sick and ageing liability.

SELECT BIBLIOGRAPHY

This bibliography is a bit peculiar because most of its books are in French. This is actually symptomatic because it reveals a problem which is so close to the bosom of the creature that it resulted in an incestuous relationship. Writing about *Françafrique* in any language other than French seems to amount to some kind of a family betrayal. Almost nobody attempted it.

* * *

Archival, *Foccart parle*, Paris, Fayard, 1995. [The confidential documents of the man who had been the publicly secret organizer of what was known under the name of *Françafrique*.]

Bromberger, Mery and Serge, *Les 13 complots du 13 mai,* Paris, Arthème Fayard, 1959. [A contemporary chronicle of the politico-military "Algerian" coup that brought General De Gaulle back to power in 1958.]

Carayol, Rémi, *Le Mirage Sahélien,* Paris, La Découverte, 2013 [The most recent book on France's war in the Sahel. The defeat, which could be predicted from the start, is now impossible to avoid.]

Cogneau, D.,*Un empire bon marché*, *Histoire et économie politique de la colonisation française,* Paris, Le Seuil, 2023, 501 pp. + maps + graphs + tables. [The colonial ground from which the post-colonial French African policies grew.]

Cooper, F., *Africa in the World, Capitalism, Empire, Nation-State,* Cambridge, Mass, Harvard University Press, 2014, 130 pp. + index. [Probably the best synthesis on the position of Africa in the world.]

Debos, M., *Living by the Gun in Chad, Combatants, Impunity and State Formation,* London Zed Books, 2016. [An astonishing book based on analyzing a society built by, for and in spite of war. The French colonial state as leader, supporter and instrument of warlordism.]

SELECT BIBLIOGRAPHY

Collective (104 contributors), *Sexe, race et colonies,* Paris, La Découverte, 2018. [An extraordinary and rather unique book. Deals not only with Africa (even if it is its main topic) but with the whole of the colonial situation from the fifteenth century till the present. Sumptuous illustrations. Dealing with Africa almost exclusively through sex (and race) it is more a study of European obsessions towards Africa than an attempt at a global vision of the continent. Strong "French" influence. From the beginning, "Africa" is defined from the outside and there is no other work so splendidly devoted to visually fascinating transcultural voyeurism.]

Deltombe, Th., Domergue M., Tatsitsa, J., *Kamerun! Une guerre cachée aux origines de la Françafrique (1948–1971)* Paris, La Découverte 2011 (Réed 2019), 976 pp. + photos + index. [An encyclopedic research on the Cameroun civil war which cemented the first *Françafrique* syntagma.]

Deltombe, Th, Borrel, Th., Boukari-Yabara, Am., Collombat, Be., *L'Empire qui ne veut pas mourir; une histoire de la Françafrique*, Paris, Le Seuil, 992 pp. + index. 2021. [By far the most exhaustive study on *Françafrique*; in fact too detailed for a non-French reader; it is also in a way a politico-diplomatic history of France in the post Second World War era.]

Deltombe, Th., *L'Afrique d'abord, Quand François Mitterrand voulait sauver l'Empire Français,* Paris, La Découverte, 2024. [A resetting of the image of François Mitterrand as an anticolonialist.]

Dumont, René, *False Start in Africa,* New York, Praeger 1966. [The French original, *L'Afrique Noire est mal partie* had been issued in 1962. Published during the enthusiastic period of the then recent decolonization this outlook was in direct contradiction with the no-nonsense approach of this French agricultural expert.]

Elgas (pen name of El Hadj Souleymane Gassama), *Les bons ressentiments ; essai sur le malaise post-colonial,* Paris, Riveneuve, 2023. [By a Senegalese intellectual, an essay on the ambiguities and specificities of decolonization in Francophone Africa.]

Georgy, Guy, *Le petit soldat de l'Empire,* Paris, Flammarion, 1992. [A well-written autobiography by one of the intellectual and practical founders of *Françafrique*.]

Glaser, Antoine and Airault Pascal, *Le piège africain de Macron , du continent à l'hexagone*, Paris, Fayard, 2021. [This shows how Emmanuel Macron's attempt at solving the *Françafrique* problem failed and made it worse.]

Gonin, Patrick, Kotlok, Nathalie and Pérouse de Montclos, Marc-Antoine , *La

SELECT BIBLIOGRAPHY

tragédie malienne Paris, Vendémiaire, 2013. [A realistic analysis of the starting point of the present Sahelian situation.]

Goya, Michel (Colonel ; ret.), *Le temps des guépards , la guerre mondiale de la France de 1961 à nos jours,* Paris, Tallandier, 2022. [By a former and very experienced French Army officer who commanded French troops in foreign operations, the history of France's nineteen small military wars since 1961 and a reflection on France's obsession with security through force].

Guillebaud, J. C., *Les confettis de l'Empire , Djibouti, Martinique, Guadeloupe, Réunion, Tahiti, Nouvelle Calédonie, Guyane,* Paris, Le Seuil, 1976. [The basic book on the floating pieces of the French Colonial Empire which represent an amazing 18% of France's landmass today, Mayotte not being included in this study since the case of the island was still "*under discussion*" at the time of the book publication. The final paradoxical decision ended up being that Mayotte was "an integral part of France" while the rest of the Comoro Archipelago became an "independent country".]

Howard, R. T., *Power and Glory, France's Secret Wars with Britain and America (1945–2016),* London, Biteback, 2016. [A little-known but nevertheless very real British point of view on the questions raised by Colonel Goya's book above.]

Laurent, S. Y., *Etat secret, état clandestin ; Essai sur la transparence démocratique,* Paris, Gallimard, 2024. [A serious essay on the notion of state secrecy; mainly focused on France, it offers a fair amount of international (European) comparisons.]

Le Floch-Prigent, Loïk, *Affaire Elf, Affaire d'Etat,* Paris, Le Cherche Midi, 2001. [By the former CEO of Elf Aquitaine, the saga of the rough dealings of the French oil giant (1989–93) which led its boss to a prison sentence which he surprisingly did serve.]

Lhuillier, Jean-François, *L'homme de Tripoli,* **Mémoires d'un agent secret,** Paris, Mareuil, 2023. [By a participant of the French intervention in Libya.]

Martinez, Luis, *L'Afrique, le prochain califat? La spectaculaire expansion du djihadisme.* Paris, Tallandier, 2023. [By a French specialist of Algerian questions, a global outlook on the growth of the African *Jihadiyya*. Detailed and clear, perhaps a little too "Arab-centered".]

Marchesin, Ph, *La politique française de coopération,* Paris, L'Harmattan, 2021. [French financial aid to Africa. Colossal (680pp.) and studded with meaningful anecdotes.]

SELECT BIBLIOGRAPHY

Merle, Isabelle, *Expériences Coloniales, Le Nouvelle Calédonie (1853–1920)*, Paris, Belin 1995 (new edn, 2020). [Looking at New Caledonia through examining the spoliation of Kanak lands by poor white immigrants backed by the administration.]

Ollivier, Jean-Yves, *Ni vu, Ni connu* Paris, Fayard, 2013. [The (carefully filtered) autobiography of one of the most high profile of *Françafrique* "businessmen" of the classical era.]

Péan, Pierre, *Une jeunesse française*, Paris, Fayard, 1994 (re-published 2011). [François Mitterrand's right-wing youth and his ambiguous relationship with the Vichy regime before he went to London and joined the Free French movement.]

Pérouse de Montclos, Marc-Antoine, *Une guerre perdue, la France au Sahel*, Paris, J.C. Lattes 2020. [The first attempt at a global view of a war which—the author insists—is more a mosaic of various conflicts than a unified Muslim insurrection.]

Pérouse de Montclos, Marc-Antoine, *'Le cul des chameaux', La Libye vue du Sahel, entre mirages et réalités*, *Hérodote* no. 182, pp. 163–177, 2021. [The impact of Gaddafi's death on the Sahel in the long range perspective.]

Pérouse de Montclos, Marc-Antoine, *Prophètes en armes,* Paris Maisonneuve et Larose, 2025. [The sociology of the "religious" Sahel war, showing how secular this ongoing insurrection actually is.]

Pascal Perri, *Comores, les nouveaux mercenaires,* Paris, L'Harmattan, 1994. [The Comoro mess left after the removal of Bob Denard and his merry outlaws.]

Peterson, B.J. *Thomas Sankara, A Revolutionary in Cold War Africa,* Bloomington, Indiana University Press, 2021. [The only biography of Thomas Sankara in English.]

Piel, Simon and Tilouine, Joan, *L'affairiste,* Paris, Stock. 2019. [A lively biography of Alexandre Djouhri following its hero from small-time street operative to a multi-million dollar go-between for *Françafrique* in international business deals; the modern inheritor of J.Y. Ollivier.]

Roussy, C. (ed.), *Afrique, un sentiment antifrançais ?* Paris, A special number of the *Revue internationale et stratégique,* no. 133 (Spring 2024). [A well-edited number of the IRIS non-governmental think tank review, trying to analyze the slow-motion cultural decomposition of *Françafrique.*]

Sardan, J.P.O. de , *L'enchevêtrement des crises au Sahel ,Niger, Mali, Burkina Fasso,* Paris, Karthala, 2023. [The recent coups marking the last stages of *Françafrique*'s political collapse and the birth of the pro-Russian EAS plug.]

SELECT BIBLIOGRAPHY

Todd, David, *Velvet Imperialism: French Informal Imperialism in the 19th Century,* Oxford University Press, 2021. [How France after its 1815 defeat made up for its lost Empire through unconventional means.]

Filmography

Kigali , des images contre un massacre, Jean-Christophe Klotz, France, 2006, 94 minutes. [A very topical documentary by a French journalist who was dispatched to Rwanda before the genocide, witnessed its beginnings, was shot and wounded by the *génocidaires,* evacuated to France and came back to Rwanda after a couple of months of hospitalization in order to pick up the interviewing of many actors of the tragedy whom he had met before April 1994.]

Mali, les Sacrifiés du Sahel , Peggy Bruguière and Marlene Rabaud, France, 2021, 60 minutes. [A sharp documentary pointing out that the basic problem of Mali is economic corruption and that this cannot be fought with guns. Motivated more by social resentment than by religion, the Jihadists, although militarily inferior, penetrate society, enabling them to often defeat the demoralized army.]

Rwanda 1994, La France face au génocide des Tutsi Vincent Nequache, France, 2024, 70 minutes. [A very tight and very dense documentary where many key actors of the tragedy are interviewed. Good, with few surviving clichés (the "artificial fabrication" of ethnic groups by the Belgians!) a summary of the many angles of the catastrophe, to be seen perhaps twice with pen and paper in hand for note-taking.]

Rwanda, La France n'a pas voulu empêcher le génocide, Maxime Cochelin, France, 2024, 80 minutes. [A long interview with Gerard Prunier giving a personal perspective and a factual account by a moderate participant in the Rwandese catastrophe.]

Colonisation, une histoire française, Hugues Nancy, France, 2025, 185 minutes. [A detailed analysis of the French relation to the notion of Empire, showing the peculiar interpenetration of the ideas of Fatherland and Empire in a structural way very different from its British equivalent.]

INDEX

Abdallah, Ahmed, 227, 228, 229, 230
Abidjan, 129
Abubakar, Sa'adu, 179
Abuja, 134
Académie Française, 62
AEF (French Equatorial Africa), 7, 139
(*Alliance des Etats du Sahel*), 209–16, 220
Africa, ix, xiv–xv, 2, 3, 49
"African democracy", 112–23
    economic changes and structural transformations, 64–8
    France's African dilemma, 100–5
    hybrid ideological confusion, 16–30
    Ivory Coast civil war in, 123–30
    Kagame and *Françafrique*, 130–42
    La Baule speech, 76–80
    Libya, intervention in, 142–51
    oil scandal, 69–70
    Rwanda disaster, 107–12
    Rwanda refuge, 80–92
    Sankara's assassination, 74–6
    see also Congo, France, Nigeria
"The African Che Guevara", 70
"African Empire", 5
"The African Ho Chi Minh", 21
African Switzerland, 79
African Union, 176, 192
Afrika Korps, 180
Ag Ghali, Iyad, 159
Ahidjo regime, 43
Ahidjo, Ahmadou, 37
Alexander VI, Pope, 2–3
Algeria, xiii, 3–4, 15–16, 37, 120, 158, 240
    "African" coup, 30–8
    France's African dilemma, 100–5
    Franco-African Summit, 60–3
    hybrid ideological confusion, 16–30
    racism, 47–51
    Rwanda disaster, 107–12
    see also De Gaulle
Algerian civil war (1992–2002), 159
Algerian war (1956–62), 155

INDEX

Algerian war model, 54
Algerian War (1954), 38
Ali (Omar's oldest son), 53–4
Alliance Démocratique des Forces de Libération (ADFL), 108–10
al-Qaeda, 159, 177–8
Americans, 140–1, 145
ANC, 73
"Anglo-Saxon mafia", 56
Angola, 109, 136
ANLK, 43–4
Antilles (West Indies), 43
anti-Nazism, 41
AOF (Afrique Occidentale Française), 6–7, 173
AQIM (al-Qaeda in the Islamic Maghreb), 160, 162, 163–4
Kati camp attack, 165
Arab Spring, 144, 158
Areva, 174
Arusha Peace Agreement, 88, 91, 92
Atlantic Ocean, 45
Atlantic Wall, 33
Atno, Idris Deby, 58–60
Aubame, Jean-Hilaire, 51
Auguste, King Philippe, 42
Australia, 40
Azerbaijan, 236

Baganda, 11, 80
Bagogwe, 85–6
Bambari, 140–1
Bamenda, 29
Bamileke, 11, 43
Bangui, 139, 141
Barcelona, 53
Barkhane Force, 165

Bassa Catholics, 17
Bassa, 24–5, 28
Bazoum, Mohamed, 173, 174, 175, 176, 177, 178
Beijing, 21, 119
Beke (Creole), 33
Belgian Africa, 62
Belgian Congo, 79
Belgian League for Human Rights, 86
Belgian Paul-Henri Spaak, 13
Belgium, 63, 79, 125
Ben Ali, President Zin El-Abdin, 144
Benghazi, 145–6
Benin, 217
Berlin Conference, 92
Berlin, ix, 4, 21, 124–5
Beshir, Beshir Saleh, 147–8
Beshir, Mohamed Omar, 58
el-Beshir, Omar, 59
Biafra, 55
Biafran, 67
Bismarck, Chancellor, 4, 124–5, 155
Biya, Paul, 46, 121–2, 190
Black Africa, 4, 139, 150
"Bloc Français de l'Empire", 6
Boillon, Mr Boris, 148–9
Boisson, Governor Pierre, 7
Bokassa, Jean-Bedel, 61, 138
Boko Haram, 197, 218
Bolivar, Simon, 12
Bolloré, Vincent, 66–7
Bonaparte, Napoleon, 2
Bongo dynasty, 46
Bongo Valentin, Nur-ed-Din, 187
Bongo, Albert-Bernard, 52, 61, 184

INDEX

Bongo, Ali, 181, 182, 188
Bongo, Omar, 182, 185–6, 206
Bongo, Pascaline, 208
Bonnecorse, Michel de, 115
Borgia family, 3
Borrel, Bernard, 114–16
Bouaké, 129
Bourgi, Robert, 25–6
Brazzaville Conference, 6, 8, 49
Brazzaville Congo, 101
Britain, 1
British (English), 11
British Mandate Zone, 37
British Raj, 40
Brussels, 148, 180
Buazizi, Muhammad, 143
Bukavu, 98–9
Burkina Faso, 196, 209, 213, 219
    Essakane village, 213
    humanitarian aid, 172
    military coups, 167–72
    "volunteer" corps, 170–1
Burkina Faso, 62, 75, 76
Burundi, 109
Byumba, 86, 95

C-47, 14
Cameroon (Cameroun), 6, 15–16, 39, 76, 114, 118, 121–2, 218
    hybrid ideological confusion, 16–30
    independences, counterinsurgency, assassinations, 42–6
    Macron visits, 122,
"Cameroonian Ho Chi Minh", 25
Cameroon base, 153
Canada, 40, 41, 133

CAR, 137–41, 150
Caracas, 12
Central Africa Economic and Monetary Community (CEMAC), 190
Central Africa, 125
Central African Republic (Ubangui-Chari), 43, 61, 196
Chad, 43, 57–60, 155, 190–4, 217–18, 210, 215
    Idris Deby's killing, 190–1, 192
    Transition Council, 191–2
Chadian case, 57
Chari (the future Central African Republic), 6
China, 21, 63, 108
    "Belt and Road" corridor, 223
Chirac, President Jacques, 107, 111, 113–16, 132, 187
Christians, 57–8, 140
Churchill, Winston, 7
CNSP (*Conseil National du Salut Populaire*), 162
Cohen, Albert, 16
Colona, Catherine, 242
Colonial Exhibition (Paris), 233–4
Comité de l'Unité Togolaise (CUT), 27
Comité Français de Libération Nationale (CFLN), 8
Comité National d'Organisation (CNO), 28
Commonwealth, 40
Communauté Européenne Charbon-Acier (CECA), 13, 21
Communism, 29, 77–8

281

INDEX

Communist International, 194
Communist Party, xii
Comoro Red Guards, 228
Comoros, 223–32
Compaoré, Blaise, 62, 75–6, 167–8, 171–2, 207
Conakry Guinea, 44
"Concert of Nations", 124
Conde, Alpha, 201, 202, 203
Conessa, Pierre, 87
Congo border, 94
Congo Brazzaville, 118
Congo Republic (Brazzaville), 43
Congo River, 125
Congo, 5, 6, 90, 222
    African dilemma, 100–5
    leaves Rwanda, 92–9
    Rwanda refuge, 80–92
Congo–Océan railway, 20
Congress of Vienna, 50
Continental Blockade (1806), 13
Cot, Jean-Pierre, 85, 186
"Council for the Defence of the Empire", 8
CPC, 140–1
Cuba, 73
Cyangugu, 94

d'Arbousier, Gabriel, 15
d'Argenlieu, Admiral Thierry, xii
d'Estaing, Valéry Giscard, 61, 66, 67, 79
Dahomey, 120
Dakar, 7, 133
"Dakota", 14
DAMI operations, 97–8
Danube, 3–4
Darfur, 141

Darfur, conquest of, 156
Darmanin, Gérald, 230, 240
De Gaulle, xi–xiii, 6–7, 15, 46–7, 90, 101, 107, 153, 184, 185, 222, 239, 241
    "African" coup, 30–8
    Brazzaville speech (1958), 200–1
    colonialism and French political tradition, 39–42
    delegation of Tuaregs met with, 157–8
    economic changes and structural transformations, 64–8
    France's African dilemma, 100–5
    hybrid ideological confusion, 16–30
    independences, counterinsurgency, assassinations, 42–6
    oil scandal, 69–70
    racism, 47–51
    see also Algeria; Cameroon (Cameroun); France
de Guiringaud, Louis, 48–9
Debarge, Marcel, 87
Debré, Prime Minister Michel, 37, 44
Deby Itno, Idriss, 190–1, 192
"decolonization", 70, 157
Delavignette, Cameroun Governor Robert, 23
Delaye, Bruno, 105
Delbos, Marielle, 58
Denard, "Bob", 48, 227, 228, 229, 230

282

INDEX

Denmark, 163, 210
Dependaud, Ndouna, 53
Desmaret, Thierry, 104
Détachement de l'Aide Militaire et de l'Instruction (DAMI), 84–7, 91
Dien Bien Phu, xii–xiii, 18, 21
Diori, Hamani, 62
Diouf, Abdou, 133
Dioula, 11
Djerma, 62
Djerou, Yahia Dillo, 215, 218
Djibouti, 43, 114–15, 218–19
Djohar, Said Mohamed, 229–30
Djouhri, Alexandre, 147
Dogon militia, 211
Douala, 23–4
Douala–Yaounde railway, 20
Doumbouya, Mamady, 202–3
DST, 37
Dumas, Roland, 103
Dutch
    independences, counterinsurgency, assassinations, 42–6

East Africa, 79
East Central Africa, 92
Eastern Congo, 92
Eastern Europe, 77
Eboué, Félix, 6, 47
Ecole Nationale d'Administration (ENA), 134
Economic Community of Central African States (ECCAF), 192
ECOWAS (Economic Community of West African States), 162, 163, 177, 179, 210

Ekite, 28
Elf Aquitaine, 56, 67
Elf, 102–4, 112, 116
Elysée, 76, 108
Eritrea, 109
"Etat Français", 41
Ethiopia, 109
Europe, 1, 41, 114
    hybrid ideological confusion, 16–30
    Ivory Coast civil war in, 123–30
    Rwanda disaster, 107–12
European Common Market!, 14
European imperialism, 1, 4
European Union (EU), 110, 127, 209
Evian, 101
Evkurov, Yunus-bek, 180
Eyadema, French Army Sargeant Gnassingbe, 44–6, 119–20

"F6F Bearcats", 14
FACT (Front pour l'Alternance et la Concorde au Tchad), 190
Fashoda + Mers-el-Kebir syndrome, 23
Fashoda Incident, 13
Faye, Bassirou Diomaye, 221, 222
Flanders, 3–4
FLN, 158
Floch-Prigent, Loïc Le, 102, 207
FNLC, 63
Foccart, Jacques, 33–4, 44, 48, 107–8, 111, 113, 153
Fontbonne, Paul, 59
Forces Armées Rwandaises (FAR), 82, 84–92, 110

283

INDEX

Françafrique ship, 51
France, decolonization process, 223–7
   The Comoros, 223–32
   New Caledonia, 233–7
France, x–xiv, 2
   "African democracy", 112–23
   African dilemma, 100–5
   "African" coup, 30–8
   Belgian Congo, 63–4
   Bongo's relationship with, 185, 186–7
   colonialism and French political tradition, 39–42
   economic changes and structural transformations, 64–8
   Franco-African Summit, 60–3
   Gabon, operating Françafrique on, 51–4
   hybrid ideological confusion, 16–30
   independences, counterinsurgency, assassinations, 42–6
   Ivory Coast civil war in, 123–30
   Kagame and *Françafrique*, 130–42
   leaves Rwanda, 92–9
   Libya, intervention in, 142–51
   racism, 47–51
   Rwanda disaster, 107–12
   Rwanda refuge, 80–92
   UN Security Council seat, 153, 222
   war in various places, 54–60
"Franco-African cooperation", 51

"Franco-African Summit", 60
Free French, 17
FRELIMO, 228
French Africa, 7–8
French Colonial Civil Service, 7
French Departments and Territories (DOM/TOM), 117
French Guiana, 43
French Secret Service (DGSE), 58–9, 98
French Special Operation Commandoes, 57
Front Populaire Ivoirien (FPI), 128
Fuchs, Gérard, 87
Fulani, 55
Fulbe Muslims, 17
Fulbe, 62

G5 Sahel alliance, 209–10
Gabon, 43, 46, 51–4, 61, 63–4, 101, 114, 121, 221
   coup (2023), 181–90, 203–9
   delegation to the Russian embassy, 181–2, 183
   Françafrique, 184
   legal action against the ill-acquired assets, 206–8
   "National Conference" (2024), 205
   party system, 182–3
Gaddafi, Muhammar, 57, 59, 71, 144–7, 148
Gallic confusion, 14
Gare du Nord, 148
Gaullism, 19, 69
Gbagbo, 128–9
Geneva, 16, 44

INDEX

Géré tribe, 128
Germanophobia, 19
Germany, x–xi, 4, 10, 210
    hybrid ideological confusion, 16–30
    Ivory Coast civil war in, 123–30
    see also World War II
Ggbagbo, Laurent, 196
Ghaddafi, Muhammar, 155 death of, 158–9
Ghana, 73
Gicongoro, 96
Gnassingbe, Faure, 45, 120–1, 217
Godfrain, Jacques, 108
Goïta, Assimi, 162, 202, 214
Gold Coast, 27
Goma, 98–9
Gorgon, 42
Governor General of Canada, 133
Governor of Chad, 6
Governor of Equatorial Africa, 6
Great Britain, 2, 7, 13, 41, 124–5
Great Lakes, 2
"Great Powers", 56, 125
Greater Comoro, 228
Grunitzky, Nicolas, 45
GSPC (*Groupe Salafiste de la Prédication et du Combat*), 159
Guadeloupe (West Indies), 6, 33
Guardian, the (newspapaer), 102, 103
Guéant, Claude, 147
Gueï, General Robert, 127–9
Guelleh, Ismail Omar, 46, 115, 218–19
Guernsey, 117
Guèye, Lamine, 10

Guillaumat, Pierre, 102
Guillebaud, Jean-Claude, 223
Guinea, 200–3
    coup (Sep 5 2021), 201–2
    "Sékou Touré Airport", 203
Guyana, 6

Habré, President Hissène, 58–9
Habyarimana, President, 82, 91–2, 108, 131
    Rwanda, France leaves, 92–9
The Hague, 115
Haïphong, xii
Harka, 37
"Harmattan Operation", 146
Hausa of Nigeria, 11, 55, 62, 175, 176–7, 178
Hemedti, 141
Himes, Chester, 97
Hindi/Sanskrit, 11
Hollande, President François, 132, 134–5, 141, 158, 160, 200
Houphouët-Boigny, Félix, 9–10, 15, 26, 34, 42, 61, 74, 100, 122–3, 126–7, 129
Hutu ethnic administration, 79, 86

Idriss Deby, Mahamat, 191, 192, 193, 215–16, 217
    meeting with Putin, 215, 216
Igbo, 55
India, 2, 11, 40
Indochina, xii, 14, 17, 120
Industrial Revolution, 4
International Court of Justice (ICJ), 115
International Monetary Fund (IMF), 73

INDEX

International Secretariat of the French Socialist Party, 81
Iranian Commission for Economic Cooperation, 211
Ireland, 11, 13
Islam, 52, 59
Islamic State (ISIS), 160
Islamic State in the Greater Sahara, 167
Islamism, 166
Issoufou, Mahamadou, 174–5, 176
Italy, 129
Itno, Mahamat Idris Deby, 60
"Ivority", 126–8
Ivory Coast, 9, 43, 61, 63–4, 107, 122–3, 195, 196, 197, 216–17
civil war in, 123–30

Jamahiriyyah (state of the masses), 144–5
Jamat al-Nusra al-Islam wa'l Muslimin (JNIM), 167
Jean, Michaëlle, 133, 135
Jersey, 117
Johannesburg, 147
Joly, Judge Eva, 102
Journiac, René, 67

Kabore, Roch-Marc, 167
Kagame, Paul, 11–12, 80, 93, 95–9, 105
Kagame and *Françafrique*, 130–42
Kamerun. *See* Cameroon (Cameroun)
Kampala, 97
Kanaks, 233–6
Kanzinga, Agathe, 108

Keita, Ibrahim, 165
Keita, Ismail Boubakar, 160, 162
Keitel, Field Marshal Wilhelm, xi
Kenya, 137
Khartoum, 58–9
Kigali, 64, 82, 87, 97
King Leopold of Belgium, 125
Kinshasa, 63, 108
Kinyarwanda, 89–90
Kirdi Animists, 17
Kisangani, 110–11
Kivu, 97
Kolwezi, 63
Konan Bédié, Henri, 126–8
Korean War, 14
Korhogo, 129
KPMG, 136

La Baule, 87–8, 123
speech in, 76–80
La Françafrique: le plus long scandale de la République (Verschave), 66
la generacion del noventa y ocho (the generation of 1898), 12
La Martinique, 15
La Réunion, 225
Lacamp, Max-Olivier, 29
Lacheroy, Colonel, 27
Lake Kivu, 79
Lamizana, Aboubakar, 62
Laurent Désiré Kabila, 109
Le Pen, Marine, 241
League of Nations (UN), x, 16–19, 79
Légion d'Honneur, 25
Lenin, 94
Léotard, François, 93

INDEX

Libreville, 184–5, 187
Libya, 73, 142–51, 158–9
    Françafrique, 154
Libyan civil war, 148
LNG, 137
London, 8, 157
Louisiana, 2
Louis-Philippe, King of France, 225, 226
Luciardi (Douala Prosecutor), 19
Lugan, Bernard, 25

M'Ba, President Léon, 51–3, 184
M62 "Movement", 177
MacArthur, General, 21
Macron, Emmanuel, 25, 59–60, 122, 132–3, 134–6, 137, 141–2, 176, 177, 178, 179, 198, 200, 205, 222, 236
    Bamako visit, cancelled, 162
    and Mahamat Deby, 215
    in Ndjamena, 191
    Ouagadougou visit, 168
    radical disengagement measure, 219
Madagascar uprising (1947), 10
Madagascar, 43
Madrid, 12
Maghrebi immigration, 155
Magna Carta, 42
Mahorais Swahili, 224
Maïga, Choguel Kokalla, 162
Mali, 42–3, 132, 142, 158, 176, 195, 209, 219
    arrests of high-ranking members, 164–5
    economic sanctions, 163
    ECOWAS lifted its sanctions on, 210
    Françafrique, 166–7
    Goïta sent an emissary to Moscow, 214
    Islamist threat and French expeditionary force, 160–1
    Tuareg Azawad movement, 166
    Tuareg revolts (1990s), 159
    UN withdrawal, 212–13
Malian Army, 161, 163, 164
    POWs, 162
Malinke, 11
Malraux, André, 47
Mandate and Territories Commission, 16
Mandate Colony, 23
Mandela, Nelson, 68, 109
Manga Bell, Alex, 26
Martre, Ambassador Georges, 84
Marx, Karl, 239
"Marxist revolutionary", 43–4
Marxist-Leninist party, 76
Mauritania, 43, 210
Mauritius, 225
Maurras, Charles, 31
Mayotte island, 223–32, 240
    citizenship, 232
    "consultation" (1974), 226–7
    Mayotte Emergency Law, 232
Mborantsuo, Marie-Madeleine, 187
McDonald, 134
McKenzie-Papineau rebellion, 40
Mediterranean shore, Roman conquest of, 156
Melnik, Constantin, 37–8
Mercier, General, 95–6

INDEX

Messmer, Pierre, 234
Metropolitan France, 35
Middle East, 138
Minister of Overseas Territories, 68
MINUSCA, 140
MINUSMA, 163, 164, 165, 166
Mitterrand, François, 26, 34, 61, 66, 68, 94, 100–1, 112–13, 131, 186
    La Baule speech, 76–80
    oil scandal, 69–70
    Rwanda refuge, 80–92
    Sankara's assassination, 74–6
    Sankara's political trajectory, 70–4
Mitterrand, Jean-Christophe, 78, 82, 99, 105
MNLA (*Mouvement National pour la Liberation de l'Azawad*), 159
Mobutu, Marshal, 108–11
Modi, Salifou, 178
Mopti, 164
Morocco, 63–4, 111
Moscow, xii, 21
    Burkinabe delegation in, 169–70
Moscow-aligned Warsaw Pact, 73
Mosley, Oswald, 40
Mossi princess, 15
Moumié, Félix, 44
Moura, 163–4
Moyen ("Middle"), 6
Mozambique, 136
MPLA, 228
MRND, 87
MUJAO (*Mouvement pour l'Unicité et le Djihad en Afrique de l'Ouest*), 160

Multinational Intervention Force (MNF), 110
Multinational Joint Task Force, 197
Museveni
    Rwanda refuge, 80–92
Mushikiwabo, Louise, 135
Muslim Sultanate, 61
Muslims, 55–8, 139

Namibia, 4
Napoleonic Wars, 225
Nation of Islam, 145
Nationalist German, 18
Native Code, 8
NATO (North Atlantic Treaty Organization), xiv–xv, 21, 146
Nazism, 20
Ndjamena, 59
"neologism", ix
"never again", 18
New Caledonia, 43, 233–7
    independence movement, 235
    population, 233
New York, 22–3, 82
Nguesso, Denis Sassou, 103, 206
Nicaragua, 73
Niger, 43, 165, 173–80, 196, 209, 210, 219
    Americans force in Agadez, 178
    coup (Jul 26 2023), 173, 175
    problem of succession, 173, 174
    three year transition program, 176
    uranium mines, 174
Nigeria, 11, 16, 55, 134, 196, 219
Normandy, xi

INDEX

North Africa, 7
North African abode, 48
Nuland, Victoria, 178
Nyerere, Julius, 109

Obiang, Theodoro, 207
Ojukwu, Colonel, 55
Oligui Nguema, Brice, 183, 184, 189–90, 204, 205, 221
  Paris visit (2024), 208
Ollivier, Jean-Yves, 147
Olympio, President Sylvanus, 44–5, 120
Omar Bongo, 52, 103, 108
Omar, Sheikh El Haj, 15
Ondo Ossa, Albert, 188–9
OPA, 104
OPEC, 52
Operation Barkhane, 197, 199, 219
Opération Résurrection, 34
Operation Sangaris, 141
Operation Turquoise, 94–5
Orban, Victor, 194
Organisation Internationale de la Francophonie (OIF), 133–5, 142
Organization for African Unity (OAU), 73
Ouagadougou, 71, 74
Ouakid, Mussa, 240, 241
Ouattara, Alassane, 126, 128, 130, 196, 216–17
Oubangui, 6
"the overseas", 17

Pakistan, 40
Panama Canal scandal (1892), 112–13

Paris Court, 147
Paris Foccart, 37
Paris, xiv, 5, 8, 11, 17, 59, 63–4, 68, 78, 95, 129, 148
  "African" coup, 30–8
  economic changes and structural transformations, 64–8
  France's African dilemma, 100–5
  Gabon, operating Françafrique on, 51–4
  hybrid ideological confusion, 16–30
  Kagame and *Françafrique*, 130–42
  Libya, intervention in, 142–51
  Rwanda disaster, 107–12
  Rwanda refuge, 80–92
  Rwanda, France leaves, 92–9
Parti Communiste Français (PCF), 15
Parti Démocratique de Côte d'Ivoire (PDCI), 127
Parti Social Démocrate (PSD), 88
Penne, Guy, 76
People's Republic of China, 119
Petain, Marshal Philippe, 6, 31–2
Pieds Noirs, 48
Ping, Jean, 183
PNDS (*Parti National pour la Démocratie et le Socialisme*), 174
Poland, 31, 46
Polynesia, 43
Pompidou, President, 60, 64, 107
Port Gentil, 186
Portugal, 1, 2

INDEX

Pré, French Governor Roland, 27
Prigozhin, Yevgeny, 138–9
Provisional Irish Republican Army, 145
Prussia, 2
Putin, Vladimir, 138, 154, 220, 236
    Mahamat meeting with, 215, 216

"Quasi-Gaullist", 67
Quebec, 2

racism, 20, 47
Raïssi, Ebrahim, 211
Ramadier, Governor Jean, 36–7
Rassemblement Démocratique Africain (RDA), 9, 14–15, 20
    hybrid ideological confusion, 16–30
Rassemblement des Républicains (RDR), 128
Rawlings, 73
RDA, 195
"real Africa", 3
"Red obsession", 24–5
Redjembe, Joseph, 186
"Referendum on Terms Extension", 141
Reims, x
Republic of Biafra, 55
République Centrafricaine, 111–12
Revolutionary Defence Committees (CDRs), 71–2
Ribadu, Nuhu, 179
Riviera, 54
RN (*Rassemblement National*), 236
Robert, Jérémie, 206

Rolland, Sonia, 241–2, 243
Rome Treaty, 13–14
Roosevelt, xi, 7
Rouamba, Olivia, 211
Rubanda Nyamwinshi, 79
Rube Goldberg, 132
Rufin, Jean-Christophe, 92–6, 111
Ruhengeri, 85–6
Russian Private Military Companies (PMCs), 220
Russians
    Bamako and, 164
Rwanda, 64, 75, 79, 129
    African dilemma, 100–5
    disaster, 107–12
    Françafrique, 154
    French leave, 92–9
    Kagame and *Françafrique*, 130–42
    refuge, 80–92
Rwandese Patriotic Front (RPF), 81, 85–92, 105, 133
    Rwanda, France leaves, 92–9
Rwigyema, Fred, 81

Sahel, 136
Sahel, unrest in, 154–61
    French Army in, 160–2
    Italian occupation (1911), 156
Said Mohamed Jaffar, 227
Sall, Macky, 221
Sanaga Maritime district, 28
Sandinista Movement, 73
Sangaré, Bakary Yaou, 211
Sankara, Thomas, 62, 167, 169
    assassination, 74–6
    political trajectory, 70–4
Santos, Eduardo Dos, 207

INDEX

Sanussi Tariqa (the Islamic Brotherhood), 157
Sarajevo experience, 96
Sargasso Sea, 147
Sarkozy, President Nicolas, 25, 147–50
Sartre, Jean-Paul, 47
Saudi Arabia, 59
SDECE, 37, 44
SDN, 27, 36
Secret Service (SDS), 115
"the Secretariat of Francophone Africa", 36
Secretary of State in Charge of Cooperation and Development, 85
Secretary of the Socialist Party International Secretariat for International Relations, 87
Seko, Congolese President Mobutu Ssese, 63
Seleka group, 139–40
Senegal, 15, 59, 64, 221–2
Senghor, Léopold Sedar, 62
September, Dulcie, 68
Sevez, General François, x–xi
Sherpa, 206
Sidi Buzid, 143
Sinistre de la Défense Nationale du Kamerun (SDNK), 28–9, 37
Sirven, Alfred, 103
Slave Trade, 3
Social Darwinism, 46
"soft Marxist", 24
Soilih, Ali, 227, 228
Somali, 11, 137
Somaliland, 11
Sommet de la Francophonie, 78
Sudan, 43
South Africa, 4, 68, 109
South America, 3
South East Asia, 17
Soviet Union, 56
Spain, 1, 2, 12
Spanish–American War, 12
Spencer, Herbert, 46
Stalin, 81
Sudan, 58–9
Suez Canal, 14
Suez Crisis (1956), 23
Survie, 206
Sweden, 210
Syrian civil war, 137–8

Takieddine, Ziad, 150
Takuba, 193
Talon, Patrice, 217
Tambèla, Kyelem Apollinaire de, 169
Tanzania, 109, 137
Tarallo, Andre, 103
Tauzin, Colonel, 96–7
Tchicot, Victorine, 208
Tebboune, Abd-el-Majid, 240
Tejero, Colonel Antonio, 12–13
Thiaroye massacre, 9
Tiani, Abdourahman, 175, 177, 179, 180
Tillinac, Denis, 25–6
Tinubu, Bola, 179
Tirailleurs Sénégalais, 9
Tiv, 55
Todd, David, 5
Togo, 43, 44, 64, 114, 120–1, 217
Tordesillas, Treaty of, 2
Total (French oil company), 104

INDEX

Touadéra, Faustin-Archange, 140–1
Touré, Sékou, 201–2
Toyota 4x4 Land Cruiser, 59
Trade Union Congress, 40
Trans-Saharan slave raids, 156
Traore, Ibrahim, 169, 170, 213
"tribalism", 25
Trudeau, Justin, 135
Truman, 21
Tshisekedi, Felix, 192
Tuareg Azawad movement, 166
Tuaregs, 154, 157, 158, 160–1, 212
Tubu, 58
Tunisia, 143–4, 148
Turuq, 157
Tutsi, 80–92, 98

Ubangui-Chari, 138
UDSR (apparentement was the Union Démocratique et Sociale Républicaine), 34
Uganda, 11
  Rwanda disaster, 107–12
  Rwanda refuge, 80–92
Ukraine, 170, 194, 212, 220, 236, 237, 244
  see also (NATO North Atlantic Treaty Organization)
Ukraine conflict, 237
Um Nyobe, Ruben, 21–5, 28, 36, 44
UN General Assembly, 50
UN Mandate, 39
UN Resolution (1973), 147
UN security Council, xi, 125
UN Special Delegate, 72

UN (United Nations), 138, 145, 164, 184, 210
  see also European Union (EU); Germany
Union Démocratique et Sociale Républicaine (UDSR), 15, 26–7
Union Française Assembly, 34
Union Française, 14
Union Générale des Pétroles (UGP), 101–2
United Kingdom (UK), 14, 40, 56
United Nations Assistance Mission to Rwanda (UNAMIR), 83
United Nations Organisation, 17
United States (US), x, 63, 118
  see also NATO (North Atlantic Treaty Organization)
UPC (Union des Populations du Cameroun), 37–8, 122
  hybrid ideological confusion, 16–30
  independences, counterinsurgency, assassinations, 42–6
Upper Volta (later Benin), 43, 62, 70, 72
US Black Panthers, 145
USAF, 33
USAID (United States Agency for International Development), 116
USSR (Union of Soviet Socialist Republics), 78, 145
VDP (*Volontaires pour la Défense de la Patrie*), 170, 171, 213

"Velvet Imperialism", 5

INDEX

Véran, Olivier, 188
Versailles, Treaty of, x
Verschave, François-Xavier, 66
Vichy, 7–8, 19, 34
Vienna, Treaty of, 124
Vietnam War, 10
Vietnamese Communists, xii

Wagner group, 136–41, 162, 163–4, 165, 177, 180, 193, 220
  delegation in Ougadougou, 170
Washington, xiv–xv, 90, 145
Weber, Max, 25
Weddeye, Goukouny, 58
Wehrmacht, 5, 30–1
West Africa, 34
West African Economic Monetary Union (WAEMU), 163

West Indian White, 15
West Indies, 33–4
"White Russian" syndrome, 82
Wibaux, Fernand, 108
World War I, x, 46, 156, 157
World War II, x, 5, 14, 19, 21–2, 28, 40, 153, 240

Yaounde airport, 37
Yaounde, 118
Yerevan Conference, 135

Zaghawa, 58, 191
Zaïre, 110–12
Zairian Army, 109
Zambia, 63
Zeitgeist, 41
Zimbabwe, 109
Zone de Pacification (ZOPAC), 29